# LAKE ERIE BARON

## The Story of Colonel Thomas Talbot

By FRED COYNE HAMIL

TORONTO
THE MACMILLAN COMPANY OF CANADA LIMITED
1955

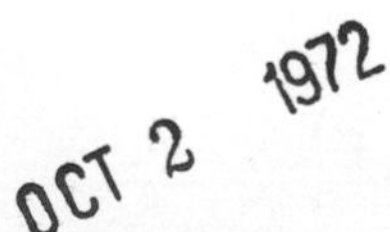

The title page of this book carries the Armorial Bearings of Colonel the Hon. Thomas Talbot which are those of Lord Talbot of Malahide with appropriate differences. The publisher acknowledges the courteous directions of Bluemantle Pursuivant of Arms, The College of Arms, London, England.

PRINTED IN CANADA

# *Preface*

A younger son of the Irish lord of Malahide, fresh from the viceroy's court in Dublin, Thomas Talbot first came to Canada in the summer of 1790 to join his regiment at Quebec. From 1791 to 1794 he served as aide to Lieutenant-Governor John Graves Simcoe, playing a minor part in the organization of the newly formed province of Upper Canada. In 1801, after an absence of nearly seven years, he returned as a private citizen, having abandoned a promising military career and the society of the Old World. The remainder of his life was devoted to the acquisition and utilization of a great landed estate for himself, and the settlement of what came to be known as the Talbot Country, which comprised parts of twenty-nine townships north of Lake Erie.

Colonel Talbot occupies an unique place among the makers of Ontario. An agent of the government, entrusted with the duty of locating settlers on the waste lands of the Crown, and of superintending the performance of the settlement duties, over the years his powers developed to an extraordinary degree. From Long Point to the Detroit River, a distance of one hundred and thirty miles, and in a range of townships north of the Thames River, his control was in some ways as absolute as that of a medieval feudal baron. From his "Castle" at Port Talbot he granted land to applicants who met with his approval, and withheld it from those who did not. When his settlers failed to comply with his regulations as to residence and labour he took away their land and gave it to others. By these autocratic methods, almost exempt from control by the provincial government, he was instrumental in colonizing an extensive territory. When he died in 1853, the wilderness to which he had come a half century before had been converted into a country of cultivated fields and comfortable homes, with numerous villages and towns and some of the best roads in Canada. Much of the credit for this development must go to him. On the other hand, there were times when autocracy threatened to become tyranny, and instances of harsh treatment and injustice were not unknown.

Two brief biographies of Colonel Talbot, anecdotal in nature, were published soon after his death: one by L. C. Kearney in 1857, and one by Edward Ermatinger in 1859. In 1904 C. O. Ermatinger expanded his father's biography into *The Talbot Regime*, which is largely devoted to the growth of the Talbot Settlement. The Colonel's personal papers, many of them from the period of the War of 1812, and a number of letters written by him to Peter Robinson and William Allan, were published with an admirable introduction by James H. Coyne in 1907-9. The authors of these works neglected most of the mass of government records concerning Talbot, as well as the local newspapers and the private collections of papers of his contemporaries. With the aid of these sources I have attempted to present a more complete account of the Colonel and his work in Upper Canada.

I am indebted to many persons for assistance in using this material. I am under special obligation to Dr. W. Kaye Lamb, Archivist of the Public Archives of Canada, and members of his staff; to Dr. George W. Spragge, Archivist, and Donald F. McOuat, Assistant Archivist, of the Department of Public Records and Archives, Ontario; to the staff of the Toronto Reference Library; to Dr. James J. Talman, Chief Librarian, and Miss Lillian Benson, of the Library of the University of Western Ontario; and to Dr. Flint Purdy of the Library of Wayne University. My sister, Miss Genevieve Hamil, gave freely of her time in investigating certain details pertaining to Talbot's residence at Niagara. From Mr. John Gray, Managing Director of The Macmillan Company of Canada Limited, I have received much encouragement and assistance.

F. C. Hamil

Wayne University, June 23, 1955

TO

BERTHA COYNE HAMIL

A Daughter

of

The Talbot Settlement

# *Contents*

# *Illustrations*

CHAPTER I

# *Malahide and Dublin*

THE Talbot name has been an honoured one among the English nobility since Richard Talbot, a Norman knight, settled in England during the reign of William the Conqueror. A century later another Richard Talbot left England to assist King Henry II in asserting his authority over the Anglo-Norman and Irish lords of Ireland, and to found the branch of the family so noted in the history of that country. In 1174, as a reward for his services, Richard received a royal grant of the important fief of Malahide, situated on the east coast nine miles north of Dublin, where he built a castle on a slight limestone elevation beside the Irish Sea. Rebuilt and extended at various times, Malahide Castle still stands after nearly eight centuries, the aged grey masonry of its turreted walls and round towers softened by the enveloping ivy. From its lofty battlements can be seen the waters of Malahide Bay and the picturesque islands of Lambay and Ireland's Eye. A half mile to the south, on the estuary of a creek, is the town of Malahide, a commercial port of some consequence in the later Middle Ages, but by the eighteenth century merely a fishing village noted for the oysters it supplied to the Dublin market. Between the rocky headland which juts into the sea below the town, and the Hill of Howth with its ancient castle overlooking Dublin Bay four miles to the south, the shore is lined with rolling sand dunes. To the north the plain of Fingal extends for fifty miles to the

Mourne Mountains beyond Dundalk. Fingal means "Land of the Foreigners"—a reminder of the Norsemen who dominated the region for two hundred years before the coming of the English.[1]

In the ruined chapel beside Malahide Castle are the tombs of some of the lords and ladies who once lived there. Still to be seen is the tomb of Maud Talbot, who lived in the sixteenth century, the tragic heroine of the ballad which begins:

The joy bells are pealing in gay Malahide,
  The fresh wind is sighing along the sea side;
The maids are assembling with garlands of flowers,
  And the harpstrings are trembling in all the glad
    bowers.

The castle and its environs have not changed too greatly since that day, when the bridegroom left the wedding feast to die in battle with the approaching foe, and the bride, meeting his corpse borne home on a shield,

Sinks on the meadow, in one morning tide
  A wife and a widow, a maid and a bride.

The moat, the drawbridge, and the portcullis have long since disappeared, but the stone barbican still guards the entrance to the courtyard, and the great oaks, chestnuts, and sycamores remain to shade the grounds. Inside the castle the carved panels and cross-beamed ceiling of the Oak Room, the Tudor dining-room with its gallery, the halls and stone staircases, are unchanged since the sixteenth century.[2]

Thomas Talbot was born at Malahide Castle on July 19, 1771, the son of Sir Richard and Lady Margaret O'Reilly Talbot. He bore the name of a fifteenth-century ancestor who received a royal grant of the customs at the port of

Malahide, as well as the judicial powers of an admiral there. At the time of the former's birth the barony had been held by the family in direct male line for six hundred years, and various members of the family had become famous as warriors, churchmen, and statesmen. His mother's father was James O'Reilly of Ballinough Castle in Westmeath, a descendant of the ancient Milesian princes of Breffney, and a relative of the noble Irish house of Nugent whose head was the Earl of Westmeath. They were members of the Roman Catholic Church, as were some branches of the Talbots, but Thomas and his sisters and brothers were reared in the Anglican faith. The Talbots of Malahide were not as much separated from the Irish inhabitants as were many other lords who did not have Catholic connections, or those whose ancestors had come from England much more recently, and who derived their lands from the still-remembered confiscations of the previous century.[3]

The Anglo-Irish aristocracy of the eighteenth century was as arrogant and oppressive as any in western Europe. A decadent type of feudalism, lingering on from the Middle Ages, bore heavily on the land. The great nobles lived in castles on their country estates, or in magnificent town mansions, supported by the labour of a tenantry scarcely removed from serfdom. Between these classes was that of the country gentry, who leased lands on long terms from the lords, and sublet to the small occupiers on short terms or at will, extracting the last farthing in rent. These were the "little country gentlemen; tenants who drink their claret by means of profit rents, jobbers in farms; bucks; your fellows with round hats, edged with gold, who hunt in the day, get drunk in the evening, and fight the next morning."[4] The labouring tenants lived in straw-thatched cottages clustered below the castles and manor houses; and there were also landless poor who lived in mud hovels built in ditches by the roads, without windows or chimneys. Domestic animals and people lived together, eating the potatoes and buttermilk that formed their staple diet.

Racial and religious differences widened the gulf between the aristocracy and the mass of the Irish people. To retain their identity most of the English conquerors had kept themselves apart as an exclusive caste; and to retain the lands they had taken from the natives they ruled tyrannically. Since the sixteenth century Anglicanism had been the religion of the alien rulers, while the conquered people clung more firmly to their Roman Catholic faith. "A long series of oppressions," Arthur Young noted during a visit to Ireland in 1776, "aided by many ill judged laws, have brought landlords into a habit of exerting a very lofty superiority, and their vassals into that of an almost unlimited submission; speaking a language that is despised, professing a religion that is abhorred, and being disarmed, the poor find themselves in many cases slaves even in the bosom of *written* liberty. . . . A landlord in Ireland can scarcely invent an order which a servant, labourer or cottar dares to refuse to execute. Nothing satisfies him but an unlimited submission. Disrespect or anything tending towards sauciness he may punish with his cane or his horsewhip with the most perfect security; a poor man would have his bones broke if he offered to lift his hand in his own defence. Knocking down is spoken of in the country in a manner that makes an Englishman stare."[5]

Thomas Talbot spent his early youth at Malahide and in the nearby metropolis of Dublin, among the highest rank of the nobility. He grew to manhood in a society accustomed to lavish entertainment, to the consumption of great quantities of claret, and to the keeping of hordes of servants, horses, and hounds. In later life he ruled his Canadian settlers like the Irish aristocrat that he was. One of them complained that he resembled his famous relative of the seventeenth century, the Earl of Tyrconnel, having inherited a great deal of the tyranny "which his family in Ireland is so famous for".[6] In Malahide Castle are three portraits of Richard Talbot, Earl and titular Duke of Tyrconnel, Roman Catholic Lord-Lieutenant of Ireland under James II. He and his brother Peter, Catholic Archbishop of Dublin, were centres of Catholic intrigue at the courts of the later Stuarts, and Peter died imprisoned in Dublin Castle after the coming of William of Orange. The Earl was the "Handsome Dick Talbot" of history and fiction, better known in the coffee houses as "Lying Dick", a notorious gallant, duellist, and swearer of oaths. After a series of noted love affairs he married "the languishing Miss Boynton". On her death in 1679 he married Lady Fanny Hamilton, the elder sister of the Duchess of Marlborough, whom he had courted in vain when she was "La belle Jennings", an outstanding beauty of her time. His niece, Frances Talbot, "a lady of strong and masculine spirit", married another Richard Talbot and became the great-grandmother of Thomas.

Mrs. Anna Jameson noted in 1837 that family and aristocratic pride was a prominent feature in Thomas Talbot's character. "A Talbot of Malahide," she wrote, "of a family representing the same barony from father to son for six hundred years, he set, not unreasonably, a high value on his noble and unstained lineage; and, in his lonely position, the simplicity of his life and manners lent to these lofty and not unreal pretensions a kind of poetical dignity."[7] She discussed with him "the exploits of some of his celebrated and gallant ancestors", and also, it may be assumed, those of his famous relatives in the English branch of the family. They doubtless talked of John Talbot, the second Earl of Shrewsbury, whose portrait hangs near that of the Earl of Tyrconnel in Malahide Castle. John Talbot was a famous captain under Henry VI in the Hundred Years War, who served as Chancellor of Ireland and later as Lord High Treasurer of England, and who was slain at the battle of Northampton fighting in the Lancastrian cause. Perhaps a reference to the story of Francis Talbot, a later Earl of Shrewsbury, and his second wife, the daughter of the Earl of Cardigan, would not have offended the Colonel. She was the "Wanton Shrewsbury" of Alexander Pope, who was said to have disguised herself as a page boy, holding the horse of her paramour the Duke of Buckingham while he killed her husband in a duel, and then clasping the blood-stained victor to her bosom.[8]

The profession of arms was an honoured one in the Talbot family, as it was among the nobility in general. One of Thomas Talbot's uncles, his father's brother, died fighting in the Austrian army. Two of his mother's brothers engaged in the same service. One of them, Andrew O'Reilly, became a dashing general of cavalry and a Count of the Empire; his wife was a Bohemian countess whom he won by killing his rival for her affections in a duel. The O'Reillys had furnished soldiers of fortune for Spain and France as well. The Talbots, as befitted gentlemen of Anglo-Norman descent, served more generally in the British armies and navies. Thomas was to become a lieutenant-colonel, his older brother Sir John an admiral, and his younger brother Neil a colonel of dragoons who fell at Cuidad Rodrigo in Spain.

Thomas Talbot began his military career as an ensign in the 66th Regiment of Foot a few weeks before his twelfth birthday. His appointment was doubtless obtained through the good offices of Lady Temple, wife of the Lord-Lieutenant of Ireland. She was a daughter of Earl Nugent of Carlanstown in Westmeath and related to Lady Talbot; and the commission was dated a few days before Lord Temple resigned his office in the spring of 1783. Such youthful appointments were not unusual at the time, when ensigns and lieutenants sometimes met death on the battlefield before the age of sixteen; and promotion was rapid for those with wealth and influence. In the fall of 1783, three weeks after the signing of the treaty that ended the war with the American Colonies, Talbot was advanced to the rank of lieutenant. Then his regiment was reduced, and the twelve-year-old lieutenant was retired on half pay. It was apparently at this time that he went, as it is reported, to complete his formal education at the Manchester Free Public School. This was the famous grammar school founded in 1519 by Hugh Oldham, Bishop of Exeter, for the purpose of teaching every child or scholar who might attend, "without any money or reward taken". In later days, besides free students, it received many children of well-to-do parents who paid fees. It was from this school, a generation later, that the young Thomas De Quincey ran away, as told in his *Confessions*.[9]

Lord Temple, now the Marquis of Buckingham, was again appointed Lord-Lieutenant or Viceroy of Ireland in the fall of 1787. One of his first acts was to provide a position for his wife's protégé by naming him one of his aides-de-camp. As a necessary preliminary young Talbot was provided with a commission as lieutenant in the 24th Regiment of Foot. Positions on the Viceroy's staff were greatly coveted, as William Grenville, the Marquis' brother, discovered to his annoyance. He was, he wrote, "pestered with applications beyond all imagination" from persons seeking places. "Every man who knows me by sight, who remembers my name at Eton or Oxford, or who voted for me in Bucks, is to be immediately made either a chaplain or an aid-de-camp, or is to have a snug place of £1,000 a year to begin with, as Sir Francis Wronghead says."[10] Among those who succeeded was Arthur Wellesley (later the Duke of Wellington), who had received the King's commission as ensign in the 73rd Regiment the previous March, just before his eighteenth birthday. At the request of Wellesley's mother, and his brother, Lord Mornington, the Marquis not only made him an aide-de-camp but assisted in the arrangements for his advancement to the rank of lieutenant in one of the regiments. "I have desired that your brother may buy his men from a Charing Cross crimp," Buckingham told Lord Mornington, "that he may not be spoilt by recruiting, and am happy that I can name him as aide-de-camp."[11] Lady Mornington was delighted. Her young son, she informed a friend, was "wonderfully lucky, in six months he has got two steps in the army and appointed Aid De Camp to Lord Buckingham which is ten shillings a day."[12] Talbot was even more lucky, being but sixteen years of age, two years younger than Wellesley.

Both young men were thoroughly familiar with the city in which they were to live as members of Buckingham's staff. Wellesley had been born there, and Talbot's home at Malahide was only a few miles away. Dublin was a splendid city, built astride the River Liffey near its entrance into the bay. As the capital of Ireland it attracted the nobility from their country estates. "It gave itself all the airs of a centre of fashion and gaiety," an historian wrote, "and so far it was in its right, for the Viceroy's Court exceeded in brilliance that of George III. Lords and commoners of distinction dwelt within its walls. They were as fine as any of the fine gentlemen in Europe—magnificent in their profuse expenditure, in their dress, their equipage, their establishments. Every nobleman had his town mansion, some palatial in size and design."[13] Outstanding among them was the Duke of Leinster's house, a very large stone edifice built in the prevailing classical style, with a spacious court and beautiful grounds. Lord Charlemont's mansion was noted for its elegant library and fine collection of paintings; he also owned the magnificent villa of Marino on the Bay.

The residences of the rich, formerly in the "Liberties" near Dublin Castle, were now in the newer sections of the city, on Mountjoy and Rutland Squares to the north of the Liffey, and Merrion Square and St. Stephen's Green to the south. The stately Georgian buildings, with their flambeaux, delicate iron grills and tracery, cornices, porticos, fanlights and pilasters, were typical of the eighteenth century. The spacious apartments within were designed for lavish entertainment. There were rich furnishings, broad stone staircases, and Italian chimney-pieces of marble ornamented in bas-relief with cornucopias and figures from mythology. Italian artists were imported to paint the walls with classical urns, trailing festoons, and elaborate medallions. Some of the finest homes faced on St. Stephen's Green, where an equestrian statue of George II stood in the centre of a meadow a quarter mile square. A double row of trees, and a dirty ditch usually containing a few dead cats and dogs, enclosed the green on all four sides. On Sundays when the weather was fine throngs of ladies and gentlemen came after church to promenade the fashionable Beaux's Walk on the north, or the slightly less favoured walks on the other sides.

Dublin was a city of vivid contrasts, especially in the old town near the Castle on Cork Hill; and along Dame Street where it widened east of the Castle to become "the focus of fashion, bustle and business", following the Liffey past bridges and quays to Trinity College and the Parliament Building on College Green. Here the long drab coats of the common people, and the filthy rags of the beggars, mingled with the elegant apparel of the rich. Hackney coaches and little wooden-wheeled carts clattered over the littered cobblestones. During the dark of the moon the streets were dimly lighted for part of the night by lanterns, and patrolled by watchmen armed with muskets and pikes. In the ancient part of the city the narrow lanes and alleys were crowded with merchants' stalls and the hovels of the poor, presenting some of the worst slums in the world. "Walking in the streets there," wrote Arthur Young in 1776, "from the narrowness and populousness of the principal thoroughfares, as well as from the dirt and wretchedness of the canaille, is a most uneasy and disgusting exercise."

During the summer, when Parliament was not in session and the nobles deserted their Dublin mansions for their country estates or villas by the sea, the Viceroy and his staff resided at the Viceregal Lodge in Phoenix Park, to the west of the city. There was then time for picnics under the spreading trees beside the Liffey, for riding on quiet paths, and for garden parties enlivened by the acting of little comedies. Gay groups rode up the river to Chapelizod and to the Salmon Leap above Lucan, near romantic Leixlip Castle with its antique tower mantled with ivy; or to Luttrell's Town, where shaded trails led through the woods and deep into a secluded glen beside a rushing stream. To the north lay Clondalkin with its round tower, and Finglas with its early church and

Irish cross. To the east was the popular resort of Blackrock, where on Sundays crowds of people from Dublin went to swim in the Irish Sea, or to drive on the hard wet sands left bare by the receding tide, past elaborate summer-houses and gardens lining the coast.

The great social season was during the winter, when the Viceroy took up residence in Dublin Castle, Parliament was in session, and the mansions of the rich were again occupied. Then the city awoke from its summer quiet and the Castle became the centre for a round of dinners, levees, balls and drawing-rooms. Silk-clad debutantes and matrons and uniformed men rode up Dame Street to Cork Hill in their coaches, to dance in the soft glow of innumerable candles at St. Patrick's Hall, or to walk on scarlet cloth up the grand staircase to the presence chamber and the drawing-room. The youthful aides-de-camp, resplendent in blue satin facings and gold furbelows, were prominent at all these affairs. Stationed at strategic points to direct the guests, or standing close to the thrones of the Viceroy and his lady, they were the objects of admiring glances of the debutantes and the flattering attentions of their mothers. Many a social climber pressed forward to talk to the aides as they basked in the reflected glory of the great couple.

"Gaiety, pleasure, luxury and extravagance" also reigned supreme in the mansions of the rich; and the presence of an aide-de-camp lent distinction to any event. Every night, somewhere in the city, there was a dinner or a ball for people of fashion. On masquerade nights the great houses were thrown open for the entertainment of the masques. Spacious apartments were crowded with ladies and gentlemen dancing, playing whist, and indulging in small talk. Dublin had a sparkling, showy character found in few other cities of the time.

The ladies were famous for their grace in dancing, the men for their courtliness, and the upper classes generally for their cultivation of social habits. They applauded good acting at the theatres with passionate enthusiasm, and held actors and painters in high esteem. A music hall, a musical academy, and a public garden for entertainments on the model of Vauxhall, testified to the widespread interest in music.

The pomp and ceremony of the Castle, reproducing on a smaller stage that of the Court of St. James's, dominated the life of the city. The Lord-Lieutenant represented the King, and round him rotated the lords and commons, bishops and judges, treasurers, chancellors, and privy councillors. From time to time he rode out from the Castle in full state, attended by his aides-de-camp and chief officials. On November 4, the anniversary of the birth of King William III of "pious, glorious, and immortal memory", the Viceroy held a levee of the nobility and gentry, and then led a cavalcade to College Green to salute that King's painted equestrian statue and attend a grand military spectacle. At other times he rode to College Green to sit upon the throne in the House of Lords, and with the usual solemnities to open or close the sessions of Parliament. He occasionally went in state to Smoke Alley Theatre, and to concerts, flower shows and bazaars. Each October, on the anniversary of the discovery of the rebellion of 1641 he went to Christ Church to hear the traditional sermon; at noon the great guns of the Castle boomed out, the church bells rang, and at night there were bonfires and an illumination. On St. Patrick's Day elaborate celebrations were held in the Castle yard for the benefit of the populace. The Lord-Lieutenant would appear on a balcony wearing the shamrock while the band played Irish airs, and the ceremonies of trooping the colours and mounting the guard were performed. At night a banquet would be given at the Castle, followed by the time-honoured St. Patrick's Ball. The common people observed it all with a mixture of amusement and resentment, of admiration and irreverence.

In April, 1789, on the occasion of the King's recovery from a period of insanity, elaborate thanksgiving ceremonies were held in Dublin. An hour before noon on the appointed day the Lord Chancellor and the peers, followed by the commons, the city officials, and the judges, moved in procession from College Green to Christ Church, where they took their seats. As the last man passed the Castle the Marquis of Buckingham appeared at the head of his aides-de-camp and officers of state, an event announced by the firing of rockets and the guns of the salute battery in Phoenix Park. Shortly after twelve o'clock he arrived at the west door of the church, where he was met by the sub-dean (in the absence of the bishop) at the head of the chapter, who conducted him to the foot of the great stairs before taking their seats in the choir. When he appeared in the viceregal closet a band of one hundred musicians began to play the overture to *Esther*, after which the services began. Most of the ladies of distinction, who were able to secure seats in the church, wore bandeaus inscribed in gold with the words "Long Live the King". The same inscription appeared in silver on blue fillets round the caps of the battle-axe guards. The day ended with a sumptuous dinner at the Castle, a prominent feature of which was a roasted warden of beef weighing more than two hundred pounds, with a huge knife and fork protruding from it.

Nevertheless, Buckingham's court was not as gay or extravagant as that of his predecessor the Duke of Rutland, which occasioned many uncomplimentary remarks from the pleasure-loving people of Dublin. The absence of the Marchioness during the winter of 1788-9 was said by some to have been because of her desire to avoid the trouble and expense "of having drums, drawing-rooms and balls at the castle". Knowing the Marquis, Lord Mornington had believed that under his eye his brother, Arthur Wellesley, would not be exposed to any of the risks that had formerly accompanied the position of aide-de-camp.[14] But even Buckingham could not prevent his aides from learning the vices of the time. They quickly spent their ten shillings per day, or gambled it away at Daly's Club, and fell into debt. They learned to drink to excess, and if need be to defend their honour in a duel. A "mischievous, reckless and jolly set", they learned all the social graces, the etiquette, and the courtly manners of a gentleman of the eighteenth century. It is not surprising that sometimes their heads were turned by the adulation showered on them, or that they became supercilious and condescending.

Thomas Talbot was sixteen years old when he became an aide to Buckingham. For two years he was moulded in the environment of the Dublin Court, which completed the work of the aristocratic society in which he had spent his earlier years. He grew to manhood in the later eighteenth century, as a member of the highest nobility in Ireland, and it left an indelible mark upon his manners and character. William Dummer Powell, who first met him in Upper Canada in 1794, wrote this description of him as he then appeared: "Mr. Talbot was considered as a gay cheerful companion whose natural selfishness and insolence of character had been improved in the best circles of Dublin and London."[15] In later years, long after he had abandoned polite society for the arduous life of a backwoodsman, his character seemed to change. To many of his contemporaries he appeared a crude and tyrannical old man who was the very reverse of a polished gentleman. But on occasion, to the end of his days, he could charm both men and women with his courtliness, his hospitality, and his ability to turn a compliment.

Buckingham's second term as Viceroy of Ireland soon ended. He had become unpopular because of his efforts to reduce extravagance and corruption in the government; and he made many enemies by his "great haughtiness, both of character and manner, extreme jealousy and proneness to take offence". His formal resignation was signed on September 30, 1789, but he did not leave Ireland until early the next January, when Lord Westmorland arrived to succeed him. "Dublin proposed to illuminate his departure. The mob designed him a rougher farewell."[16] But the Marquis slipped away quietly and embarked at Blackrock for England, in striking contrast to his arrival two years before, when the people of Dublin drew his carriage through the streets amidst universal acclamation. Talbot had only a few miles to go to reach Malahide Castle. In the spring of 1790 he sailed to join his regiment, which was then doing garrison duty at Quebec.

## CHAPTER II

# *Governor Simcoe's Secretary*

The landscape along the St. Lawrence below Quebec, as Lieutenant Talbot and his companions saw it in the summer of 1790, was wild and beautiful—a wilderness of rocks and trees. But within a few miles of the town, where the river narrowed, white farm-houses and cultivated fields began to line the banks, with here and there a tiny French village, its church spire pointing heavenward. Just beyond the verdant Island of Orleans, where the St. Charles River flowed into the St. Lawrence from the north, the lofty promontory of Cape Diamond, crowned by the citadel of Quebec, towered more than three hundred feet above the water. At its base, towards the east, lay the Lower Town, a jumble of wharves and jetties, warehouses and stores, crowded along narrow streets and almost engulfed in mud during wet weather. At the western end, where only a narrow pathway lay between the cliff and the St. Lawrence, iron bolts imbedded in the rock provided moorings for some of the many ships that crowded the harbour and the river beyond. Steep streets and tiers of tin-roofed houses, some bright in the sunshine but most rusted and dull, climbed upward from the water to Upper Town, where the citadel, the barracks, and the Governor's house were backed by residential sections of wood and stone buildings, all enclosed by a strong stone wall. The general type of architecture, as well as the dress of the women and the wooden shoes of the lower classes, gave evidence that this was still very much a French town.

If the appearance of Quebec from the river was somewhat disappointing, the view from the top of the promontory was magnificent. Below lay the St. Lawrence and the wide mouth of the St. Charles, dotted with sailing ships and *bateaux*. Behind Point Levis on the opposite side stretched the vast forest of the south. To the east was the Island of Orleans, with its precise fields and vineyards, and in the distance the white ribbon of the Falls of Montmorency, sparkling in the sun. To the north across the valley of the St. Charles, wooded hills swept to the purple mountains on the horizon; and over the new Dorchester bridge clattered the wooden carts of the habitants, filled with provisions—sometimes only a basket of eggs, or firewood from the forests of Charlebourg and Beauport—or with dung from the town. Westward herds of cattle grazed on the green fields of the Plains of Abraham. It was still a primitive land, on whose borders civilization had gained no more than a narrow foothold.

Nevertheless, in a smaller way, Quebec society was as gay as that of Dublin. Here also winter was the season of festivity. By December the last ships had departed for Europe and business was at an end. Then began a round of balls, concerts, plays, and dinners, with officers of the garrison and officials of the government mingling with the local seigneurs and wealthy merchants. Governor Dorchester held his levees at the Castle of St. Louis in a style worthy of Dublin Castle; they were always held in the forenoon, on such occasions as the King's birthday. Then the principal gentlemen of the garrison came to pay their compliments to the Governor. At noon a royal salute was fired from the citadel and the Grand Battery on the ramparts, which was answered from the Lower Town. The troops of the garrison, drawn up on the parade, then fired three volleys of musquetry. In the evening the élite attended a splendid supper and ball at the Castle of St. Louis.

During winter mornings it was a common amusement for the young officers to go carioling over the ice or snow in a sleigh, drawn by a single horse equipped with tinkling bells and fancy trappings. "Thus appointed," wrote a visitor to Quebec at this time, "a Canadian cavalier dashes through the snows, and solicits some fair dame to participate in the pleasure of the day. Races are run, and emulative happiness is everywhere visible."[1] In the summer the cariole gave way to the *calèche*, in which the officers explored the environs of the town and the more distant points of interest along the rivers. The gay circle of the town held parties of pleasure to such places as the picturesque Falls of Montmorency, a favourite spot for picnics.

Late in May, 1791, the 24th Regiment, under the command of Colonel Richard England, was transferred from Quebec to Montreal, after a grand review on the Plains of Abraham by Lord Dorchester, followed by a dinner for the officers. Lieutenant Talbot remained with his regiment at Montreal until the following December, learning to know this commercial entrepôt of the West, where Indians, voyageurs and fur-traders jostled soldiers and habitants in the busy streets below the Mountain. Built on an island, the town was smaller than Quebec, but its flagged streets were cleaner, and the stone houses, although in the French style, were generally much lower and neater in appearance.[2]

It may have been a desire to penetrate farther into this new and exciting land that prompted Talbot to seek a post with Colonel John Graves Simcoe, the first Lieutenant-

Governor of the newly created province of Upper Canada that lay to the west of Montreal and the Ottawa River; or he may have become tired of the routine of garrison duty and wished to obtain more active employment, with a chance for advancement. Whatever his motives, he enlisted the aid of his patron, the Marquis of Buckingham, who recommended him to Simcoe as a former member of his staff in Ireland, and requested the Colonel to take him into his official family.

Simcoe arrived at Quebec from England in November, 1791, and early the next month went to Montreal on the business of his government. When he returned to Quebec a few days later he brought Talbot with him as his assistant private secretary and aide.[3] The young lieutenant was then twenty years of age, of medium height and robust constitution, with a handsome, intelligent face that gave no hint of the harshness and eccentricity he was to exhibit in later years. He was known as "a gay cheerful companion", fastidious in dress, with courtly manners, a cool and confident air, and an active interest in everything going on about him. Perhaps the "natural selfishness and insolence of character" described by Powell was recognized by some, but Talbot was a great favourite with Governor and Mrs. Simcoe. As a member of their "family" he accompanied them everywhere, and guided them on their walks about the town. His official duties included the writing of Simcoe's first proclamation, dated February 7, 1792, which set forth the rules for granting the Crown lands of Upper Canada.

It was at this time that Talbot came to know James Archibald Stuart, an ensign in the 7th Royal Fusiliers commanded by His Royal Highness the Duke of Kent, which had arrived at Quebec in August, 1791. Stuart-Wortley, as his name became in 1795 after his father inherited the Wortley estates in Yorkshire and Cornwall, was raised to the peerage in 1826 as Baron Wharncliffe of Wortley. In 1791, however, Ensign Stuart was but fifteen years of age, five years younger than Lieutenant Talbot. Nevertheless, a friendship was formed that was to endure until the former's death in 1845; they carried on a correspondence for many years, and on his visits to England Talbot always remained for a time as a guest at Wortley Hall.

The Simcoes and their staff first lived in a house on St. John Street, but in March they moved to a larger one whose back windows overlooked the gardens of the Ursuline Convent. A partition on the second floor was removed to make a room forty-five feet long in which to dance. Adjoining it was a tea room and card room, with a room below for dining. Mrs. Simcoe, finding that Talbot was, as she expressed it, "*au fait* in all those points which give weight in matters of no moment", gave him the management of the etiquette of the house.[4] The lessons learned at the Viceroy's court in Dublin enabled him to carry out his duties to her entire satisfaction.

At last the vexatious delays which had kept the Lieutenant-Governor at Quebec were ended, and the time came to leave for Niagara, which was to be the temporary capital of Upper Canada. Early on the morning of June 8, 1792, the Simcoes with their children and Lieutenants Grey and Talbot walked through the St. Louis Gate and down the hill to the river, where they embarked with their servants and baggage in three large *bateaux*. The long and arduous journey up the St. Lawrence to Kingston did not end until early July, after a stop of ten days at Montreal, and days of walking and riding around the rapids above. Talbot was particularly attentive to Mrs. Simcoe, doing what he could to ease the discomforts and irritations of the trip, as at Cap de la Magdeleine when he gave the owner of some trapped wood pigeons a shilling to release them, because she was disturbed by their frantic efforts to escape. At Rivière du Loup she laughed to see him attempt to paddle a canoe across the river, a bright-coloured handkerchief tied round his head in French-Canadian fashion.[5] It might have been said of him then, as it was later, that he was "the prettiest, the neatest and the most active of the whole party".[6]

Three weeks were spent at the bustling town of Kingston, in the ceremonies incident to the inauguration of the new government. Then the journey was resumed by sailing vessel across Lake Ontario to Niagara. On July 26 they arrived at Navy Hall, a mile or so up the west bank of the river, where a ruinous group of buildings stood near the water, but separated from it by a marshy piece of ground, a breeding-place for malarial mosquitoes. The necessary alterations not having been completed, Simcoe ordered a marquee or field tent set up for himself and family on the hill above Navy Hall, with two others for Lieutenants Grey and Talbot. Long grass and scattered oak bushes covered the hill, which commanded a fine view of the river one hundred feet below, as well as the old French fort occupied by British troops lower down on the opposite side near the lake.

Between Navy Hall and Lake Ontario there were only three habitable houses among a number of "cabbins, skeletons, or ruins", some of which were being repaired for the use of the government officials.[7] A short distance below Navy Hall was the encampment of the Queen's Rangers, soon to be moved to "The Landing" at Queenston. To the south lay a wide tract of land reserved for the Crown, which extended westward as far as the Four Mile Creek; and from this reserve to the great escarpment below the Whirlpool the land had been granted for eight concessions from the river. Only scattered clearings lay along the back concessions, but on the road to the Falls, near the bank of the river, log houses and small clearings were spaced at intervals of less than a mile. Such was the capital of Upper Canada in the summer of 1792. Simcoe planned to establish his permanent capital in the "very heart of the country, upon the River La Tranche", which he had just renamed the Thames. He realized that the future lay in the great peninsula between Lakes Huron, Erie and Ontario, which was still untouched by the axe or plough of the pioneer, except at the eastern and western extremities; north of the River Thames and Burlington Bay on Lake Ontario nearly all of it was still the property of the Indians. Kingston seemed the obvious choice for a temporary capital, as most of the population was concentrated in that region, but Simcoe planned to settle the fertile lands of the southern peninsula with Loyalists, and he wished to be as close as possible to them.

There was much work to be done in building the machinery of government. But there was also time for pleasure, as when the Simcoes and the aides drove in *calèches* up the river road, stopping for breakfast at Robert Hamilton's large stone house at The Landing, and for picnic lunch at Table Rock on the brink of the Falls. Their dining-room at Navy Hall was a large bower made of oak boughs, which one day caught fire and burned to the ground, the only casualties being some of Mrs. Simcoe's new English dishes. Despite this mishap, and the blowing down of the tents during a thunderstorm, the summer passed pleasantly. Talbot and Grey were among those who frequently dropped in to drink

MALAHIDE CASTLE, CO. DUBLIN, IRELAND, c. 1783
From T. Milton *Select Views* 1788-93

tea at the house of Peter Russell, the Receiver-General, and his attractive sister, Elizabeth.[8] Nearly half a century later Talbot spoke of "the summer of 1792 at Niagara, when we were all young and gay".[9]

The first meeting of the Parliament of Upper Canada was held in the fall. People were then arriving daily from the United States to settle in the vicinity of Niagara or Detroit. The Simcoes and their aides had taken up quarters a short time before in Navy Hall, where they dined sumptuously on whitefish which the soldiers caught in the river with nets. In November Talbot went with Colonel Butler to distribute presents to the Indians at Buffalo Creek, and to attend an Indian Council to discuss the matter of a peace between the Indians and the United States. On his return he presented Mrs. Simcoe with a fawn skin and a cake of dried huckleberries, which he had bought from the natives.[10]

Simcoe had informed the Colonial Secretary soon after his arrival at Niagara that he hoped to visit the Thames region before winter set in. He also wished to inspect Long Point on Lake Erie and Toronto Bay on Lake Ontario preparatory to establishing military posts at those places. The press of business, however, prevented him from leaving until February 4, 1793, when he set out by way of the Thames River for Detroit, which was under his jurisdiction, not yet having been handed over to the United States as agreed upon by the treaty of 1783. Accompanied by Lieutenant Talbot and five other officers, as well as a party of soldiers, Simcoe travelled by sleigh to Forty Mile Creek, thence over the "mountain" to Nellis's on the Grand River, and up that river on the ice to the Mohawk Village (Brantford).[11] The Indians greeted them with a salute from their guns, hoisted their flags and trophies, and entertained them for three days. Chief Joseph

Brant and a band of Indians then guided them on foot along the trail through the Burford plains and the forest to the River Thames below the site of Woodstock. Fording the river they followed the trail westward to a point about half way to the "Forks". The trail then turned southwest, crossing the river again and cutting through the woods to the Indian village on the Thames at Delaware. Here the party remained for a day, as guests at an Indian council, before taking the Longwoods trail to the Moravian Indian village thirty miles below. Stopping briefly with the Moravian missionaries and their charges, they then continued down the river. A few miles above the site of Chatham they were pleasantly surprised to be met by a number of men from the new white settlement below, who carried them in carioles to Dolsen's, one of the principal inhabitants, and later to Detroit.

On February 23 Simcoe left Detroit, having spent several days reviewing the 24th Regiment, Talbot's regiment, which was in garrison there, and examining the fort and adjacent country. On the return trip stops were made at Dolsen's and the Moravian village. The fifth night was spent in an abandoned Indian hut below Delaware, where the men ate a supper of pork and venison, and lay down to rest on boughs after singing "God Save the King" as was their custom. Three days later, having followed the river above Delaware, they stopped to examine the "Forks", where Simcoe planned to establish his capital, to be called London. Here one of the officers killed a porcupine, which provided a meal for the hungry travellers—an incident recalled by Talbot nearly sixty years later.[12] At the Grand River the Indians danced for their entertainment, and the officers, attired in Indian dress, were adopted as chiefs.

On this trip Talbot first saw part of the fertile country that was one day to bear his name. The whole region from the Niagara River and Lake Ontario to the lower part of the Thames and Detroit rivers was still an uninhabited wilderness of forest, plain and swamp, except for a few Indian villages and the occasional hut of a trader. The only roads were the Indian trails and the waters of the lakes and rivers. Here was an abundance of rich land, sufficient to form scores of great feudal estates. As a member of the Irish aristocracy, whose wealth and power was based on land, Talbot was stirred by the thought of acquiring an estate for himself. He seems also to have been attracted by the life of a woodsman. He learned from the Indians how to hunt, to cook his meals over an open fire, and to make a shelter for the night with the bark of elm trees.

Soon after his return to Niagara Talbot was employed by Simcoe as an official courier between himself and the British Minister at Philadelphia, bearing letters and oral information too secret to be committed to paper. Towards the end of June he sailed for Miamis Bay at the western end of Lake Erie, a region still under British control, with letters and confidential instructions for the Indian agent, Alexander McKee. On July 7 he attended a council at Navy Hall, where it was decided to have the Indians meet the American commissioners at Sandusky to treat for peace. Named to accompany the deputies of the "Seven Nations", Talbot was forced to remain with his charges for three weeks at Fort Erie, until a ship was available to take them up the lake. Immediately after his return from Sandusky he was despatched on another mission to Philadelphia, and before the end of August he sailed once more for the Miamis. On September 5 he was back with the news that negotiations had been broken off while the American commissioners were still at Detroit, because of the Indians' insistence that the Ohio River should be the boundary between them and the United States.[13]

Talbot played a rather important role in this first attempt to end the conflict between the western Indians and the Americans. On his first trip to the Miamis he bore a letter from Simcoe informing McKee that the young lieutenant was "much in my regard and confidence and is fully instructed in my opinion on many important subjects."[14] Some years later, when Talbot was applying for a grant of land, Simcoe recommended him to the Colonial Secretary in the following words: ". . . he not only conducted many details and important duties incidental to the original establishment of a colony in matters of internal regulations, to my entire satisfaction, but was employed in the most *confidential* measures necessary to preserve that Country in Peace, without violating, on the one hand, the relations of unity with the United States, and on the other alienating the affection of the Indian nations, at that period, in open war with them. In this very critical situation I principally made use of Mr. Talbot for the most confidential intercourse with the several Indian Tribes and occasionally with His Majesty's Minister at Philadelphia; these duties without any salary or emolument, he executed to my perfect satisfaction."[15]

When Talbot returned from the Miamis in September, the Lieutenant-Governor and most of his officials were residing in tents on the shore of Toronto Bay, where a town to be called York was being surveyed. "There is a most magnificent city laid out here which is to be begun in the spring," Talbot wrote to McKee. This was the post that Simcoe had planned; and he now decided to make it the temporary capital of the province. The Executive Council met at York from the end of August through the early part of September for the purpose of receiving petitions for land. On October 12, a month after it suspended operations until the following spring, Lieutenants Grey and Talbot petitioned for grants of one hundred acres of land in the first concession of the Township of York. When the Council met again it was known that Grey and Talbot were about to leave the province, and their petition was never read or acted upon in Council, although their names remained on the Surveyor-General's map for the desired lots for several years.[16]

During the fall of 1793 Mrs. Simcoe and Talbot often rode together on the peninsula at Toronto, racing their horses over the sand, or stopping to pick wild grapes. They also took long walks in the woods, especially in the region of the lovely Don River. There the Simcoes built a summer house, on a steep high bank covered with trees and overlooking the valley of the Don. They moved into it early in 1794 while it was still unfinished, naming it Castle Frank after their young son.[17] Nine years later, long after it had been deserted by the Simcoes, Talbot paid a visit to it and reported that some rascals had recently entered by breaking the shutters on a window, after which they had destroyed the lower part of the chimney in order to steal the supporting iron bar.[18]

In the winter when the ice was hard and clear on the bay and the River Don, Talbot skated, while most of the others went down to watch him. When the weather was mild they went horseback-riding on the sands, or walked through the snow in the woods. One day they went down to the bay to watch the Indians fishing through the ice. While the Governor steadied himself by pushing a large branch of a tree in front of him, Talbot gallantly assisted Mrs. Simcoe across the slippery surface.[19] Not forgetting the comely Elizabeth Russell at Niagara, Talbot sent her, with his respects, "a small tin case containing a most *uncommon* and *beautiful Animal* which was taken in the woods adjacent to York."[20]

On March 17, 1794, a St. Patrick's Day dance was held at Castle Frank. It was also a farewell to the Lieutenant-Governor and his suite, who early the next morning set out for Detroit by way of the Thames River. Simcoe had just received orders from Lord Dorchester to build a fort on the Miamis as a protection against the advance of the American army under General Anthony Wayne, who was carrying on the war against the Indians and showing a disposition to establish American control over the whole region south of the lakes. Simcoe spent several days at Niagara, while Talbot made arrangements with the Iroquois at the Grand River to build canoes by the Thames.[21] When they finally embarked they were carried swiftly down-stream on the waters swollen by the melting snows, through the dense forest and tangled brushwood that crowded close upon the winding river, or past "fertile flats of meadow-land, more thinly wooded with the stately and widely-branching sycamore, and here and there willows and bushes of alder, with the wild vine twining about them".[22] In four days the travellers completed the descent of the river from Oxford to its mouth, skirted the southern shore of Lake St. Clair, and beached their canoes at Fort Detroit. After a short stay there they went on to the Miamis River. The return trip was made on board a sailing ship across Lake Erie.

On May 9, one week after his return to York, Simcoe took his family and aides to Niagara in an open boat. At Burlington Bay a stiff breeze forced them to put ashore for the night, and Talbot exhibited his skill by barking elm trees in the Indian fashion to cover his tent to keep out the falling rain.[23] In the evenings at Niagara he amused himself by paddling his canoe to The Landing, or he drove Mrs. Simcoe up the road while the Governor employed himself in writing. On one of these occasions the gig almost upset when one wheel ran over a cow lying in the road; with his usual confidence Talbot had not turned aside, expecting that the cow would get out of his way. When a sudden thunderstorm came up to drench them Talbot remarked, as Mrs. Simcoe noted in her diary, "that the rain had been the pleasantest mode of taking a shower bath."[24]

By this time Talbot knew that he had been promoted to a captaincy in the 85th Regiment of Foot, which was then stationed in Ireland, but it was not until June 22 that he said good-bye to his friends and sailed for Kingston, on the first stage of his journey to England. Four days later he wrote to Simcoe from Kingston: "Fearing that I might have been somewhat deficient in expressing my gratitude to your Excellency and Mrs. Simcoe on my departure I beg to assure you by a few lines that I felt so sensibly the many obligations that I am under to you that my disposition would not allow me to acknowledge them as I ought, but believe me that I am most unfeignedly thankful and that I shall ever entertain the most sincere interest in every event that concerns you and your family's happiness, and trust that my conduct through life will be such as not to make me unworthy of the continuance of that protection which Your Excellency did me the honor of granting when not personally acquainted with me."[25]

Detained at Kingston for nine days, Talbot found it "many degrees warmer and duller than when I was here before, although I must acknowledge that the Commandant and natives pay me every respect due to my rank and fortune." Three days were spent getting to Montreal, another three days at that place, and five days on a wearisome progress down the St. Lawrence in a sloop to Cape Santé, where he disembarked and completed the journey to Quebec in a *calèche.* He called on Lord Dorchester to secure permission to join his new regiment, and at the same time answered the Governor's queries concerning Simcoe's conduct of affairs in Upper Canada. When he informed Simcoe of all this in a letter dated July 17,[26] Talbot told him, "with infinite pleasure", that he had just learned of his promotion to "the second Majority of Colonel Nugent's Regiment". He was eager to get to England, he wrote, but could not obtain passage for another three weeks. His friends dissuaded him from embarking on a ship that sailed for Lisbon a few days after his arrival at Quebec, because of the danger of capture by the French, and the length of time it would take to reach England. He therefore waited until he could secure a berth on a ship bound for London.

## CHAPTER III

# *The Charter of Liberties*

THE Marquis of Buckingham had worked long and hard to secure a captaincy for his former aide. Early in the year 1792, when war with France was imminent, he undertook to recruit a company for him in Ireland, but finding this a slow and expensive process he asked Lord Amherst, the Commander-in-Chief of the army, to give Talbot a commission in an established company. Although Amherst's reply seemed encouraging months passed without tangible results, and finally the Marquis asked his brother, William Grenville, the Secretary of State for Foreign Affairs, to speak to their relative, Prime Minister William Pitt. Companies were being given "right hand and left to different officers, without any attention to Lieutenant Talbot," Buckingham complained, and unless they could carry this point for him the boy would be "quite undone". He was extremely anxious to secure the commission for Talbot because, as he explained, "my wife presses much for it, and the delay is ruin."

Writing in September, 1793, in reply to the Prime Minister's letter on the subject, Amherst said that he could not advance Talbot in his own regiment over the heads of a captain-lieutenant and two lieutenants who were above him in rank, even if a vacancy should happen to occur, because the regiment was on service abroad and "the successions must go on". This rule did not apply to the regiments stationed in England, but at the moment all were out on active service. Amherst therefore recommended that the Marquis complete the raising of the independent company he had begun, as several others were doing, as the only way to secure a promotion for his protégé. But the Marquis termed this "a heap of nonsense and of falsehood"; the promotion should not have cost him a second letter, "particularly when I stated the strong reason I had to wish, for my wife's sake, that it should be done." But he refused to press Pitt or Amherst further for "this very small civility", and he returned to his original plan of recruiting an independent company, which was completed some weeks later. By this means Talbot secured his captaincy in the 85th Regiment of Foot, which was under the command of Colonel Nugent, a distant relative. His promotion to major came even before he left Canada to join his new regiment.[1]

In September, 1794, Talbot arrived in London with letters of introduction from Simcoe to Colonial Secretary Dundas and Under-secretary King, which described him as capable of supplying any information they needed on Upper Canada.[2] He probably remained there for some days or weeks before joining his regiment, which was fighting the French in Holland. He must have been with the Duke of York's army that winter when it was forced to retreat across the frozen lands between the Zuider Zee and the North German ports, during which thousands of men died of famine and cold. Either at this time or during the campaign of 1799 Talbot received a mild reprimand from the Duke of York for marching his men by a different route from that ordered, to avoid exposing them to what he considered unnecessary danger.[3]

In the spring of 1795 the army was evacuated from Germany to England, and Talbot was sent to do garrison duty at Gibraltar. One year later, having purchased a lieutenant-colonelcy in the 5th Regiment of Foot, he again returned to England.[4] William Dummer Powell stated years later that, during his own visit to London at this time, he was engaged by the person who had sold the commission to Talbot to aid in realizing the price, "which was an equivalent in Commissions in new Corps". The sale of these commissions proved to be so slow and troublesome that the seller's agent told Powell "he hoped never again to have anything to do with Gentlemen!"[5]

Later in this year, 1796, John Graves Simcoe was appointed Governor and Commander-in-Chief of the British possessions in the island of San Domingo in the West Indies. He asked to have Colonel Talbot as his Quartermaster-General, but for some reason the Duke of York refused his consent,[6] and during most of the next three years Talbot remained on routine duty in England, mingling with the fashionable society of London and the royal court. There is, however, some indication that he was the Talbot mentioned by his fellow-officer, Charles Stevenson, in a letter to Peter Russell dated March 7, 1798, as having been taken prisoner by the French while on his way to Upper Canada.[7] In January of that year the Council of Upper Canada had ordered the erasure of his name from the Surveyor-General's map of the Township of York.[8] It is possible that he had set out for Canada in an attempt to save the valuable farm lot reserved for him by Simcoe. He must soon have obtained his freedom, for he was living in the English town of Boston in the spring of 1799.[9]

In September, 1799, Talbot went to Holland in command of the second battalion of the 5th Regiment; on October 10 it was attacked by the French, but it held its position until ordered to retreat. For his part in this action Colonel Talbot was commended by Prince William in a general order.[10] This second campaign in Holland under the Duke of York was as disastrous as the first, and the British army was soon forced to withdraw. Talbot spent one more year in England. Finally, on Christmas Day, 1800, he surprised everyone by selling his commission for the sum of 5,000 guineas and soon after taking ship for America.[11] Before leaving he applied to the Colonial Secretary for a grant of 5,000 acres of land in Upper Canada, but was told that it would be necessary for him to apply to the Lieutenant-Governor of the province.[12]

This decision to quit what appeared to be a most promising career in the army, and to take up the rough and solitary life of a pioneer farmer, occasioned much speculation. There were persistent rumours that he was disappointed in love. It was said with some degree of plausibility that he wished to marry the Princess Amelia, a daughter of King George III, whose exalted station in life precluded such an alliance. Long afterwards one of his settlers, a former employee of the Earl of Ellesmere, stated that Talbot had been a suitor for the hand of Lady Ellesmere before her marriage to the Earl. Talbot was certainly a friend of the Ellesmeres, and visited with them while on a trip to England in 1849.[13] Much has been made of his jocular statement that the only girl he ever loved was one of Sir John Johnson's daughters, whom he had courted at Niagara while aide to Simcoe, and who would not marry him.

The suggestion that Talbot was dissatisfied with his military or political advancement receives some support from an undated letter addressed to him by his sister, Lady Barbara Young, which was probably written not long before he quit the army. In this letter she made reference to some very desirable position which the Duke of Cumberland had obtained for him, although the King favoured another.[14] In the end Talbot failed to get the appointment. Could it have been the position of Lieutenant-Governor of Upper Canada? It is possible that he used his close associations with the royal princes to seek this high honour; and his disappointment when it went to Major-General Peter Hunter in the spring of 1799 may have been one of the reasons why he decided to bury himself in the woods of Upper Canada. Perhaps failure in love and in political advancement both contributed. That the Duke of Cumberland took a keen interest in him is shown by his offer to assist in any way possible the new career that Talbot had chosen.

The Colonel's own explanation for his move, given at various times, was merely that he had become attached to the country while on Simcoe's staff, and that he wished to assist in its settlement and development.[15] In the summer of 1837, in answer to a question asked by Mrs. Jameson, he said lightly that the writer Charlevoix was the true cause of his coming to Upper Canada, because he described the region north of Lake Erie as the "Paradise of the Hurons", and he wished to get to paradise. He then went on, however, to speak bitterly and with scorn of "the follies and falsehoods and restrictions of artificial life",[16]—which lends support to the view that he had suffered some deep hurt and disillusionment with the society of the Old World. This is further strengthened by his letter to the Duke of Cumberland, written in May, 1801, a few weeks after his arrival in Upper Canada, in which he stated: "I am out every morning at Sun-rise in my smock frock felling and burning the Forest to form a farm; could I but be seen by some of my St. James's friends when I come home to my frugal supper—as black as any chimney sweeper—they would exclaim, 'what a dam'd block head you have been, Tom'—but I say, no, as I actually eat my homely fare with more zest than I ever did the best dinner in London. . . ."[17]

In this letter Talbot referred to his arrival in his "favourite settlement", but he did not identify the place except by the words "Skitteewaaba, Upper Canada", at the top of the page. He made it clear that this was not a mailing address by stating that any communications to him from the Duke should be sent to his sister Barbara, who would know how to forward them. This secrecy seems to point to a desire to keep his exact whereabouts unknown even to his friends. He apparently wrote to none of them during this first phase of his retirement, except to the Duke, whose assistance he wished in securing a grant of land. It was not until his return to England in the fall of 1802 that he told Simcoe some of the details of his reception by Lieutenant-Governor Hunter on his arrival at York the previous year. Even then, and in all his subsequent letters, the location of his farm was not given. It has generally been supposed that Skitteewaaba, which is Ojibway for "firewater", was at the mouth of Kettle Creek (now Port Stanley), in the southwest corner of the Township of Yarmouth on Lake Erie. There is, however, no basis for the tradition that he chose this spot for his future settlement while on a trip to Detroit with Simcoe; it is certain that he never visited this region until after he settled in Dunwich in 1803.[18]

There is strong evidence that Skitteewaaba, the name Talbot gave to his farm in 1801, was near the government reserve lying north of Navy Hall and the Town of Newark. The Indian word for firewater may have been originally associated with the foaming Niagara River as it came through the gorge below the Falls. The Colonel knew this region well, and it had become his "favourite settlement" during the years he spent there as Simcoe's secretary. The best evidence of this is his official description in the spring of 1802, as "Thomas Talbot of the Township of Niagara in the County of Lincoln in the District of Niagara".[19] In October of the same year, while in England, he spoke of his "return to Niagara", as though that place was where he had been living.[20] That he was located near the government reserve north of Navy Hall is also indicated by a few brief notes made in his diary during September, 1801, which refer to the loan of his oxen to his neighbour, Billinger, in payment of which he went with William Powers and another servant to collect a load of hay.[21] This appears to be a reference to Michael Bellinger, who at that time owned Lots 68 and 69 in the third concession from the Niagara River, on the edge of the reserve.[22]

Talbot may have leased land either from Bellinger or from others near him, with the expectation of buying it later, or possibly for the purpose of acquiring a knowledge of the business of farming while looking about for a larger tract. Some light appears in a memorandum made at Niagara in May, 1802, by William Dummer Powell, concerning a subversive movement designed "to dissolve the Government and declare the Province part of the U.S." Powell was told that the information about the plot came from John Backhouse, who gave it to Richard Addison and Colonel Talbot, and that the latter took it so seriously that he decided not to buy land in the province.[23] After his return to England the following September Talbot remarked that he could have purchased 15,000 acres from Robert Hamilton, Peter Russell, "or other land jobbers", for the expenses attending his journey there and back—which suggests that he may have considered buying property.[24]

By the middle of May, 1801, when he wrote from Skitteewaaba to the Duke of Cumberland, Talbot was already at work felling and burning trees to form his farm. He spoke of himself as "the once gay Tom Talbot", who was happy with his new life. Confident that his own labour would provide him with the necessities of life, he felt that the small income he possessed would suffice for the few luxuries he desired. Indeed, he said, he looked forward to the enjoyment of every comfort, "excepting that material one, of seeing those I most respect and love."[25] After his return to England a year and a half later he stated that during his stay in Upper Canada he had "remained in perfect retirement, employing myself bona fida in the laborious occupations of a farmer."[26] In a letter to Lord Hobart, some months later, Simcoe noted that he had been "very successful in the cultivation of Hemp on the proper principles and to a greater extent perhaps, than any other settler in the province."[27] As a farmer possessing some capital and a number of hired labourers it was natural that he should have turned to this crop, which the government was attempting to encourage by the payment of premiums and bounties.[28]

On the day that Talbot wrote to the Duke from Niagara, Lieutenant-Governor Hunter arrived back at York from a visit to Quebec. Two days later the Colonel was at York seeking a grant of 5,000 acres of land as a field officer. "I experienced very little disposition on the part of General Hunter to forward my wishes," he informed Simcoe, "and indeed he carried this so far as to grant me with the utmost reluctance the usual quantity of twelve hundred acres in separate lots upon my paying the fees."[29] Talbot selected four lots in Townsend Township, one in Woodhouse Township, and one in Charlotteville Township, all in Norfolk County east of Long Point.[30]

In his letter to the Duke of Cumberland, written two days before, Talbot asked him to procure a royal patent for an entire township, exempt from fees and the obligations of settlement, which the Duke could then transfer to himself. This was all that was necessary to complete his "happiness in this world", he declared. "I flatter myself," he wrote, "that Your Royal Highness will admit that I am as loyal a subject and equally entitled to the Degree of *Hidalgo* as other *adventurers* in a new country." Writing to Simcoe in 1802, he said that his request for an entire township was made because he thought "when I had recourse to so high an authority, that it ought to be for something considerable, sufficient to induce me to prosecute my prospects with spirit, and by affording me the facility of putting those plans in execution, authorize me to look forward with satisfaction to the ultimate establishment of a comfortable and respectable tenantry around me. My great plan was to embark largely in the culture of Hemp, and I flattered myself that such an undertaking would meet with every encouragement from Government."[31]

This plan seemed simple, but as the Duke of Kent commented, Talbot was ignorant "of the difficulty there is for any of His Majesty's Sons to address him with a request of any sort, but more especially of the nature of *that* which *he* points out. . . ." Cumberland therefore turned to Simcoe, who, the Colonel declared, had made a grant to him of 5,000 acres while Lieutenant-Governor of Upper Canada, but had neglected to have the necessary warrants made out to make it official. Simcoe replied that Talbot's services merited such a grant under the principles he had laid down for officers, and that he would have made it as Lieutenant-Governor. "But," he added, "it would appear extra-official and *not* serve him, if I did it without authority. . . . Talbot of course must pay the Fees, the order should be sent from home, and I think forwarded at the Duke of Cumberland's request to the Duke of Kent, stating his being confidentially employed by me, his Military Rank or Services with my confirmation thereof, and the Duke of Kent as Commander in chief, to make application to the Secretary of State."[32]

Acting on this suggestion Kent wrote to the Colonial Secretary asking him to instruct Lieutenant-Governor Hunter to make the grant of a township, on the ground that Talbot's services merited it, and that Simcoe had "omitted doing what was necessary to complete his promise". No distinction was made between the reputed promise of 5,000 acres of land and the present request for a township of ten times that amount or more. Cumberland was extremely anxious, Kent wrote, "that whatever indulgence can be shown Colonel Talbot should be afforded him", but he did not want his own name to appear further in the transaction.[33]

Colonial Secretary Hobart was reluctant to order Hunter to revive, for Talbot's benefit, the old and discredited system of grants of townships to "leaders" and their associates, and the matter was quietly shelved without a definite answer being given. Impatient at the long delay, Talbot set out for England in the fall of 1802 to see what he could do there. Calling first on the Duke of Cumberland, he received from him a letter of introduction to the Colonial Secretary. Lord Hobart received him graciously, "professed great inclination to serve" him, and arranged an interview with Under-secretary John Sullivan, who listened attentively to his views on settlement and appeared to approve most of them. "He went so far indeed," Talbot told Simcoe, "as to propose to me without any suggestion on my part, to take out settlers from this Country. Upon my representing the risk and heavy expense of such an enterprize for an individual, he gave me to understand that Government would probably defray their charges to the place of their destination."[34]

The day following this interview Talbot put his proposals on paper, stressing those points which he thought would be most acceptable to the government. It was important, he wrote, to divert the flow of emigration from the United States to Upper Canada, where it would add to the strength of the Empire rather than that of its enemies. In addition it would check "the growing tendency to insubordination and revolt already manifested by persons brought up in the wilds of America, unaccustomed to any manner of control and ignorant of almost every religious duty." It was essential also to have in the province persons of superior social rank, who could protect the common people from the exactions of their magistrates. Most of the present magistrates lacked the education and "liberality of sentiment" for the proper exercise of their functions, and the best of them were business men who furnished the settlers with necessities at an exorbitant rate, "securing payment by mortgages upon their grants whereby a great portion of the cultivators are held in such subjection that their exertions are much cramped and discouraged."

Lacking the means to bring out emigrants from the British Isles, Talbot planned in the settlement of his township to employ persons who were already in the country but had not yet received Crown lands. He offered, however, in the event the home government would agree to pay their passage and supply them with farm implements, to procure settlers in Britain, take charge of them to their destination, and superintend the distribution of the implements. In return for these services he asked only a free grant of land, so that he might employ all his capital in the cultivation of hemp, on which he solemnly promised to embark to the utmost of his means.[35]

Sullivan agreed to lay these proposals before Lord Hobart; and he suggested that it would be proper for Talbot to give each of his settlers fifty acres of land out of each 200-acre lot, keeping the remainder for himself. But when he next saw Sullivan Talbot was surprised to find him "much cooled in his manner, and without assigning any reason for this change in his sentiments, put every obstacle in the way of compliance" with his proposals. Sullivan had apparently learned for the first time that the British government did not wish to encourage emigration, and that Hobart hesitated to make such large grants to individuals in opposition to the wishes of the provincial government. In addition, Lord Selkirk was also seeking the grant of a township in which to settle Irish or Scottish emigrants, and obstacles having been placed in his path they could not be removed from Talbot's. The most that Hobart might be induced to agree to, Sullivan thought, was Talbot's original request for 5,000 acres. But Talbot was now after a much bigger prize. The fees on such a grant, he said, would be almost as much as the cost of buying the land in a good location; and the expenses attending his trip to England were sufficient to buy three times that amount.[36]

Once again Talbot had to turn to Simcoe and the Duke of Cumberland for help. The Duke promised to approach Prime Minister Addington on his behalf. Simcoe wrote to both the Prime Minister and the Colonial Secretary describing Talbot's services in Canada. In an interview with Lord Hobart in February, 1803, Simcoe attempted to meet all the objections to Talbot's grant. He said that the Colonel knew of some 1,000 Welsh and Scottish families in New York State who had emigrated in the summer of 1801, several of whom wished to return under British rule but lacked the means to buy land or even to pay the fees on government grants. These people would be glad to remove to Talbot's township, where they would each receive fifty acres free of fees or other expense. Once settled they would attract their friends from the United States, as well as most of those who would emigrate later from Great Britain. Thus emigration would not be encouraged; it would merely be diverted from the United States to Canada.

Talbot had learned by this time that a large part of the Township of Houghton, which he had first sought, was reserved for the support of schools, and he now asked for a grant of 5,000 acres in Yarmouth, the next township to the west, with a reservation of the remainder of the township, to be granted to him at the rate of 200 acres for each family to whom he assigned fifty acres—all of these lands to be subject to half fees only, which he would pay. His object, Simcoe told Hobart, was to grow hemp, and to encourage its cultivation throughout the township. He hoped also to develop by precept and example the principles of loyalty, obedience, and private industry among his settlers.[37]

In a despatch dated February 15, 1803, and addressed to Lieutenant-Governor Hunter, Lord Hobart outlined the terms of an arrangement with Talbot. He was to receive an outright grant of 5,000 acres of land in Yarmouth or any other available township he might select. At the same time "a proportion of the said Township immediately contiguous" to this grant was to be reserved "for the present", for the future appropriation to him of "a further quantity at the rate of two hundred acres for every family he may induce to settle there either from the Continent of Europe or America, provided he shall have surrendered fifty acres of his Original Grant" to each such family.[38]

At first glance this "charter" might seem to convey all that Talbot had asked for; but actually it was worded in such a manner as to alter and seriously limit the system as proposed by him. His settlers had to be placed on fifty-acre farms within his original grant of 5,000 acres, which limited their number to one hundred. Instead of the remainder of the township only a "proportion", or 20,000 acres, was reserved for him; he would receive this after giving up all his original grant. What he had sought was 5,000 acres and an additional two hundred acres for each settler that he placed on fifty acres in the reserve, until the whole township was exhausted, which would give him a personal estate of at least 50,000 acres. Besides, because the government did not wish to encourage emigration from Great Britain, his settlers could not be drawn from there, but had to come from the continents of Europe and America. Finally, no mention was made of any reduction in the established fees; and Hobart's reference to Talbot's plans for the cultivation of hemp implied that the arrangement was made chiefly for that purpose.

Having given in to the pressure exerted on Talbot's behalf, the Colonial Office could no longer resist Lord Selkirk's proposals. Two weeks later a similar agreement was made with the Earl; but there were a number of important differences. Selkirk's original grant was 1,200 acres of land in any unappropriated township that he might select. The "remainder" of the township was to be reserved for five years only; and his settlers were not restricted in origin and did not have to be placed on his original grant. The only requirement was that he must surrender fifty acres of land to each family that he brought into the province, before claiming an additional two hundred acres in right of each.[39] It was this arrangement that Talbot had sought in vain from Hobart but which he was eventually to acquire from a later Colonial Secretary.

CHAPTER IV

# *Founding the Talbot Principality*

LIEUTENANT-GOVERNOR HUNTER received Colonel Talbot coldly and did not attempt to conceal his displeasure when the Colonel arrived at York about May 1, 1803, to present Lord Hobart's despatch to him. He announced that he was left with no discretion in the matter of the grant, but that Talbot would find his support of considerable assistance in the carrying out of his plans. This support, Hunter said, would not be forthcoming if Talbot should persist in the manner of life he had formerly led in the province, "to *cook your own dinner and wear a smock frock* practicing all the menial offices of a Peasant. Such a mode of life might suit a Republic but is not fitted to a Monarchical Government."

Smiling at this pompous speech, Talbot nevertheless replied respectfully but firmly that however much he valued the Governor's protection and support he would have to "forego both sooner than relinquish a talent which Heaven had" most liberally endowed him with—the ability to cook a good dinner. He lamented the suggestion "that the possession of a disposition and genius to furnish within myself the requisites of an Infant Country was incompatible with the duties I owed my King." He concluded by assuring the Governor that he "would continue to cook or do any other work that I might find necessary through life without considering for a moment the light in which it might be seen by His Excellency or the world at large."

"This determined language," Talbot informed Simcoe, "had the desired effect, and from the harsh, vulgar Northern Chief he became sweetly serene, professed the warmest friendship for me, nothing that could possibly be done for me he would not do, ordered the Surveyor's office to be at my disposal, promised that all recommendations of mine should be attended to, and that whenever any troops were to be discharged, that he would not only acquaint me therewith but recommend to them to become settlers on my land. What return could I make for so much kindness, but condescend to accept the Lieutenancy of a County, the Command of the Militia and Judge of the District Court, etc., so that you are now my dear General aware of the growing consequence of your correspondent."[1]

Having found that most of Yarmouth and Southwold—like Houghton—was already granted or reserved for the support of schools, Talbot decided to accept the southern halves of Dunwich and Aldborough, the next townships to the west. He informed Simcoe that the area available to him extended twenty-one miles along the coast of Lake Erie and was about nine miles in depth, which was a larger tract than that contained in a single township. Some time later, however, he discovered that the unsettled parts of Dunwich and Aldborough were not as large as he had thought; consequently Dunwich was widened by moving its boundary eastward to take from Southwold a strip three lots wide from the Thames River to Lake Erie, while Aldborough was widened in the same way at the expense of Orford on the west, by a strip four lots wide. Although Hobart's despatch had indicated that a reservation of 20,000 acres was all that was necessary, Talbot succeeded in tying up three times that amount.

After a week at York the Colonel departed for Niagara, accompanied by his servant, Corporal William Powers, two hired men named Patrick Whealand and George Crane, and Deputy Surveyor William Hambly. Another hired man, Samuel Rogers, was engaged at Niagara, and a few days later all set out by boat for Dunwich. On May 21, as captain of his little "Mayflower", Talbot directed his men to row into a small harbour at the mouth of a creek near the eastern boundary of the township. The French had called this stream the Rivière de Tonti in honour of La Salle's lieutenant, who probably encamped there in 1679 during his passage up the lake in a canoe. In 1765 the trader John Porteous, travelling in a *bateau* along this shore, noted that the "River Tentin" had "a fine opening to eastward with a very good beach". For miles on both sides the high clay banks of the lake, broken occasionally by small runs and gulleys, or by larger creeks such as Kettle Creek eight miles to the east, rose perpendicularly from the waves a hundred feet or more. Three miles to the west of the River Tentin or Tonti the shore curved out in a wide sweep to Pointe au Fort (now Plum Point), which Porteous described as "a double Point very high with a small creek and beach in the middle."[2] Inland the unbroken forest clothed the steep banks of the ravines and the rolling hills.

Talbot's choice of this creek, which soon came to be known as the Colonel's or the Talbot Creek, as the site of his future home, was made primarily on the advice of William Hambly, who had surveyed the township and was impressed with the beauty of the place. Well satisfied with what he saw on this delightful spring day, when the stream ran wide and deep, and the towering trees on the hills above seemed to touch the sky with their green branches, the

Colonel decided to look no further. Climbing up the western side of the steep ravine he ceremoniously cut down the first tree on the top of the cliff which overlooked the lake. During the next few days a space was cleared, and then a small log house was built. "Where I have fixed my residence," Talbot informed Simcoe in a letter dated July 17, 1803, "is six miles to the westward of Kettle Creek in Dunwich in a fine Bay where vessels can come to an anchor with safety within 20 yards of the shore. The site of my hut is elevated 150 feet above the water having a view of the Lake in front; on my left flank a beautiful river flows and empties itself into the Bay navigable for large boats 3 miles and for a short distance a sufficient depth for vessels, but like the other Rivers on these Lakes is shut up with sand when the wind blows strong into the Bay. However it is the opinion of many that have been here, that by a trifling expense the mouth could be kept open enough to admit vessels."[3]

The Colonel called the place Port Talbot. "Mark the sound of the capital," he wrote, "is it not grand?" It was the capital of what he now called, for the first time, his "principality", no idle term in the light of his successful struggle through the years ahead to maintain for the Talbot Settlement a position that was almost independent of the provincial government. But his fief was as yet only an uninhabited wilderness. The nearest white settlement on the east was forty miles away at Charlotteville, beyond Long Point. Westward, the forest clothed the shore almost to the mouth of the Detroit River. Settlement along the Thames River had not yet advanced above the Moravian village in Kent County, or below Oxford Township on its upper reaches—except at Delaware Village, about twenty miles northeast of Port Talbot by Indian trail. At points the trail was so indiscernible that in December of this year the Colonel became lost while returning by land from Niagara. He wandered for five days, the last three without food, in the forest south of Delaware, before he was rescued by a band of Indians.[4] Failing to have the winter expresses that passed through Delaware carry his mail to Port Talbot, he had it addressed to Moses Brigham at the former place.[5]

While William Hambly surveyed the lots that Talbot selected in two blocks about his home, the work of clearing the land went forward rapidly, with the aid of two new men, William Caffry and Daniel Walker. By July 17, when he wrote to Simcoe, several parties of applicants had come to see the tract and inquire about the terms of settlement, and Talbot was confident that his colony would make "a formidable figure" before a year had passed. His friend Charles Broke wrote from England in answer to his enthusiastic letter: "The picturesque beauty of your castle view is quite enchanting. I should like, were the fates so to will it, to see you in your domain. By the time that happens the woods will have yielded to Husbandry and the Lord of the Country, with nature for his Artist, will have perfected the beauty of his place."[6]

While at Niagara on business in the fall of 1803, Talbot met Lord Selkirk. He told the Earl that four or five settlers had already promised to come, and he expressed optimism for the future; but Selkirk found others who thought that his offer of fifty acres of land would "be no great temptation and will not bring him Settlers—none will be satisfied with so small an allotment unless they have the promise of more on fixed terms."[7] To overcome this difficulty in the settlement of his own townships of Dover and Chatham, Selkirk was bringing out a group of poor families from Scotland, who had bound themselves to work a number of years on his personal farm on the Chenail Ecarté, in return for their passage to Canada and the promise of a gift of fifty acres of land, and the opportunity to buy more on reasonable terms, at the end of their period of indenture.[8]

Talbot soon realized that he would be unable to attract settlers to his isolated part of the province unless he provided mills for their convenience. On June 4, 1804, while on a visit to Niagara, he wrote to Simcoe:[9]

> I have remained almost constantly at Port Talbot, actively employed in clearing land and laying the foundation of a great settlement, and which I have every reason to think will, in the course of a very few years make as distinguished a figure in population and wealth as any other Township in Upper Canada. But to forward these expectations I am under the immediate necessity of sinking for the present more than £2,000 in the erection of Saw and Grist Mills, as I found that the first enquiry of those disposed to become Settlers was, "When they could depend upon having the convenience of Mills"; and in fact it is a matter of great moment to the farmer, to have the means of converting his produce into a merchantable state contiguous to the place of his residence.
>
> The further I explore my estate and consider the natural advantages that Port Talbot derives from being so placed between Lake Erie and the River Thames as that the traverse from water to water does not exceed ten miles, the more I am satisfied with my *pitch*; and to establish its fame, I am now waiting the arrival at Fort Erie of His Majesty's Ship Camden (the largest vessel on the lakes) in order to pilot her in person to Port Talbot.

The Colonel had gone to York the previous month to secure patents for the 5,000 acres of land that he had chosen for himself in the southeast corner of Dunwich.[10] Before leaving York he purchased from the government stores the machinery for his mills. Late in June he went to Niagara and hired a woman named Ann Lawler to assist his housekeeper, Mrs. Powers; at the same time he engaged a carpenter named James Whitten, and his apprentice, James Newlands, who began work on a larger log house, which was completed that fall. Work on the mills then began, and these were finished two years later.[11]

In the meantime, Selkirk's first settlers from Scotland arrived in the summer of 1804. In June Talbot informed Simcoe that he knew nothing of the Earl's plans, but that he had heard unfavourable accounts of the low and marshy tract in Dover.[12] It is probable, however, that he knew of Selkirk's plans to build a road along the north shore of Lake Erie, for the surveyor Augustus Jones had explored for the road during the winter.[13] On August 30 Selkirk presented to the government a proposal to open a road all the way from York to Amherstburg along the southern route, in return for a grant of land three concessions deep on both sides. His plan was to have most of the work done by settlers, who would be given lots on the road subject to this obligation. Lieutenant-Governor Hunter at first expressed himself in favour of the project; but on September 18 it was rejected in Council.[14]

Selkirk was greatly disappointed at this unexpected check to his designs, the more so because the Council on the very next day approved a report recommending that a new road be built with government funds approximately on the route planned by him.[15] The report had been drawn up by Colonel Talbot, William Spurgin, John Bostwick, and Nathan Barnum, all living in the Long Point or Port Talbot regions, who were among the commissioners appointed the previous April to superintend the expenditure of £250 on the existing east-west highway along the Thames River in the London District. After describing the disadvantages of the northern route, they strongly advised spending the money on a new and "infinitely more eligible" route estimated to be thirty miles shorter. Beginning at the eastern boundary of the Gore of Burford (now Oakland Township), it would follow a good road leading south to Sayles Mills in Townsend, thence along an old Indian trail north of Long Point and through the townships along Lake Erie to the western boundary of Aldborough, where it would turn north to the Thames River Road near the Moravian village. The commissioners also recommended that Colonel Talbot be given charge of the money appropriated for the road, and that he hire men by the month rather than contracting for the work to be done.

Talbot began the work immediately after the acceptance of the report, and by the early part of 1806 all the money was expended,[16] although the road through the unsettled townships west of Long Point was still far from complete. As no additional government funds were forthcoming what had been spent appeared in danger of being wasted, and Port Talbot, which might have been linked to the settlements on the east and west under Selkirk's plan, remained isolated, attracting few settlers. It was not until three more years had passed that the Colonel was able, under a system remarkably like Selkirk's, to revive the project of the road that was to bear his name.

The four settlers who had promised to settle in Dunwich arrived in September, 1805, adding to the population that had previously consisted of the farm workmen, carpenters, and house servants at Port Talbot. Probably most of these had large families, so that the Colonel may not have exaggerated in his letter to James Stuart-Wortley in December, when he said that his "subjects" numbered about one hundred souls. He then had forty-three acres of land sown in wheat, and was clearing another forty acres to be ready in the spring for the planting of Indian corn, barley, and potatoes. These crops, he estimated, would bring him a return of £400. The grist mill, which had cost much less than expected, would be ready for grinding by fall, and then the great expense of bringing in provisions from Long Point for his settlers and for his own household would be ended; and by the time he had forty industrious settlers about him the mill would produce an income of at least £225. Optimistic as always, he expected to have an annual income of £1,000 from his mills and farm within two more years. Most of this he would save, he wrote, "as my Farm will furnish every necessity excepting Wines and Groceries, and the former I am not without my expectation of making at home as the soil and climate appear most genial to the Vine, but to enjoy all these blessings a person must divest himself of the Society of the Great World and feel the inward gratification that *I do* of being the founder of this little Empire."

Elsewhere in this letter Talbot expressed his satisfaction with the new life that he had chosen for himself. "The fact is," he told Stuart-Wortley, who was now a Tory member of the British Commons from the family borough of Bossiney, "that you are growing so bad in England that had I but the power of drawing your house and a very few of my other friends to this country, I never would feel the least inclination to cross the Atlantic. I frequently flatter myself in my solitary rambles through *my* Forests that the downfall of Great Britain will some day throw you within reach of this place, for as far as life can be peaceable I enjoy it, and the

A ROAD IN THE TALBOT SETTLEMENT, c. 1838
From the painting by P. J. Bainbrigge, courtesy Public Archives of Canada

more I labour the more I become attached to the spot I have chosen for my retreat.[17] Perhaps he was whistling to keep up his courage and to convince his friends that he did not regret his move, but some of his letters in much later years sound the same note of disillusionment with the political and social scene in England, and on the continent, where the French Revolution and then Napoleon had arisen to disturb the established order. At the same time his own empire-building engaged his interest, and the future of his adopted country appeared bright.

Wortley replied that by the time he should be forced to emigrate he supposed Talbot's farm would present a model for all to copy, and "the border of Lake Erie as highly cultivated as the banks of the Tweed".[18] But in the meantime, the Colonel had few comforts, and he lived in a way hardly to be distinguished from that of the meanest farmer. Amelia Harris as a child saw him about this time, and in later life wrote the following account: "When in the Army he was looked upon as a dandy, but my first impressions would place him in a very different light. He had come to Port Ryerse with a boat-load of grain to be ground at my Father's mill. The men slept in the Boat with an awning over it and had a fire on shore. In the front of this fire Col. Talbot was mixing bread in a pail to be baked in the ashes for the men. I had never seen a man so employed and it made a lasting impression upon my childish memory. My next recollection of him was his picking a wild Goose which my father had shot, for my mother to dress for dinner."[19]

Although the Colonel usually had women in his household who could perform such tasks there were times when he had to do them himself, and he delighted to boast of his ability to make the bread and butter, milk the cows, and act as a servant for his own hired men. He once told an anecdote concerning one of his settlers named John Barber, a strict Presbyterian who came to Port Talbot each Saturday evening to remain until Monday morning, doing little except to read his Bible and help the Colonel make their week's supply of bread. One Saturday evening in the fall of 1809, as Talbot related it, "Johnny did not arrive at Port Talbot, as usual, by sunset, and I began to fear all was not right with him. I prepared some food, and carried it through the woods to Johnny's shanty of bass-wood bark, where I found him hale and sound. To my question, why he did not come home as usual, I received for reply, that he had worked till sunset on the Saturday, and of course, would not break the Sabbath by walking to Port Talbot. I cursed him for his prejudice, threw down the provisions, entreated him not to overwork himself any more on the Saturday, as he was fool enough to starve, in preference to coming home as he ought to do."[20]

Colonel Talbot made application for 1,200 acres of land in right of his first six settlers, under the arrangement with Lord Hobart, on April 3, 1806. It was perhaps fortunate for him that Lieutenant-Governor Hunter had died the previous fall, and that the easy-going Alexander Grant, president of the Executive Council, was administrator of the province. Talbot received his grant without any vouchers except six certificates signed with the settlers' names, stating that each had received fifty acres of a certain lot within the Colonel's 5,000-acre domain.[21] Thus the precedent was established of accepting his settlers without requiring their personal appearance before the Council, and without check upon their eligibility.

The certificates indicate that Talbot's first settler was Charles Scarlet, who was located on part of Lot 18 in the 11th concession of Dunwich on September 2, 1805. He was followed by Mark Chase, John Craford, James Whitten (the carpenter), John Dunbar Davis, and Daniel Kingsland, who received parts of the lots numbered 17 to 20 in the same concession, just west of Port Talbot. But the local registry office, established in 1811, contains no record of these transactions; all the lands involved remained in the Colonel's name until his death, with the exception of three sales made in 1823 and 1824. There is evidence that the six men named were living at Port Talbot at this time, but by the close of the War of 1812 all had moved away. Two of them, Mark Chase and John Craford, settled on farm lots in Kent County. Thus none of these first settlers was a permanent acquisition to the settlement. The suspicion arises that they were fictitious settlers, perhaps the Colonel's employees, who were used by him to acquire more land for himself and to save his monopoly of Dunwich and Aldborough. At a time when two hundred acres of land could be obtained by application at York, and the payment of the fees, it was difficult to find men who had not yet received any Crown land and who were willing to accept fifty acres in bar of any future grant. But Talbot's influence with the provincial government, and his unchecked power over the granting of Crown land outside his two townships, which he acquired a few years later, made it possible for him to reward the people who did his bidding. Some of his own employees might be willing to accept his fifty-acre lots, do some work on them in their spare time, and sell them back to him later, when they found that he would give them a two-hundred-acre lot in some other township.

Several more settlers were recorded by Talbot during 1806, but of his purported gifts of land to them only those to Joseph Smith, his foreman, and William Crane, are recorded in the registry office. Through Talbot's influence with Lieutenant-Governor Gore, Smith also obtained grants of several hundred acres of the Crown lands.[22] After 1806, when Talbot placed his settlers on his recent acquisitions outside his original grant, nearly all his gifts of land are registered. It seems clear that he was determined, despite Lord Hobart's despatch, to keep his original 5,000-acre block practically intact—that he had no intention of giving it all away in order to secure less desirable lands within the reserve. Until the outbreak of war in 1812 he had claimed 5,400 acres in right of twenty-seven settlers, but in return for this cost to the province it failed to profit by the permanent establishment of even half of these persons.

No comment was made by the Council in the spring of 1807 when the certificates produced by the Colonel showed that half of a second group of ten settlers were not placed on his original grant.[23] He had, however, complied with Hobart's instructions to the extent of giving these settlers title to fifty-acre lots. It was in this respect that Lord Selkirk failed to satisfy the Council one month later, when he applied for 2,800 acres in right of fourteen families that he had brought over from Scotland. Having only 1,200 acres of his own, which he kept as his personal farm, he had established his settlers on land reserved but not yet granted to him, so that he was unable to give them titles. It was not until a year had passed that the Council finally granted him the land.[24]

In the fall of 1808 Judge William Dummer Powell became a member of the Executive Council. During that and the following year Talbot acquired an additional 2,200 acres of land in right of eleven settlers.[25] Many years later, after his final break with the Colonel, Powell wrote:[26]

> At the period of Mr. Powell's admission into the executive Council his duty first led him to any concern with Mr. Talbot's land affairs, when upon his application for a Grant to be made to him in compensation, Mr. P[owell] as a man of business requested to be informed on the subject he was called to advise on, and finding that the proceeding had been too loose to justify he suggested first, that the land to be conveyed to settlers to entitle Col. Talbot to compensation was limited to parcels of his original Tract of 5000 acres and consequently limited his compensation to 20,000 acres. This construction was over ruled chiefly on the ground that it had not hitherto been adhered to, and in consequence the limit to Colonel Talbot's demand became the quantity of land reserved in the Townships of Dunwich and Aldborough amounting to sixty five thousand acres.
>
> The second suggestion of Mr. Powell was that some assurance beyond the certificate of Colonel Talbot should be required by the Board of the actual conveyance of fifty acres to a settler, before it assented to the grant in remuneration and as there is a registry of all liens upon lands in every county it was proposed to require the certificate of the registry of such conveyance, which was the only security to the settler from any future act of Col. Talbot or his heirs.
>
> This was thought reasonable and adopted but Colonel Talbot found means to evade it. . . .

Talbot held many important offices in the London District. Soon after his arrival in 1803 he was appointed a justice of the peace and Lieutenant of the County of Middlesex, an important position containing the charge of the local militia. Three years later he was named one of the commissioners for administering the oath of allegiance to half-pay officers. In 1807 he became a trustee for the public schools in the London District, and a commissioner to carry into effect "An Act for better securing this province against all seditious attempts or designs to disturb the tranquillity thereof."[27] In 1810, as one of the commissioners appointed the previous year to purchase hemp, he received from the Receiver-General the sum of £100 for the purpose.[28] He appears to have taken most of his duties seriously, except those associated with the Legislative Council and the office of magistrate. Probably the only occasions on which he ever attended the general quarter sessions of the peace at Charlotteville were in 1806 and 1815. It is said that he never issued a warrant for an arrest; and it is uncertain whether or not he ever attended the court of requests for Middlesex, to which he was appointed in 1807. His activities as a magistrate were confined to administering oaths and taking testimony, and in the early years performing marriages for his settlers.

Lieutenant-Governor Gore was a visitor at Port Talbot for a time during his tour of the western part of the province in the summer of 1806. The friendly relations established at that time prompted him to recommend that Talbot be appointed to the Legislative Council.[29] Although Viscount Castlereagh made the appointment in September, 1809, giving the Colonel the coveted title of "Honourable", Talbot appears never to have attended the meetings of the Legislative Council. This may have been the result of his disappointment at not having been appointed to the Executive Council as well—a desirable position for him because this body controlled the granting of the Crown lands. In 1804 he had written to Simcoe: "Mr. Alcock is very desirous that I should become a Legislative Councillor and that I should request of you to recommend me to the Secretary of State for the Colonies for that situation, as he wishes to check the *Scotch* faction. I must beg to observe, that I do not like working for nothing, and that if you should think it advisable to recommend me, that I would also wish to be recommended for an Executive Councillor, as the £100 is as well to have as not."[30] As late as 1817 it was rumoured that Talbot had sent for his commission with the intention of attending the Legislative Council, but there is no evidence that he ever took his seat.[31]

CHAPTER V

# *The Talbot Roads*

May 21, 1808, marked the end of the fifth year of the Colonel's residence at Port Talbot. During those five years he had been able to establish only twenty settlers on his lands; and the cultivation of hemp, which was a primary purpose of his grant, had been almost forgotten. The Earl of Selkirk's experiment in Dover and Chatham had been limited to five years; and the term would not be extended. Lord Hobart's despatch had limited the period of Talbot's agency only by the phrase "for the present", but he had been little more successful than the Earl, and the Executive Council was considering the advisability of recommending that the reserve lands in Dunwich and Aldborough be thrown open to general settlement.[1]

To forestall this threatening action Talbot approached Lieutenant-Governor Gore in February, 1809, with a scheme for completing the road from Long Point to Dunwich, on which he had expended the government money a few years before. He pointed out that this would not only connect his settlement with the eastern part of the province and thus attract settlers, but it would enhance the value of the school reserves in the townships of Middleton, Houghton, Yarmouth, and Southwold, through which it would pass. His plan was to employ the system used successfully on Yonge Street by Simcoe: settlers placed on lots along the line of the road would be obligated to clear it of timber and make it passable for vehicles. To do this the reserves would have to be removed from a range of lots on each side and placed somewhere else.[2]

Although impressed by the Colonel's arguments, Gore feared that the Council would oppose a measure which would cause delay in the taking out of patents and the payment of fees until the completion of the settlement duties. However, William Dummer Powell was soon won over to the view that it would be "beneficial not merely to Colonel Talbot but to the purposes of the Reserve", and it was he who "suggested, advocated, and finaly [*sic*] carried an order of the Governor in Council", dated February 15, 1809, for the road.[3] It was also provided that the Lieutenant-Governor should appoint two commissioners, whose duties were to determine the exact route of the road and to see that each settler performed the prescribed work within two years of his location. The commissioners' reports would determine whether a settler would receive his patent at the end of two years or be deprived of his lot.[4]

The Lieutenant-Governor at once appointed Robert Nichol of Port Dover (near Long Point), and Colonel Talbot,[5] as unpaid commissioners, and directed the Surveyor-General to begin the survey of the road. Many years later Talbot stated that he undertook this arduous assignment at Gore's suggestion, and "for the benefit of this part of the country, in order to prevent improper characters from getting possession of the Crown Lands and to see that each Lot should be occupied by an actual settler, having been aware of the serious injury that many parts of this Province has sustained in consequence of Individuals holding large tracts, who never intended to be actual settlers, and by which means the extents they own remain unimproved, so that the Roads, a primary object of importance, cannot be worked to any general advantage."[6]

Deputy Surveyor Mahlon Burwell surveyed the line of the road, with a range of lots on each side, from Dunwich to Middleton, during the summer and fall.[7] On December 6 he came before the Council with his plan of the road—soon to be known as the Talbot Road East—as well as with petitions signed by Daniel Rapelje, David Mandeville, and himself, asking for grants there. At Talbot's request the Surveyor-General reserved certain lots for them in Yarmouth and Southwold; a few days later warrants of location were issued for these lots, the first to be located on the Talbot Road.[8]

In March of the next year the Colonel was visited by Simon Zelotes Watson, a surveyor from Montreal, who spent several days at Port Talbot enjoying the "great hospitality and friendship" of his host. Watson was engaged in exploring the London District for a suitable place in which to form a settlement of his followers from Lower Canada, Lieutenant-Governor Gore having promised each of them the usual two hundred acres of land, and up to 1,200 acres for Watson himself.[9] It was doubtless on the advice of the Colonel that Watson now chose the southern part of the township of Southwold, adjoining Dunwich on the east, and suggested to the Council that his settlers could be used on the Talbot Road there, as well as between it and the lake. However, because this tract was largely reserved for the schools, the Council recommended "that a Road should be made through the Township of Westminster, and Settlement Duties performed by the said Mr. Watson and his followers, for the making of that Road", under the same conditions as applied for the Talbot Road.[10] Watson accepted this arrangement, and was appointed a deputy surveyor to lay out two concessions for his people south of the River Thames in Westminster, a township situated to the north of Southwold and Yarmouth.

By the end of June Watson had completed the survey, and he returned to Port Talbot for another visit of three days.[11] Delighted with the "friendly attention" he received there, he asked his host if there was any way in which he could be of service to him. Talbot replied that it would help him greatly if Watson could bring in enough settlers for the Talbot Road as well as for his tract in Westminster. Watson said this would not be difficult if he were permitted to bring in settlers from the United States. The Colonel assured him that Americans made excellent settlers, and had always been welcomed in Upper Canada. "We then agreed," Watson testified later, "that all my Lower Canadian followers, as well as those I might engage in the States, should be informed by me of the Tracts on the two Streets, and be at liberty to settle on which they pleased until the whole was occupied."[12]

Talbot was unaware that the government considered Watson bound to employ only those people whom he should bring in from Lower Canada, or that Watson required each settler to give him a bond for $100, out of which he would pay the land fees of $37.50, keeping the remainder for himself. Thus Talbot was placed in the position of being a partner in a speculative scheme which reflected adversely upon his honour. What proved particularly embarrassing to him was a letter he wrote for Watson at this time, designed to be shown to prospective emigrants from the United States to encourage them to come to the London District, and which Watson employed to prove that Talbot was his partner in a mercenary enterprise.[13]

On August 10, 1810, a few weeks after Watson's visit to Port Talbot, an order-in-council greatly enlarged the duties of the commissioners for the Talbot Road.[14] It was, no doubt, at the Colonel's request that Chief Justice Thomas Scott, chairman of the land committee of the Council, had written to Lieutenant-Governor Gore:

> The Committee of Council are anxious that no delay should take place in the settlement of the Road which is to pass thro' the lands reserved for the Schools, but a standing order requiring the personal appearance of such Persons as petition for grants of 200 acres from the Crown, stands in the way.
>
> I therefore suggest if your Excellency thinks fit, that you refer to the Committee to consider whether from the great respectability of the Commissioners appointed for that Road, and the very great distance of the place of Settlement from the seat of Government, the above standing order with respect to such persons as have obtained their Recommendation might not be dispensed with.

Gore complied at once, and the order was passed the same day. Thus the commissioners, whose duties had consisted solely of supervising the performance of the settlement duties, were now empowered to interview and select the settlers for the Road, as Talbot did for those in Dunwich and Aldborough. The Council could not have foreseen the manner in which Talbot would use this prerogative of the government to magnify his authority, until he became almost independent of the provincial officials. But the concession had the immediate and desired effect of hastening the opening of the Talbot Road.[15]

The two commissioners were by no means equal. Some years later Nichol asserted that for nearly four years as commissioner he had had "a great deal of trouble, while Colonel

Talbot received *all* the credit", and he himself "received nothing but blame". His chief duty, Nichol said, was to receive the fees, while the Colonel kept for himself the task of selecting and locating the applicants for land. At that time the fees had to be paid to the Receiver-General at York as soon as the settlers' petitions, endorsed with Talbot's recommendation, were laid before the Council. Nichol resigned as commissioner during the War of 1812, but the difficulty experienced by dispossessed settlers in getting a refund of their fees caused him embarrassment for several years.[16] After the war, when Talbot was the sole commissioner, he stopped collecting the fees, which were not paid by the settlers until they had completed their settlement duties and were ready to apply for their patents.

In February, 1811, during his customary winter visit to York, Talbot proposed to the Lieutenant-Governor that his road should be continued westward from Dunwich to the Detroit River, and that it should be connected with Watson's settlement by a northern extension through Southwold and Westminster. He also suggested, solely for the purpose of seeing that the settlement duties were performed, that the new townships of Bayham and Malahide (formed from the western part of Houghton), as well as all the unreserved and unlocated lots in Yarmouth, should be put under his superintendence on the same plan as the lots on the Talbot Roads.[17] Gore consented to these proposals; and on February 12, without submitting the matter to the Council for its approval, he ordered Surveyor-General Ridout to proceed with the survey of the new roads—Talbot Road West and Talbot Road North—and to furnish the Colonel with a list of the vacant lots in Yarmouth, which were to be reserved for persons recommended by him.[18] But, unfortunately for Talbot,

Gore's written directions to Ridout did not mention Bayham and Malahide, and Gore left the province in the fall without bringing any of Talbot's proposals before the Council.

It was while he was in York on this business that Talbot first learned of Watson's speculation with his settlers, and of the requirement that they had to be from Lower Canada. During the previous August and September Watson had travelled nearly 700 miles through the eastern part of the United States, searching for settlers. He then went to the Montreal District to explain his plans to his followers there. A few went on with him to settle in the Westminster tract, but most decided to wait until the spring. When Watson arrived in York on personal business about the middle of February he was astonished to learn of the change in Talbot's attitude towards him. "I was informed by a friend," he testified some weeks later, "that the Colonel had reported that I was settling the Tract ordered to myself and followers in Westminster with people belonging to this Province; that I was speculating on the Crown Lands; that I had no right to settle any person but those who came direct from Lower Canada, and that none of my followers should pay me anything for the time and money I had spent or might expend in Settling and obtaining Titles for them."[19]

Going to the Colonel's lodgings, Watson held a lengthy and sometimes heated discussion with him, at the end of which it was agreed that Talbot would pass upon the Westminster settlers, with the consent of the Council, in the same way he did his own. The Council at first insisted that Watson could not make use of immigrants from the United States, but this limitation did not appear in the order that finally issued, and Talbot agreed that it gave him authority to approve Americans for the Westminster tract. Convinced that his troubles were over, Watson departed for Ancaster, where he remained for some days before going on to his settlement.[20]

Not long after Watson had taken leave of him Talbot also left for home, travelling by way of Westminster, where he stopped to tell the settlers "that no extraordinary charges are to be imposed upon them, as His Majesty will in every instance prevent all manner of speculation upon the Crown Lands."[21] Watson complained that he told the settlers "not to pay me a farthing for all my time, trouble and expense, and ordered them in an authoritive [*sic*] manner to bring the fees for granting and surveying to him, observing at the same time that I had not anything more to do with them regarding the Settlement."[22] Even the Lieutenant-Governor felt that this was going too far, although he had asked Talbot to tell the settlers that only those from Lower Canada would be recognized by the government. Talbot was highly incensed at Watson for concealing the fact that each settler was forced to pay Watson a large sum of money; and in answer to Talbot's question Gore said that the government had nothing to do with such private contracts, and would not enforce them by withholding the settlers' patents. The Colonel then informed the settlers of this in such a way as to lead them to believe they did not have to pay Watson anything. "I hope you perfectly understand," Gore told Talbot after he heard what he had done, "that this Government never intended to interfere with Watson's private arrangements with those Persons, who he may bring from *Lower Canada* as settlers."[23]

When Watson arrived home and learned from his settlers, and from a letter left for him by Talbot, what had transpired, he hurried to Port Talbot filled with anger. "Watson attacked me in a most insolent tone," the Colonel informed Secretary Halton, "asked me 'how I had dared to go amongst his settlers and desire them not to pay his demands on them of 100 Dollars, that he would take out a bench warrant against me and compel me to pay him 100 Dollars for every person that refuses to give him that sum, in consequence of my advice—that neither the Governor, Government or any individual had a right to interfere with his private contracts, that the lands were assigned to him to settle and he would shew the world that he would make such bargains as he thought fit and he was not apprehensive of consequences, as he was certain of the support of an honest jury'—his passion increased to so abusive a strain, that I ordered him out of my house and by that method got rid of the fellow."[24]

Watson's anger had been increased by the arrival of some of his settlers, who paid their fees to the Colonel rather than to himself. Retiring to the home of a nearby settler he wrote to demand that Talbot come to Westminster and retract what he had done, under penalty of a vague threat of death.[25] Talbot replied contemptuously that he had no intention of complying with his demands, and that Watson was also mistaken if he expected that he would "enter the lists with you, for believe me, I value my life too highly to hazard it in your speculations. Should you further intrude yourself personally upon me with threats, I will employ the Constable to deliver the necessary reply."[26]

Although Gore decided later that the Colonel had misunderstood his instructions, his immediate reaction was favourable. "Do not let that Rascal Watson slip through those delicate hands of yours," he wrote. "You acted most prudently and judiciously by warning him of his danger in my name. Would to God every one in the Province would use it to so good a purpose."[27] Secretary Halton told Talbot that Gore "approves *entirely* of what you have done, and requests you will continue rigidly to enforce *His orders* as contained in your Letters."[28]

Watson wrote once more to Talbot demanding a retraction and uttering open threats against his life. Receiving no reply, on April 27 he addressed a memorial to the Lieutenant-Governor and Council asking for justice. In a report on the memorial the Council admitted that it had no right to interfere in private contracts between Watson and his followers, and that it should have demanded a list of those from Lower Canada in the beginning, so that he could be held to his agreement. But it was incensed at his statement that he had not known he was restricted to immigrants from Lower Canada. It therefore recommended that his agency in Westminster be terminated at the end of the year, which would allow sufficient time for all his Lower Canadian people to come in. In view of his threats against Talbot it also recommended that he be bound over to keep the peace.[29]

When he informed the Colonel of this decision Gore said that Watson had been threatening to prosecute him if he continued to interfere in his business. "You will laugh at and despise all such puerile nonsense," Gore wrote, "and I feel assured that you will protect the character of the Government, both as to its faith with Mr. W. and the treatment of his Settlers." He suggested, however, that since Watson had much altered his tone recently, Talbot might show his "magnanimity by continuing to pass his Recruits", for if he refused to do so all the Westminster settlers would have to appear before the Council at York.[30] Talbot agreed, to prevent the province from losing a number of valuable immigrants from Lower Canada, and because to decline "would have the appearance of timidity".[31]

Complying with directions from the Council Watson gave it a list of 140 of his followers who, he expected, would come in from Lower Canada; but by the end of the year only three of these had arrived in Westminster and claimed warrants of location.[32] On February 8, 1812, the unoccupied lots in the tract were declared open for general location. In April the surveyor, John Bostwick, was sent to Westminster to inform the settlers that Watson was no longer authorized to make locations. Bostwick reported the settlement in a very promising condition, but said that several of the settlers had paid the amount of their fees to Watson, who showed no disposition to refund them. Watson was also threatening to drive off any persons who presumed to settle on his tract, and seemed determined, now that he had lost control, to throw every obstacle that he could in the way of its settlement.[33] Colonel Talbot continued to locate and recommend applicants for land there, so that in effect it became a part of his settlement.[34]

His difficulty with Watson had scarcely abated when new ones arose between Talbot and the provincial officials, resulting from Gore's failure to secure an order-in-council for the Talbot Roads and for Talbot's jurisdiction in Bayham, Malahide, and Yarmouth, which he had authorized verbally. In the spring of 1812, after Gore left the province for an extended vacation in England, Surveyor-General Ridout wrote to Talbot to tell him he had just discovered that the Council had not confirmed the new roads, and that no more settlers should be placed on them until this was done.[35] Ridout had directed Burwell to begin the surveys the previous June; by the fall of 1811 the Talbot Road North, as the road to Westminster was called, was surveyed, and Burwell had also completed the survey of the Talbot Road West from Dunwich to the middle of Howard Township in the County of Kent, before quitting for the season. But the Colonel had not even waited for the surveys to be begun. On June 1, 1811, he informed Secretary Halton that he had placed a number of young men from Nova Scotia along the line where he had decided the road to Westminster should go. He had been very successful, he wrote, "in procuring settlers and filling this part of the province with a most industrious description of inhabitants. . . . For my own part, I cannot describe the happiness I enjoy from being instrumental in adding to the strength and prosperity of this valuable part of the world."[36]

Settlement on Talbot's own land in Dunwich had been almost at a standstill since 1809, but now that the danger of losing his agency appeared temporarily at an end, he was content to occupy himself with his work as superintendent of the Roads, knowing that they would ultimately bring settlers to his property. Now, with the receipt of Ridout's letter in the spring of 1812, all his plans were placed in jeopardy. Writing in alarm to Isaac Brock, administrator of the province in Gore's absence, he said that if the Council were to refuse to confirm the new roads it would place him "in a most humiliating and contemptable [*sic*] light", and make the rest of his life unhappy because of a breach of faith with the settlers whom he had established.[37]

Another blow struck the Colonel almost immediately, when Ridout wrote to say he had just discovered from Burwell's notes that instead of surveying the connecting road from Westminster to the Talbot Road at Kettle Creek, he had turned west about two and a half miles from Kettle Creek and run the road to the western boundary of Southwold

Township.[38] This part of the road was parallel to the original Talbot Road and broke in on the Crown and clergy reserves; and it was here that the Colonel had placed most of his settlers from Nova Scotia. Ridout thought there could be no justification for this parallel road, but Talbot claimed a verbal permission for it from Gore because the old Talbot Road there was wet and unfit for settlement.[39]

Despite the Colonel's anguished pleas the Council now appeared determined to withhold its consent for any of the new roads. By order of April 17, 1812, it directed him to make a return of his locations on them so that the settlers might receive compensation for their labour.[40] Brock expressed his regret, but he told Talbot he would continue to do all he could "to enable you to fulfil your engagements, being satisfied that, however premature you may have been, you acted from the best motives." He hoped the Council might still be induced to meet his wishes in every particular, if Talbot could make it appear that Gore had been "privy and sanctioned the measure".[41] However, the Council in June demanded that Talbot report on his locations throughout the whole settlement, and ordered him not to place any more settlers until further notice.[42] This, and the outbreak of war with the United States about the same time, effectively blocked all further activity in this direction until 1815.

When Talbot made his report the Council was astonished to learn that he had placed a number of Nova Scotia settlers in Bayham and Malahide. Gore's verbal authority for this had never been confirmed by the Council, and Surveyor-General Ridout had told Brock that these townships were open for general location. Knowing nothing about the locations made there by the Colonel, Brock had then made several large grants, some of which conflicted with these locations, and had issued the patents without requiring the performance of settlement duties.[43] Talbot was enraged at this new development, and demanded that the patents be revoked. In March, 1813, he wrote a lengthy account of his troubles to Gore, who was still in England, and urged him to send some authorization confirming his verbal assurances. It was at Gore's suggestion, Talbot wrote, that he had undertaken the task of land superintendent, which had caused him "much expense and trouble, by having my house constantly filled with applicants for land". He concluded: "To describe the distress of mind that has almost continually harassed me since your departure is beyond my ability, arising from the joint *impertinence* and *contempt* of the late General Brock and Ridout, the Sur. Genl., to your orders and arrangements in respect to the Lands which you were pleased to place under my care."[44]

The Lieutenant-Governor was disturbed by the turn of events. "I am vexed," he wrote to Powell, "that my friend Talbot should commit himself, nor, can I admit it, that the verbal assurances of the Lt. Governor can be binding on his successors."[45] The war prevented Talbot from carrying his appeal in person to the Colonial Secretary, but the problem remained to plague Gore after his return to Upper Canada in the fall of 1815.

## CHAPTER VI

# *An Interlude of War*

"THE District of London," wrote Judge Powell on returning from the western circuit in the fall of 1809, "heretofore the most turbulent and apparently dissatisfied (with they know not what), having lost by death and removal the instigators of Discontent, appears now to be in harmony and perfect good will to the executive Government, and exemplified it in the most respectful and decorous attention to the Commission, the Bearer of which has been supposed, from former reports, to be personally obnoxious."[1] Nevertheless, much discontent remained hidden, and it continued to develop during the next three years. When war with the United States began in June, 1812, Simon Zelotes Watson and some of his Westminster settlers deserted to the enemy. In Delaware the notorious Ebenezer Allan and Andrew Westbrook were the leaders of the renegades, although Allan died a few months later. There were many others in the London and Western Districts who joined General William Hull's army when it occupied Canadian soil at Sandwich. The more desperate of these led raiding parties against their former neighbours. "The enemy's cavalry," General Brock reported to Sir George Prevost on July 26, "amounts to about 50. They are led by one Watson, a surveyor of Montreal, of a desperate character. This fellow has been allowed to parade with about 20 men of the same description as far as Westminster, vowing as they went along the most bitter vengeance against the first characters of the province."[2]

Colonel Talbot, the particular object of Watson's vengeance, was in command of the first regiment of Middlesex militia, and had supervision over all the militia regiments of the London District. On July 25 he went to Long Point to raise one hundred volunteers from the Norfolk militia as reinforcements for a detachment under Major Chambers, who was at Oxford waiting to proceed down the Thames River to the Moravian village, where Brock had decided to establish a strong post against the raiders. When the volunteers learned that they would have to leave their farms during the harvest, and face the enemy at such a distance from their families, most of them refused the Colonel's command to march. He finally dismissed them and proceeded to Oxford, where he found Chambers with fifty men of the 41st Regiment and sixty volunteers from the Oxford militia. The rest of the Oxford militia could not be relied upon, Talbot reported to Brock, and no more than sixty men could be furnished by Middlesex. To make matters worse, many of the inhabitants of Delaware and Westminster had sent a petition to General Hull asking for protection, and enemy agents had so influenced the Indians of the Grand River that only forty or fifty could be expected to join the British forces.

Talbot's despair at the "dismal prospect" is shown in the concluding part of his letter to Brock. "I'm most anxious," he wrote, "to know your determination if you should be forced to send to Genl. Hull. Do let me know as those in promise of land on performing their settlement duties should be included in such condition as may be entered into, and something relative to myself."[3] Brock was not pleased at this suggestion of surrender. Years later Powell wrote that the

General "lost all confidence in the gallant Colonel", when he suggested capitulation and a special protection for Port Talbot.[4] The plan for a post at the Moravian village had to be abandoned, but as soon as the meeting of the legislature was over Brock proceeded to Long Point with several officers and a detachment of York and Lincoln volunteers. At Port Dover they were joined by Colonel Robert Nichol and two flank companies of the Norfolk militia. On August 10 the fleet of small boats stopped at Port Talbot, where additional recruits were obtained, many of them through the exertions of Colonel Talbot. Under the energetic leadership of Brock confidence was restored, and a sufficient force was raised to proceed to Amherstburg and secure the surrender of Hull's army and Detroit. Talbot did not take part in the expedition, having remained behind on routine business of the militia.

Early in September, after holding a general inspection of the militia regiments of the London District, Talbot assembled several companies and sent them to Fort George on the Niagara River, where an attack by the enemy was daily expected.[5] The danger passed for the time, and on September 12 Lieutenant-Colonel Macdonell sent word for Talbot to recall his men. At the same time Macdonell congratulated him "on not having been torn or driven away from your household Gods (and Goddesses, if any you have), and I assure you that I feel a friendly and anxious desire that ye should all remain quietly under the same roof, undisturbed by Hulls or Watsons or any of their wicked works."[6]

Watson escaped from Detroit just before the capitulation, and fled to the south; but the Colonel was not able to remain quietly at home. At the request of General Sheaffe, who succeeded as administrator of the province after Brock's death at Queenston Heights, he established his headquarters at Dover Mills, east of Long Point, in October. About the middle of the month, expecting an attack at any moment, Sheaffe sent urgent orders for Talbot to send four companies of militia to the Niagara frontier, but before these could be despatched Sheaffe had arranged an armistice with General Smyth of the American army. As a result Talbot received orders to distribute the companies between Long Point and Point Albino, stationing strong detachments at Long Point, Dover Mills, Grand River, and Sugar Loaf, with a small party to patrol the region between Sugar Loaf and Fort Erie. The militia remained on duty until December 11, when most were permitted to return to their homes for the winter.[7]

Sheaffe had complete confidence in Colonel Talbot. In April, 1813, while stationed at Niagara, Colonel Nichol wrote to Talbot: "You are so much better acquainted with the localities of the country than the General himself, that everything in your District is left to your discretion."[8] His duties throughout the war were chiefly routine—calling up or dismissing the militia as he was ordered, or sometimes at his own discretion, directing the patrols and detachments established at various points, and collecting and forwarding supplies. In May, 1813, he reported that the people of the County of Oxford, with a very few exceptions, were a "violent and systematic band of enemies", and he advised sending all aliens out of the province, as they were "indefatigable in spreading discord and alarm".[9]

The danger increased greatly towards the end of September, when General William Harrison's American army landed below Amherstburg and forced the British to retreat from the Detroit region. On September 23 General Henry Procter, in command at Malden, acknowledged the receipt of 150 barrels of flour sent by Talbot, and asked him to have two huts and a shelter for horses built at the Fourteen Mile Tree in the Longwoods wilderness, to assist him in his retreat up the Thames River.[10] Two weeks later Procter and his army were overtaken and defeated near the Moravian village. The American army then withdrew to Detroit, but the western part of the province was left open to its foraging and raiding parties. In the spring of 1814 their inroads were coming dangerously close to Port Talbot. One day while the Colonel was at home on a brief visit, word came that the enemy was about to strike. He departed hurriedly in a skiff belonging to one of his men, to the concern of Mahlon Burwell, who arrived just too late to use the skiff in evacuating his family.[11] However, the alarm proved groundless.

The first attack came from across the lake and was directed against Port Dover. The militia barracks, six mills, and many private houses and other buildings in the vicinity were burned by the Americans. Colonel Talbot was at Port Dover at the time, but he did not attempt to oppose their landing. Concentrating the militia thirty miles away at Brantford he marched to Turkey Point, arriving the day after the enemy had sailed away. Talbot incurred considerable criticism for this decision.[12]

Five days later, on May 20, Port Talbot was raided by thirty riflemen under the command of Andrew Westbrook. The band probably included Daniel Norton, Samuel Doyle, and James Pelton, who had previously been associated with Westbrook as scouts for the Americans. Simon Zelotes Watson may have helped to plan this raid against his old adversary, but as a topographical engineer attached to the general staff he was unable to lead it. Finding the Colonel absent the raiders retired, after forcing a number of the inhabitants to take the oath of neutrality. In July a much larger force again missed the Colonel, who was accustomed to visit Port Talbot from time to time to attend to his personal affairs. On this occasion the raiders did not leave until they had destroyed a great deal of the farmers' crops. Getting word from an informer that Talbot was at home, they struck again on August 16, and almost succeeded in capturing him.[13]

In later years the Colonel never tired of telling the story of his escape. Mrs. Stewart recorded the following account, as he told it to her at Peterborough in 1826:[14] "One day as he was looking out of his log-house drawing-room window he saw an Indian coming towards the house. He thought at first it was a messenger from some other officer and called to his servant to go out to him, then went on writing a letter. But his servant stood petrified looking out of the window. 'What is the matter?' said the Colonel. 'The Indians, they are coming,' was the answer. The Colonel looked again and saw them coming two or three in advance of the rest. One opened the door and walked in. The Colonel with much composure welcomed him and gave him something to drink. Another followed. With the same composure and hospitality he received him, pretending to consider them friends, he then said he would go out and welcome the rest of the party whom he saw at a little distance outside of the house. He walked leisurely round making signs of welcome and unconcernedly examining the posts of his verandah which had been hurt by the cattle, all the time edging on and on by degrees till he had turned the corner of the building, and was hid from their view. Then he jumped into a ravine behind the house where he knew he could run without being seen and set off with all speed to the woods. He wandered on till night and then climbed into a tree. He heard the party in search of him come to the foot of the tree and talk, wondering which way he had gone. As they were about to find him they went away. On his return to his house he found they had carried off almost everything. He had nothing left but the Russia duck jacket and trousers in which he had run off. They had set fire to the house; but one good-natured Indian returned to tell him where the concealed fire was, and warned him in time to put it out."

It is probable that the Colonel, an excellent raconteur, embellished the actual facts with some fancies of his own. Many years after, his account of the event, as told to Sir James Alexander,[15] differed in considerable detail. Another account, given by Captain Leslie Patterson to Edward Ermatinger,[16] was also different. Talbot told Alexander that he was out in a field when the Americans arrived, and that his servant told them he was only an old fellow who tended the cows. The raiders ordered him to drive in the cows, and departed without suspecting his identity. Patterson told Ermatinger he had come to the house to warn the Colonel that the enemy was approaching, whereupon the Colonel left and was just crossing the bar at the mouth of the creek when the Americans, disguised as Indians, came up. One of them levelled his rifle at Talbot, but when told by Patterson that he was only a poor man who looked after the sheep he did not fire, and so Talbot's life was spared.

Ten days after his escape the Colonel arrived at Fort Erie with the information that his horses and nearly all the rest of his property had been carried off or destroyed, and that the raiders had threatened to return in a few weeks to take away the inhabitants' cattle and complete the destruction of the settlement.[17] It was at this time that Colonel Mahlon

Burwell and several other inhabitants were taken to Ohio as prisoners, and fifty settlers were plundered of their horses, wearing apparel and household furniture. True to his promise, Westbrook returned on September 19, burned the Talbot mills, and killed several of his cattle and sheep. The band then advanced along the Talbot Road for fifteen miles, plundering and burning. The final attack came early in November, when General MacArthur's troops camped for the night at the site of St. Thomas, destroying grain and sheep in the neighbourhood.[18]

Talbot was eventually awarded £3,630 by the government for his personal losses, but it was not until 1824 that he was paid the first quarter of this sum.[19] He received some assistance from the Loyal and Patriotic Society of Upper Canada, which also sent about £750 for his destitute settlers.[20] But with his farm devastated and his mills destroyed he found himself financially embarrassed, and unable to give his customary aid to the needy immigrants who began to arrive in ever increasing numbers with the cessation of hostilities. The task of reconstruction was further complicated by the work involved in his public duties. In May, 1815, he was appointed a road commissioner for the district, and also a commissioner to carry into effect the provisions of an act for the confiscation of the property of aliens who had deserted to the enemy. A few weeks later he was named to a committee to superintend the building of a district gaol and court-house at Vittoria.[21] At the same time all his difficulties with the provincial government concerning his work as land superintendent again came to the fore.

CHAPTER VII

# *The Struggle for Independence*

LIEUTENANT-GOVERNOR GORE, who had been in England since 1811, returned to Upper Canada in the fall of 1815. In his absence the Council had refused to renew Talbot's authority to make locations outside his own townships of Dunwich and Aldborough. In February, 1815, however, after hearing testimony from him and the Surveyor-General, it decided that he had been justified in thinking he had such authority in Bayham and Malahide, where he had placed eighty-three settlers, some of them on lots granted by Brock to two officials, William Stanton and John Hale. In view of this, and to compensate the settlers whose locations conflicted with these grants, the Council recommended that each should be given a double allotment of land in some other place.[1]

This solution failed to satisfy the settlers, and when Gore arrived at York in September he was greeted by a lengthy letter of complaint from the Colonel. He immediately returned the Talbot Road East to the latter's control;[2] but because of the difficulties that had arisen from his verbal authorization for the other roads and townships he decided to refer it to the Colonial Secretary for confirmation. He also suggested to Lord Bathurst, because of the heavy settlement duties involved, that Talbot should be permitted to continue making locations of 200 acres on his roads, rather than 100 acres as recently decreed for ordinary settlers by the Colonial

Office.[3] Bathurst concurred in these recommendations in his despatch of February 10, 1816. Six months later an order-in-council at last gave official confirmation to Talbot's superintendence of Bayham, Malahide, and Yarmouth, and to the Talbot Roads West and North—including the parallel road through Southwold.[4] During the summer and fall Burwell carried the survey of Talbot Road West from the middle of Howard to the western boundary of Mersea in Essex County.[5]

In confirming the Colonel's jurisdiction in Bayham and Malahide, Bathurst directed that Stanton and Hale be asked to give up the lots on which his settlers were located, in exchange for other grants. If they refused, Bathurst wrote, the necessary legal measures for revoking their grants should be taken, on the ground that they had made no improvements, or that the lots were previously occupied.[6] John Hale was induced to surrender his deeds in the summer of 1817; but Talbot had already bought the Stanton lots so that his settlers might remain. The Council refused to reimburse him for this expense until positive orders from Bathurst finally forced it to do so.[7]

In the spring of 1815 the Council had requested that the Surveyor-General prepare a report on all lands available for the settlement of the immigrants, who were expected to begin arriving soon from the British Isles. Ridout's report included a reference to the 139,000 acres of surveyed lands under Talbot's control; but because the latter had not made a return of his locations for three years Ridout did not know how much of this was still unsettled.[8] The following October, in answer to a request from the Lieutenant-Governor, Talbot submitted a list containing about 350 names, of which only 77 were found to have deposited warrants for land in the Surveyor-General's office, as they should have done before being located. Ridout's complaints about this lack of orderly procedure, and the confusion that it caused in his office, fell on deaf ears.[9] On the other hand he made no comment on the Colonel's assertion of a *de facto* power to dispossess settlers—a power that had always been exercised by the Council alone. "In many instances," Talbot wrote when sending in his report, "it may be proper to remove names where the party is dilatory in commencing and performing the settlement duties, as I have found it absolutely necessary to be thus rigid to enforce the exertions of the settlers." He suggested that Ridout follow his example and insert the names on his maps in pencil, so they might be easily erased.[10]

The other government officials were much more concerned with the fact that Talbot's settlers did not now pay their fees until they were ready to take out their patents, which many neglected to do. In the spring of 1817, when the government was in great financial straits, the Receiver-General estimated that nearly £1,200 in fees was due from those settlers reported by Talbot two years before.[11] At his suggestion Lieutenant-Governor Gore asked Talbot to make out a new return, and to notify his settlers they must pay their fees at once, even if they had not completed the settlement duties.[12] The Colonel's return, dated August 5, 1817, listed the names of 804 settlers, and he again emphasized that it was liable to alterations.[13] Six months later, despite Gore's order, 545 of these settlers had still not paid their fees, which now amounted to a total of £4,324.[14] For a government dependent on land fees for much of its income, this was a serious problem. On the other hand, Talbot well knew the difficulties that would arise if the fees were paid and the money used by the government before the settlers took out their patents. The resulting confusion, where dispossessions occurred, would seriously hamper his freedom to exercise control over the settlers.[15]

Meanwhile, the Colonel had been able to attract a few settlers to his own lands in Dunwich and Aldborough. In the summer of 1816 he applied for a grant of 5,000 acres, in right of twenty-five settlers who had come in since the close of the war. Some difficulty arose when it was found that eight of these had previously been given 200 acres on the Talbot Road or elsewhere. This was clearly a violation of the rules laid down by Lord Hobart, but on Talbot's insistence that he had never considered himself restricted in this respect the Council accepted all his settlers, with the condition that in future he was not to employ anyone who had already obtained a grant of more than fifty acres of land.[16]

It is possible that Talbot regarded this as permission to tell all the settlers on his lands that they would receive, in addition, fifty acres of the Crown lands. A few years later he asserted that Lieutenant-Governor Gore in 1816 had given him a verbal authority to make such a promise. Whatever the reason, when a number of Scottish Highlanders from Caledonia in New York State came to Aldborough in that year, Talbot told them they were not eligible to obtain grants of the Crown lands because they had lived in the United States during the late war; but he would give them each fifty acres of his own land without cost, and when the existing regulation against Americans was repealed, they would then be able to draw the usual amount of Crown land. About the same time a number of Highlanders from Lord Selkirk's Red River Colony, who had been forced by the North West Company to go to Upper Canada, received land from Talbot in Aldborough and Dunwich. Wishing to remain neutral in the dispute between Selkirk and the Company, the government of Upper Canada had refused to grant land to these people; but Talbot assured them that the acceptance of his land would not prevent them from obtaining Crown land if the government should change its mind.[17]

While Gore was still in England in 1815 William Dummer Powell wrote to tell him that the Colonel was much annoyed at the disclosure that Hobart's despatch limited the number of his settlers in Dunwich and Aldborough to one hundred, and the amount of his own lands to 20,000 acres. His pretensions, Powell declared, extended "ad infinitum —for he now contends that the Minister's design was not to limit his settlements to parts of his original Grant, but to give him claim for 200 acres in respect of every 50 acres he may convey to actual Settlers." If this were countenanced the whole province would eventually be at his disposal.[18] In a memorial thirty years later Talbot stated: "The tenour of Lord Hobart's instructions does not admit of any doubt, but that I have an unquestionable right to claim an equal percentage for all the Townships I have settled as for the Townships of Dunwich and Aldborough, which I commenced with, and that it is altogether forbearance on my part not having done so. . . ."[19]

By June, 1817, Lieutenant-Governor Gore felt compelled to submit the question of Talbot's authority under Hobart's despatch to the consideration of the Council. The resulting report, drawn up by Powell, stated that progress in the settlement of Dunwich and Aldborough had been very slow, so that thousands of acres of surveyed lands there remained unoccupied, although needed for the large number of immigrants arriving from the United Kingdom. Most of Talbot's settlers had formerly come from the United States, but since the war Americans could not receive land grants in Canada.

Under Lord Hobart's instructions immigrants from the United Kingdom were not eligible to become his settlers. Finally, the Colonel had given up his plans for the cultivation of hemp, which was the primary reason for the arrangement with him. For these reasons the Council recommended that his agency be terminated at once, by giving him an outright grant of an additional 4,200 acres of land, which would complete the 20,000 acres to which he was entitled.

Gore concurred in this, but he decided to refer the matter to the Colonial Secretary, on the ground that the provincial government could not make an ordinary grant of more than 1,200 acres. Until the Secretary's decision could be learned Dunwich and Aldborough were to remain under reserve, but none of Talbot's settlers was to be accepted until examined personally by the Council.[20] Gore notified the Colonel of this by letter on June 7,[21] and four days later set out for England. "It certainly may wear the air of duplicity which he gives it," he admitted later, "a blow and then running away. I might as well have left the odium to my successor. I do not feel quite satisfied with myself."[22]

This blow struck at the Colonel's authority came only three months after he had been honoured at a meeting of his settlers held at Lee's hotel in Yarmouth, at which arrangements were made to hold a celebration on May 21 of each year, to commemorate the beginning of the settlement. An address of gratitude to Colonel Talbot was prepared, and it was decided that at each Anniversary dinner a chair should be reserved for him, to be left empty when he was unable to appear. On May 21, 1817, the first Talbot Anniversary was held at Lee's hotel. The Colonel was deeply touched by the honour done him; and during the remainder of his life he looked to the Anniversary as the major event of the year.[23]

The following August Talbot met at Fort George John Savery Brock, a brother of Sir Isaac, whom he had known in Holland during the campaign of 1799. Brock thought him "a wonderful character". He was told that Talbot had 5,000 "children" in his settlements, and "a fine farm of about five hundred acres *cleared*". Having once made his own butter and cooked for himself, he was now assisted in this work. Brock later went to Port Talbot, where he remained for eleven days as the Colonel's guest. He learned that there were then 1,315 families living in the settlement, all but 187 of them on the Talbot Roads. "It is not surprising," he wrote to his brother, "that in so fine a Country many settlers come up. Col. Talbot, however sanguine he may have been at first, could scarcely hope for the success he has met with, all flock to his reputation. He has acted from the first on a well organized system—the public good being the sole advantage at which he aims—all things go well. What consoling reflections to his superior mind! how delightful the thought of so many men made happy by his talents and active exertions. Could his Prince behold all he has done, he would bestow thanks and honors on him, he has settled the country with judgment, zeal, and activity, and of a perfect wilderness, he has laid in seven years the foundation of a populous and interesting country."[24]

If his host talked of his difficulties with the Executive Council, Brock did not mention it in his letters. But Talbot was preparing to go to England to present his case to the Colonial Secretary. A few weeks after Brock's visit John Strachan, then a member of the Council, wrote to tell Gore that he had advised Talbot "to go home at once and get the matter settled, if he considered himself aggrieved". Strachan agreed with the other members of the Council that the

Colonel's agency in his two townships should be ended. "This mode of settling," he declared, "makes the Gov't odious and the inhabitants dissatisfied. I like the Col. very much and wish him as much success as he desires, provided it be not the continuance of that imperium in imperio which he has so long exercised."[25] Talbot was at York on his way to England on November 6, when he requested that no locations should be made in the lands under his superintendence during his absence.[26] The Council agreed to this only until steps could be taken to learn what settlers had not yet paid their fees, and for a further period of six months, after which all lots on which the fees had not been paid or the settlement duties were not in progress were to be opened to general location by the Surveyor-General.[27]

Arriving in London early in January, 1818, by ship from New York to Penzance, Talbot called briefly on Gore and then spent an hour with Mrs. Gore, during which he complained of the treatment he had received.[28] "Talbot came home excessively enraged with [the Council] and I believe with Governor Gore too," William Halton wrote to a friend, "and I really was sorry to hear Talbot speak of him in an uncivil and very slighting manner after all his efforts to serve Talbot and all his private attentions to him."[29] Gore did what he could by explaining the situation in a letter to the Colonial Office, and expressing a desire that Talbot's superintendence be continued.[30] On February 8 he informed Powell that he had not been consulted by the Colonial Office, but that he and the Colonel were "very good friends".[31]

By the early part of March Talbot had completed his business in London. "Colonel Talbot leaves town to-morrow or next day," Gore told Powell on March 7, "to return via Boston—he says he has succeeded every way—I told you he has powerful interest, which I believe has been exerted manfully—five years is to terminate his settlements—his settlers are not to proceed to York for *approval*—and the Fees are not to be paid till the settlement *duty is performed*—and he may (he says) admit Americans."[32] Halton informed his friend: "Talbot has good interest: and whether it was that or the justice of his cause I do not know, but I believe he carried all his points in Downing St.—but notwithstanding, the Executive Council will be able to plague him much if they think fit to do so."[33]

Gore explained that when Talbot first arrived in London, Under-secretary Goulburn had seemed determined to limit his grant in Dunwich and Aldborough to 20,000 acres, "but in a very few days the state of affairs altered, the Colonel was received with open arms, and everything, short of an Act of Parliament in his favor, complied with." This change, Gore heard, was brought about by an opposition member of Parliament named Brand, who threatened Goulburn with a parliamentary motion.[34] Although Talbot had dined with the Gores once or twice, and they had chatted pleasantly about old friends in Canada, Gore was completely disillusioned. "I do consider him," he wrote to Powell, "the most selfish man I ever yet met with, not one expression of acknowledgment to me for former kindness has passed his lips, even his friend Mrs. Gore is disgusted with him."[35]

The Colonel's helpful friend was Thomas Brand, a Whig member of Parliament, who a year later succeeded to the title of Lord Dacre, married, and settled down to become, in the words of Fanny Kemble, the "ideal of an English country gentleman". These events caused him to discard plans which he had made to found a colony in Canada in association with Colonel Talbot, "where Arcadia was to revive again, at a distance from all the depraved and degraded social systems of Europe, under the auspices of these two enthusiastic reformers." In love with liberty, Mrs. Kemble declared, Brand "embraced with the most ardent hopes the scheme of emigration of Colonel Talbot for forming in the New World a colony where all the errors of the old were to be avoided." Perhaps the practical Colonel was secretly relieved when his liberal friend gave up his plans to come to Canada.[36]

Lord Bathurst's despatch of February 26, 1818, which Talbot presented to President Samuel Smith on his return to York, confirmed the powers that the Colonel had been assuming gradually during the previous fifteen years. Bathurst agreed that Hobart's instructions limited Talbot to 20,000 acres of land, but he thought that his "successful exertions" entitled him to something more. He directed, therefore, that all the vacant lands in Dunwich and Aldborough should be continued at Talbot's disposal for a further period of five years. In addition, to further the settlement of all the roads and townships under his superintendence, Bathurst decreed that his settlers were not to be restricted as to country of origin except as any settlers in the province might be, and that they did not have to appear before the Council or pay the fees before they completed the settlement duties.[37]

The Colonel's return to Upper Canada put a stop to the efforts of the Council to collect the unpaid fees from his settlers or to declare their lots open for re-location. On April 6 it had recommended sending a special commissioner to visit each location in the Talbot Settlement to check on the character of the settlers and the progress of settlement duties. All those who had not taken the oath of allegiance or paid the fees were to be ordered to do so within a limited time, or forfeit their lots.[38] Acting on this advice President Smith appointed Duncan McDonell, who visited each settler on the Talbot Road from Middleton to Dunwich before receiving orders to quit. He found that the settlers had been carefully chosen, with due regard for all the requirements except, in some cases, the oath of allegiance.[39]

The provincial officials were astonished and indignant when they learned how far the Colonel had succeeded on his mission to England. Powell spoke of his "palatinate", and of his final emancipation from all provincial control. Ridout complained again about the removal of so much surveyed land from general location, and about the unpaid fees amounting to £4,000.[40] Strachan declared that most of Dunwich and Aldborough was now virtually recognized as Talbot's private property. Within a year or so it would all be settled, and then he would have a "Princely domain and a princely fortune".[41] Gore advised Powell to withdraw from all political business, "and let them see how the government will be conducted under the advice of Supt. Small and Talbot".[42] This may have been a reference to the rumour, soon to be proved unfounded, that the Colonel intended to take his seat on the Legislative Council.[43]

The provincial officials were also uncertain as to the extent of Talbot's powers as superintendent in the townships outside Dunwich and Aldborough. In December, 1819, after considering an appeal made by a settler whom he had dispossessed, the Council reported that, if the settler's allegations were true, "they would entitle him to the interference and protection of the Executive Government, was the original location under its immediate contract, but the locations having been made by Colonel Talbot, it is doubtful how far that Gentleman may consider himself exempt by the late instructions from His Majesty's Government from any accountability to this Board." Talbot resolved the dilemma by offering a full explanation, which convinced the Council he was justified in his action.[44]

A difficulty of another sort arose in the case of Peter Montross, Jr., whom Talbot had located in Malahide previous to his trip to England. In 1821 Talbot erased Montross' name from his map for failure to live on the lot or do any work there, unaware that during his absence in England the Council had interfered, permitting Montross to take out his patent without completing the settlement duties. Talbot then gave the lot to Thomas Hodgkinson, who soon performed the required work and applied for his patent. When the conflict was discovered the Lieutenant-Governor and Council tried desperately to induce Montross to agree to the cancellation of his deed, but he stood firm for three years before giving up the lot in exchange for a larger grant.[45]

Talbot was on hand to greet the new Lieutenant-Governor, Sir Peregrine Maitland, who arrived in August, 1818, to succeed Francis Gore. Maitland was charmed by the courtly and persuasive Colonel, and not only complied with his request to place the Township of London under his superintendence but a few weeks later accompanied him to Port Talbot as his guest.[46] It was on September 9, while still at York, that the Colonel met his distant kinsman, Richard Talbot of Cloghjordan, who had brought out a group of settlers from southern Ireland. Richard accepted his advice to locate in London; and late in the fall he and twenty-one followers were established in the fifth and sixth concessions there. The following spring Mahlon Burwell finished the survey of the northern part of this township enabling the Colonel to locate many of the applicants who had been clamouring for land since his return home.[47]

Immigrants were "pouring in to this portion of the Province at a great rate", Burwell had written in February, 1819. Already Talbot was beginning to find the lands under his superintendence inadequate for the horde of applicants. To relieve the pressure, and to settle the country close to him, he suggested to Maitland that portions of the school reserves in Southwold, Yarmouth, and Houghton be surveyed into lots and sold at public auction under his supervision. Maitland agreed to this, and the first auction sale of school lands was held on July 1 of that year.[48] Many people were eager to buy,[49] but few lots were sold because Talbot had set a minimum price of ten shillings per acre, which was considered too high. "If I had not been present and no minimum price," he reported to Secretary Hillier, "I do believe that the land would not have brought more than two or three shillings the acre, as the Vagabonds think the Government have not any right to sell for more than 6d. or so." There would always be "a combination against the value of the land" at auctions, but he thought he could sell all of it at a fixed price of three dollars per acre.[50] The government soon discontinued the sales altogether. A year later Talbot declared that he could have sold hundreds of lots before the present scarcity of money.[51]

Maitland was much impressed by the success of Talbot's system, which depended upon local supervision and strict enforcement of the settlement duties before the issuance of the patent. By order-in-council of March 13, 1819, he established a similar system throughout the province, with a land board in each district empowered to examine applicants and make locations, thus relieving the Council of much of this work. These boards were similar to the land boards that had been in existence from 1789 to 1794, although they had powers of supervision that the earlier boards did not. But for various reasons the system did not work well. The board for the Western District never became effective. Talbot was appointed chairman of the board for the London District, and during the year that he acted in that capacity there was no apparent change in his routine. After he resigned in April, 1820, because of a dispute with the Council, he was given the powers of a land board throughout his whole settlement, which occupied much of the London and Western Districts.

The trouble with the Council, which resulted in Talbot's resignation, had its origin in 1816 when he placed a number of settlers along the Talbot Road in Harwich Township, on land long since deeded to non-residents. When this conflict was discovered he explained that the plan of the township which Burwell had used for the survey did not show any prior grants, and that he assumed lots could be laid out on the road and given to his settlers as in the other townships. Surveyor-General Ridout admitted that such a plan had been given to Burwell in 1811, but Burwell had reported this lost during the war, and had been given a new plan on which all the old grants were marked, before beginning the survey in 1816.[52] The government attempted to remedy the situation by offering the Harwich settlers larger grants in another township, but neither they nor Talbot wished to accept this solution. While Talbot was in England in 1818 he convinced Lord Bathurst that the Surveyor-General was at fault, and that the provincial government was in justice bound to secure his settlers by inducing the non-resident owners to exchange or sell their lands.[53]

At first William Dummer Powell supported this position, but when he learned the facts about the two plans he was convinced that Burwell, at least, had practised deception, and that Talbot was aware of it. His indignation was aroused when the Colonel, while waiting in the Council room for the opening of the meeting on April 1, 1820, showed him the 1811 plan of Harwich to support his claim. It was not until Talbot presented a list of his new settlers in Dunwich and Aldborough, and objected to furnishing any proof that they had received lands from him, that Powell permitted his feelings to show. He could no longer, he explained to Secretary Hillier, "withhold the Term of Reprobation which, however, did not apply to anything but his gross misrepresentations and the consequent instructions [from Lord Bathurst] so offensive to the provincial executive Government."[54] Retorting angrily that the Council was attempting to interfere with his rightful authority, Talbot left the room after declaring he would no longer act as chairman of the London District Board. Powell felt obliged to make a full explanation to Hillier, to prevent, he said, any misrepresentation by the Colonel "to justify his extraordinary resolution to withdraw his services at a Post, which however he might grace, was not thought degrading to him."[55]

A few days later Talbot refused to accept the plans for the townships of Nissouri and Zorra, saying he would have nothing to do with them.[56] However, when Maitland asked him for a return of the locations he had made in the township of London, which had been placed in his charge as chairman of the board rather than as part of the Talbot Settlement, he said he could not make an accurate return because of the frequent casualties and changes in locations resulting from his system. It would only result in "a multiplicity of confusion, and a continual recurrence of references, so that the trouble of the land granting department would be increased beyond my ability to encounter."[57] Hillier reminded him that he had resigned from the District Board, and that whoever undertook the work in the future would have to know what locations had been made.[58] But Talbot neither made the return nor gave up his control of London Township. On June 21, 1821, he was invested with all the powers of the land boards for the various Talbot Roads, as well as for the townships of London, Malahide, and Bayham.[59] This authority was extended from time to time to other townships as they were placed under his superintendence. Nevertheless his quarrel with Powell caused him the loss of Nissouri and Zorra and several other townships in the London District; and his Harwich settlers were forced to move to new but larger locations on Big Bear Creek, which prevented the opening of the Talbot Road across Harwich.[60]

CHAPTER VIII

# *The Highlanders of Aldborough*

By the close of the year 1819 Talbot had more than sufficient settlers in Dunwich and Aldborough to enable him to apply for all the remaining reserved lands in those townships. His success was largely due to his assurance to those who accepted fifty acres of his land, that they would still be eligible to receive fifty or even one hundred acres from the Crown. In the fall of 1818, after his return from England, he issued a public notice to that effect. Powell believed he did this because he regarded Lord Bathurst's despatch as "a total relaxation from all restraint"; but Talbot insisted that his action was based on a verbal authorization given him in 1816 by Lieutenant-Governor Gore.[1]

Some of the Scots from New York State, and from Selkirk's Red River Colony in the West, who had settled in Aldborough in 1816, wrote letters to their friends in Scotland praising the place and telling of the Colonel's promises. This had a great effect on the poor land-hungry Highlanders. In the fall of 1818 thirty-six families from Argyllshire came to join their relatives, and many more followed during the next two years.[2] Tragedy struck some of them at the very moment of their arrival. In 1819 the York Society of Friends to the Strangers in Distress sent the sum of twelve pounds ten shillings to Colonel Talbot, "for the relief of some widows, whose husbands (emigrants) were drowned as they were landing their baggage at Port Talbot."[3]

In the fall of 1819 the Highlanders were surprised and disappointed to find that Talbot would no longer give away any land in Dunwich or Aldborough, and that he would sell it only at the exorbitant price of six dollars per acre. He still had Crown lands to dispose of in other townships, at the rate of one hundred acres to each settler, but the fees were high, and the Scots wished to remain together. They therefore proceeded to draw up a petition asking the provincial government for a grant of the Township of Mosa, directly behind Aldborough, which was part of the Longwoods tract recently purchased from the Indians. This would enable them, they said, to support a minister of the Gospel who spoke their language, and to enjoy the fellowship and assistance of their friends in both townships.[4]

It was while considering this petition that the Council first learned of Talbot's promise to his settlers of an additional fifty or one hundred acres of the Crown lands.[5] The Colonel explained that Francis Gore had given him a verbal authority to do so; and he remarked that grants of one hundred acres had already been made to a number of his people. These, it was soon revealed, were the former Red River settlers, to whom the government had just given lots in ignorance that they had received land from Talbot. Indignant at this "fraudulent concealment" the Council immediately rescinded the warrants that had been issued in their favour.[6] After further consideration, however, it reluctantly agreed that each settler in Dunwich and Aldborough should receive an additional grant of one hundred acres from the Crown. Noting that Talbot would receive a grant of two hundred acres in right of each, the Council decreed that the fees on these additional grants would be the same as those paid by persons who had already received that amount, which were higher than the fees on primary grants.[7]

The Council had remarked on Talbot's memorial of November 6, 1817: "When an Emigrant possessing an authority to receive one hundred acres of land finds himself limited to the possession of fifty, and that the Government actually bestows on a stranger 200 acres on that account, no reasoning can remove the impression of something worse than mere absurdity." John Strachan declared that this method of settling made "the Gov't odious and the inhabitants dissatisfied."[8] The truth of this was soon to be made clear to all. The Council felt that it had raised an "invidious distinction" in favour of the Dunwich and Aldborough settlers, who could now acquire one hundred and fifty acres of Crown lands instead of the one hundred acres to which the ordinary settler was limited.[9] But the Highlanders were displeased to find that they had to pay higher fees when they had never received the two hundred acres referred to by the Council; and they soon became convinced that Talbot was illegally keeping part of their lands.

On April 1, 1820, occurred the quarrel between the Colonel and William Dummer Powell which resulted in the former declining to act further as chairman of the London District Land Board. Powell was indignant when Talbot tried to justify his actions in Harwich, but he said nothing until Talbot applied for two hundred acres of land in right of each of more than two hundred settlers whom he said he had established in Dunwich and Aldborough. He produced nothing but a bare list of names in support of his claim. It was then, as Powell explained to Secretary Hillier, that "the whole job, from the first proposition to raise hemp, through all its encroachments on Justice and Decency, worked so strongly on my mind, that, upon the Colonel's reprobating the trouble and expence of further evidence than his list, I could not withhold the Term of Reprobation. . . ."[10]

It was not long before Powell discovered why Talbot was so reluctant to produce evidence that he had actually conveyed fifty acres of his own land to each of the settlers named: he had put them on land reserved but not yet granted to him, probably because the lots he already owned were more desirable. But he was now placed in an embarrassing position because the Council would not grant him the land on which these people were, and thus he could not give them title to it. Many began to fear they might lose their land; and when the elections were held the following July they found they were prevented from voting because they did not have deeds. In a memorial addressed to the Lieutenant-Governor a short time later, they stated that Mahlon Burwell and John Bostwick "sent hand bills among us to see if we would vote for them to be members of parliament for this County, and about a hundred and fifty of our Highlanders went about a day's journey to the place appointed with their usual music, the bag pipes, but when they saw that we were not to vote in their favour they rejected us for being on Talbot's land."[11]

Powell was convinced that, in justice to the settlers, Talbot should be given a deed in trust for the land on which they were established, in order that he might make conveyances to them. "There can be little doubt," he wrote while making this recommendation to Maitland, "but that at no distant period, the progress of Col. Talbot towards the acquisition of his Palatinate on Lake Erie will incite Enquiry and possibly some Censure on the executive Government of Upper Canada, which during successive administrations has not merely acquiesced in the orders of his Majesty's Secretary of State, but with an indifference which may be thought blameable, has yielded to the unreasonable pretensions of Colonel Talbot, in no manner authorised by the most indulgent consideration of the Instructions." Maitland replied that he was extremely anxious to get rid of Talbot's business, even if it meant overlooking his irregularities, and he saw no point in refusing to permit him to convey land to the people he had already located, which would only result in "dissatisfying a whole population".

On March 12, 1821, nearly a year after the Colonel's quarrel with Powell, a warrant was issued for the deed in trust, to be given Talbot after he had deposited with the Surveyor-General a plan of the locations and a signed statement that each settler named was in actual occupation, and had never received any other lands from the Crown. But to show, in Powell's words, "that there was nothing personal to Col. Talbot in this proposition", it was also provided that the remainder of the reserved land in the two townships should be granted to him outright. Nevertheless, Talbot felt that it was an insult to his honour that the government should feel it necessary to thus guard the interests of his settlers. But he agreed to the arrangement because his Highlanders were clamouring for their deeds. Having given the Surveyor-General a plan of locations containing 186 names, he received fifty acres in trust for each of them. The remaining 40,420 acres of the reserve were granted to him for his own use.[12]

The deed in trust seemed to confirm the suspicions of the settlers that Talbot was simply an agent of the government to deliver their patents, that he had no right to the land on which they were located, and that he was keeping part of their lands. In July he appealed to the Council for permission to surrender the deed in trust in exchange for a regular deed. This the Council refused to do, but it was more receptive to the Colonel's request that his settlers not be charged the higher fees on their additional grants. The discontent in Dunwich and Aldborough was now so great, he said, that he feared for his own safety unless the fees were lowered. The Council agreed to this—although realizing that this new concession would expose it to the "reproach and murmurs" of less favoured settlers—because of the "notoriety of the agency of Col. Talbot, and confidence reposed in him by government, almost identifying his acts with those of the provincial administration."[13]

Instead of being content with this liberal treatment, the Highlanders of Aldborough addressed a new memorial to the Council, stating their determination to claim as a legal right the full two hundred acres that the Colonel had received for each of them. They charged that he had taken advantage of them as strangers, had "blinded their eyes, lead them astray and endeavoured to swindle them of their rights, and to settle them on a plane that was inconsistent to the order of Government and against the prosperity of settlers." The Council indignantly rejected these assumptions. No one, it replied, had any "right" to the Crown lands, grants were purely a matter of grace, and the memorialists had falsely represented Talbot's actions and promises. Unless they made a proper acknowledgment "for their false statements and indecorous language" they would not receive the additional grants already sanctioned.[14]

Malcolm Robertson, who had drawn up and presented the memorial, hastened to assume full responsibility for it. Many of the Highlanders had feared it might cause offence, and others had signed their names without knowing what was in it, he wrote. The inhabitants of the two townships, who had signed the memorial, presented a collective apology for their "expressions of warmth" in telling of Talbot's conduct, and for appearing to demand as a right what they knew to be a free gift of the King. But both Robertson and the settlers repeated most of their old charges against Talbot, and added a new complaint: the reduced fees on their additional grants were still higher than they would have been at the time of their first arrival, and which they would have paid if not misled by the Colonel into accepting his land. They asked that the fees be reduced to that level.[15]

Maitland rejected this complaint, as well as the collective apology. A year later Secretary Hillier informed Talbot that not many of his settlers had apologized for the language in the memorial and obtained their additional lands.[16] It was not until the spring of 1824 that the stubborn Highlanders made their submission.[17]

In the meantime, the Colonel found himself in serious financial difficulties. To obtain his personal grant of 40,420 acres of land he had paid fees amounting to £1,260, at the rate of £31/3/9 per thousand. But at his urgent request the Council reluctantly agreed to let him pay only the land officers' fees of £5/11 per thousand on the 9,300 acres included in the deed of trust, deferring the Crown and survey fees of about £25 per thousand until he could appeal to the home government for their remission.[18] Early in 1822 Talbot went to England, where he had a series of interviews with Lord Bathurst, the Colonial Secretary, and with his Under-secretary, Wilmot Horton. He now sought not only the remission of the Crown and survey fees on the deed of trust, but the return of all those he had already paid. He also asked for sufficient assistance from the government to enable him to have the help of a clerk, and to "support the rank and influence which he has hitherto maintained". In support of his claim Talbot cited the great expense and labour involved in his superintendence of a successful settlement which now included 12,000 souls. Before the outbreak of war in 1812 he had already spent about £15,000 of his own money in this work, but during the war his fields were laid waste, his mills burned, his effects destroyed or carried off, and his settlers reduced to poverty. Since the war he had struggled in the work of reconstruction, and his house had always been open to new settlers until they were able to support themselves. But now his capital was exhausted and he could no longer give assistance to the many poor immigrants who came to his settlement.

There were a number of other problems that had brought the Colonel to England. The provincial government had refused to grant him 10,000 acres of land in right of a group of fifty Highlanders, beyond the number required to complete his obligations in Dunwich and Aldborough, whom he had settled on his own land. His other interests were revealed in conversations with Wilmot Horton. He urged the renewal of the sale of school lands under his supervision, as well as the lands reserved in the Longwoods tract for the endowment of a military hospital. To prevent the provincial government from interfering with his work, he asked that definite instructions be given it limiting its power to that of a reporter for the home government; and he should be relieved of the necessity of furnishing it with regular returns.[19]

Just before leaving London, about the middle of April, Talbot called on Mrs. Gore to say good-bye, leaving her with the impression that he had "not succeeded to that extent which he was boasting of".[20] Bathurst's despatch to Maitland, which Talbot carried with him, expressed approval for everything he had asked for except the pension; but it had one fatal defect—Bathurst merely recommended that these be carried out, thus giving the Lieutenant-Governor an opportunity to voice his objections.[21] William Dummer Powell, who was in England at this time, was not sorry to hear that his enemy was probably "less elated than he appeared to be at the thought of carrying powers with him to dictate to Sir P M[aitland] and the executive Government, every member of which but one is honored here with the most virulent, malicious and malignant abuse." At one time, Powell informed his wife, the Colonel exulted "in the assurance that he was made practically independent of the Governor and the Council, and I know rejoiced in the expectation of insulting the Board on his return, but the despatch which he relied on was countermanded, and so modified as to damp his spirits. . . ."[22]

Although, as Powell told his wife, he had never mentioned Talbot's name at the Colonial Office, Talbot appeared to believe that he was responsible for the change in the Secretary's despatch. It was now Powell's turn to suspect that the Colonel had spread "malevolent reports" about him, and that this had "made some unfavourable change in the Under Secretary of State, who from the warmth of youthful friendship suddenly has transformed himself into a cold, distant and important statesman, transferring his attentions to the Attorney General [John B. Robinson] and Mr. Talbot."

In an attempt "to confute the malice of Col. Thomas Talbot", Powell prepared "a concise sketch of that person", for the Colonial Office. He was "credibly informed", the sketch begins, "that Colonel Thomas Talbot of Port Talbot has allowed himself to assert in public and private that he had used his influence with the under Secretary of State to counteract Chief Justice Powell, and probably adverted to the infamous calumny circulated against that officer thirty years past, which he asserted to Mr. Nichol and Mr. Swazie was never discredited by Lieut. Governor Simcoe, as he had reason to know from having been in his family at the time. . . ."[23] This charge was first made at Detroit in 1792, and was based on an anonymous letter addressed to the Secretary of War for the United States, which suggested means by which Detroit might be seized from the British, one involving the spread of deadly diseases among their Indian allies. The handwriting, as well as references in the letter, obviously point to Powell as the author, but Lieutenant-Governor Simcoe called it "a most atrocious and artful Forgery", which indeed it appears to be, and expressed his complete confidence in Powell. There can be no doubt but that it was a clumsy attempt on the part of the justice's enemies at Detroit to get rid of him. Talbot must have known this, and about Simcoe's support of Powell, but it seems that he was the first to revive this long dormant charge in an effort to discredit his principal opponent in the provincial government.[24] Two years later it appeared in the notorious Spanish Freeholder letter published by William Lyon Mackenzie in the *Colonial Advocate,* which caused so much anguish for the ageing chief justice.

CHAPTER IX

# The Pension and a Larger Domain

SOON after his return to Port Talbot the Colonel wrote to James Stuart-Wortley: "I am again safe in my old Log House on the top of my own high Hill, after a very tedious passage from England and journey from New York, occasioned by the quantity of baggage and the three great Dogs that I brought, which forced me to travel slow in a common farm waggon the most part of the way." Although glad to be home he was not so satisfied as formerly with his "retirement". He frequently wished, he admitted, that he was amongst his friends at Wortley Hall.[1] The passing months did not relieve his "gloomy feelings" and his sense of his "solitary situation". "You are quite correct," he told Stuart-Wortley in October, "in your suspicions as to my enjoying the civilised society around Port Talbot. Not one of my trees grew, and the Spanish Dog is dead. The Lady has produced 3 but unfortunately they are the consequence of an *illicit* amour carried on with a Dandy Lurcher during the voyage."[2]

The prime reason for the Colonel's dissatisfaction was the realization that his trip to England had not been entirely successful. When he arrived at York in June, 1822, he had met with a cool reception from Sir Peregrine Maitland, who could not conceal his displeasure at the contents of Lord Bathurst's despatch. He told Talbot that he would answer it immediately, but it would probably be three or four months before he would be able to do anything to carry out its instructions. He then demanded to know why Talbot had not delivered a letter of introduction and explanation to Bathurst which he had written for him. Talbot replied that Bathurst had received him so kindly he did not think it necessary to use it; but this excuse did not deceive Maitland, and the Colonel admitted to Stuart-Wortley that his real reason was the suspicion that his views would be in opposition to those expressed by the Lieutenant-Governor.

Immediately after his interview with Maitland, Talbot wrote to Wilmot Horton to present his side of the case. "It is really most vexatious," he told Stuart-Wortley, "after the assurances that Wilmott gave me that I would not meet with any difficulty in this Province, to find myself placed in the situation I am thro' the caprice of such a little genious as you and myself recollect Maitland to have been." His spirits had been "a little invigorated", however, by learning from a friend in Montreal of a rumour that Maitland was about to be transferred to another post, and that "your humble servant was to be elevated to the Government Chair of this Province." Professing to give little credence to the report, Talbot admitted he would "like it very much, as it would afford a comfortable provision and enable me to render essential benefit to a part of the world that has taken up so many years of my life in endeavouring to serve."[3] The vision of such an avenue of escape from his present difficulties must have been very attractive to him. If there was any chance of fulfilment, perhaps a word to Stuart-Wortley might be helpful.

This bit of cheerful news was offset by information from England that a banking house with which he had deposited nearly £1,200 had failed. Although his fears eventually proved unfounded, Talbot made use of the prospect of loss to urge Stuart-Wortley to intercede with the Colonial Office in the matter of his pension, which he thought should be £800 per annum, and certainly not less than £500. The proper procedure, he said, was for Bathurst to order Maitland to send a message to the provincial legislature asking for the pension. His situation was desperate: he did not think that all his landed property would sell for more than £3,000, and he was in debt to that amount.[4]

Writing to Bathurst on June 29, 1822, Maitland said that he wished to explain certain things which Talbot had either passed over in silence or represented erroneously. Until the previous year Talbot had paid without question the Crown and survey fees of £25 per thousand acres on all his grants. Before leaving for England he had declared he was seeking only the return of those he had paid on his last deed, and the remission of those due on his deed of trust. This money still remained untouched, and could be refunded to him, but the fees paid on his various grants since 1804 had long since been spent, and there was no fund available for them. Talbot also sought 10,000 acres of land in right of fifty Highlanders, although his agency under the agreement with Lord Hobart had ended. Maitland suggested he be given a grant of 2,500 acres only, an amount equal to what he had given to the Highlanders.

Turning to the question of Talbot's superintendence, Maitland wrote that he had no reason to complain about having to make returns to the Surveyor-General, and he disagreed with Talbot's statement that his system was much more successful than that of the provincial government. Talbot's was not a new system, nor was it confined to his settlement. The government under the present administration also enforced the performance of settlement duties before issuing deeds; and this, with the establishment of the land boards, had caused such rapid progress that several districts now surpassed the Talbot Settlement. The Lieutenant-Governor further disagreed with the Colonel's suggestion that all reserves should be removed from roads throughout the province so they might be completely settled and opened. He was much more concerned with the rapid increase in value of reserves left on the roads, which brought in much income to the government.

Despite these criticisms Maitland concluded by praising Talbot for his generous assistance to new settlers, his punctuality in the enforcement of settlement duties, and his success in opening and improving roads. He was in agreement on the question of selling the school lands, and noted that he himself had asked and been given permission to sell part of them. If the sale were advertised in England, and only the annual interest had to be paid by buyers, he thought a sufficient revenue could be obtained for the support of the schools.[5]

Lord Bathurst was displeased to learn that Talbot had not delivered Maitland's letter to him, and that he had not been entirely candid in his representations. He fully approved of all Maitland's recommendations but told him the Colonel must be given to understand that the refund of the extra fees, on his last grant only, was "a pure matter of grace and favor, and in no way whatever countenancing the pretensions he had advanced".[6] When informed of this Talbot signed a statement agreeing to the condition; but he refused to accept the "illiberal" offer of a mere 2,500 acres of land in right of his fifty Highlanders.[7] It is likely that these were among the Scots who left Aldborough to settle in Lobo

Township. Talbot never forgave the Lieutenant-Governor. "The truth is," he had written to Stuart-Wortley in the fall of 1822, "that he is jealous and annoyed at my having acquired so much credit for the improvement of so extensive a portion of the Province, and to hear from every person who visits the Talbot Country, that it infinitely surpases [*sic*] any of the settlements formed under the auspices of the Colonial Government."[8]

Writing again to Stuart-Wortley the following June, Talbot said: "How delightful are all your accounts of every one of my dear friends belonging to your family. I can't describe the pleasure I would feel from seeing you all again, but Missy I fear will be so grown, before I can pay my way to England, that she will *cut* the Knight of St. Thomas. . . . I need not apprize you that I passed a devilish Winter, besides it has been the most severe that I have known in U. C. and the spring the most backward and cold. I went for a month to York, our Metropolis. Maitland and myself corresponded with the frigidness of the Season, but I was received in as friendly a manner as possible by Lady Sarah, who is a dear good person and I pity her from my heart in having so frozen a helpmate. I am now busy ploughing and getting in my Spring crops and superintending my flock (settlers); by the way, there was a most gay *anniversary* on the 21st May and 'the Old Colonel' kicked his heels from 8 in the evening to 8 in the morng, so that you may appreciate his merits."[9] In England, the Gores learned of the difficulties between Maitland and Talbot with a certain amount of satisfaction. "We are very desirous," Gore wrote to Powell, "to know how our *excellent* friend Talbot is getting on, and if it has yet come to a decided blow-up with the Lieutenant-Governor."[10]

In his next letter to Stuart-Wortley, written in September 1823, Talbot spoke of a visit he had had from an agent for a group of farmers of Fifeshire, Scotland, who were thinking of emigrating to Canada. "With me," he said, "it continues as dull as last year, that is, as bad as possible, no money. I wish that a company of rich Fifeshire farmers would come out and purchase all my lands, if so I would soon be amongst you and enjoy the remainder of my days in Gentlemanly Society. Here I scarcely see one of that description in 12 months, even when I visit York, our seat of Government, the Noblesse, some of whom are good sort of people, but in point of refinement, not a little deficient. . . . Now I must beg of you to write to me as often as you can as I really have no other pleasure in this wilderness than your letters."[11]

Having heard that Wilmot Horton wished to know how the Assembly of Upper Canada would view the question of his pension, Talbot turned to his friend Christopher Hagerman, one of the leading members. Hagerman's reply seemed to convey a favourable prospect, and he suggested writing to the Lieutenant-Governor on the subject. This the Colonel would not do, as he told Stuart-Wortley, because he believed Maitland was "of so cold and unforgiving a nature" that he would be most likely to oppose any measure for his relief.[12] A few months later, in the fall of 1823, he was disappointed to learn that Bathurst would not consent to instruct Maitland in the matter. Talbot blamed this on the latter's opposition, but Horton declared that Maitland had not said a word about the pension; Bathurst was angry at Talbot, being "*strongly* of the opinion" that he had done wrong in withholding Maitland's letter of recommendation while in London. Horton thought that Bathurst might be disposed to sanction the pension if Hagerman volunteered to introduce a bill for that purpose, but it would have to take its chance of passing.[13]

Talbot refused to follow this procedure. "I would not for a moment," he told Stuart-Wortley, "think of exposing myself before such a body as a Colonial House of Assembly is composed of, upon such slender encouragement as was held out by Lord Bathurst and Wilmot Horton."[14] He and his friends continued to urge the pension on the London government. Lewis McGillivray wrote of him in April, 1824: "He has devoted the labour of a life 25 years, and shown a degree of energy and perseverance, which in any pursuit would have ensured success. He has succeeded—he is a Patriarch—surrounded by a thriving, increasing population. . . . Now look at the *real* result. Colonel Talbot has expended in this pursuit the labour of his life—the sacrifice of comfort and society—and about £20,000. He has got about 60,000 acres of land, which in the time of his Brothers' Grandchildren may be valuable but which *he could not now sell for* £12,000. The enthusiasm which gave energy to his early efforts is worn out and he is tied for life to a scene now become irksome to him, because having expended all his money, and being unable to get it back, he cannot afford to live in England."[15]

Early in 1826, when the groundwork for success had been completed, Talbot prepared a new memorial on the subject. The Lieutenant-Governor, now on much better terms with him, forwarded it to Bathurst with a strong recommendation in its favour. There was no provincial revenue then available for the pension, he said, but he suggested that it might be paid out of the proceeds of the sale of the Crown reserves to the Canada Company.[16] Bathurst agreed, and in a despatch dated June 8, 1826, authorized a pension to Talbot of £400 annually, retroactive to the first of the year.[17] The provincial Assembly was not consulted, a fact to be listed as a grievance in future years. The pension was not as large as the Colonel had hoped for, and he did not give up his efforts to obtain further government assistance.

The sale to the Canada Company of a million acres of land to the east of Lake Huron, known henceforth as the Huron Tract, provided part of the funds from which Talbot's pension was derived, but it also put an end to his hopes of forming a great new settlement in that region. Writing to Hillier in August, 1824, Talbot expressed regret that the negotiations with the Indians for the purchase of the immense territory north of the London and Western Districts had not yet been completed. The land there was of excellent quality, he said, and was well watered by Big Bear Creek (now the River Sydenham) and the River Sable. If it were open for settlement he "could make a delightful one of it, having lately had an intimation from upwards of sixty Welsh families now in the United States, that they would remove into this neighbourhood, if they could obtain land, and my object would be to place them immediately north of my friend *Squire* Matthews' little Welsh colony in London. Besides, Mr. Matthews proposes going to England the next autumn for the purpose of bringing out some more of his relations, and I have not any doubt but that he could induce a large emigration from South Wales, who are a very orderly and industrious people."[18]

Later in the month Talbot went to Queenston to meet four young members of the British House of Commons, who were on a tour of North America. They were John Evelyn Denison, Henry Labouchere, John Stuart-Wortley (eldest son of his old friend), and Edward Geoffrey Stanley (son of the Earl of Derby). Two weeks were spent as the guests of the Lieutenant-Governor at Stamford Cottage, his delightful summer home midway between Queenston and Niagara Falls,[19] interrupted by a three-day trip by land to Rochester in New York State. Early in September all accompanied Maitland to Quebec. Later in the month Talbot and his four "travelling companions" returned to Niagara Falls, whence they set out on a tour of the western part of the province. About a month later, after a stay at Port Talbot, they came back to Stamford Cottage for another brief visit with Maitland before the young Englishmen left for the United States.[20]

The Colonel took advantage of his stay at Stamford to discuss his plans for the new tract. On a map of the province he marked four townships immediately to the north of Lobo, London, Nissouri, and Zorra, which he suggested should be named Stanley, Wortley, Denison, and Labouchere in honour of his friends, and put under his superintendence for settlement. Maitland seemed friendly to the plan, perhaps in deference to his distinguished visitors from England, but nothing could be done until the purchase was completed.[21]

Nearly a year later, in June, 1825, having heard rumours that a bargain had at last been made with the Indians for "that delightful part of the province",[22] Talbot wrote to tell Secretary Hillier that he was anxious to begin the settlement of the Township of Wortley, which was to be north of London Township, as soon as it could be surveyed. Squire Matthews had lately returned from England with a number of his Welsh friends, and was about to visit the large Welsh settlement in New York State to invite the people there to emigrate to Wortley.[23] The following spring Talbot was

BARRACKS, CHATHAM, c. 1838

From the painting by P. J. Bainbrigge, courtesy Public Archives of Canada

still optimistic about getting control,[24] but by fall he had begun to despair. "I must beg of you," he wrote to Hillier in November, 1826, "not to let the Company get my four townships, Stanley, Wortley, Denison, and La Bouchere. . . ."[25] In April, 1827, he wrote to say that he had almost given up hope, and to warn Hillier that the Canada Company's officers were "a troublesome gang". He had heard while at Quebec that they expressed dislike for Commissioner of Crown Lands Peter Robinson, "and the Administration in general of the Province".[26] Soon afterwards his fears were confirmed when he learned that the Huron Tract, which included his prospective townships, was to be sold to the Company.

Meanwhile, on January 1, 1826, a change had gone into effect in the provincial land-granting system, by which Crown lands were no longer granted on the payment of fees, but were sold at public auction under the direction of a commissioner. Talbot was now put in the anomalous position of still granting lots under the old system; and there was danger that pressure might be exerted to end his superintendence and put the Talbot Settlement under the control of the Commissioner of Crown Lands. The Colonel decided to attack first by going again to England and presenting a plan which, if accepted, would have greatly enlarged the area under his jurisdiction. But he was "most savagely in want", as he wrote to Hillier in September, 1827, and he could not make the trip until he received the first payment of his pension, which depended on when the Canada Company should pay the first instalment on its debt to the government. A month later he received the amount due on his pension for the first year and a half, amounting to £600 sterling.[27]

Leaving home about the middle of January, 1828, Talbot went to New York and from there sailed for Liverpool in the packet ship *William Thompson*.[28] He arrived in London in March to discuss his plans with Under-secretary Robert Hay. On April 28 he submitted to Secretary William Huskisson a map of Upper Canada, on which he had marked the boundaries of the tract which he wished to have called the Talbot Settlement, and within which he would control the location of all vacant Crown lands. In a later letter he said that the tract was about three hundred miles in length and from fifty to one hundred miles in breadth, which would appear to cover most of the province west of Lake Simcoe. Huskisson submitted the request to Maitland for his opinion, and at the same time told him to instruct the Commissioner of Crown Lands not to sell any part of the tract until a final decision was made.[29]

During the remainder of the year Talbot visited old friends in England, and his brother at Malahide Castle in Ireland. In January he returned to London, but soon after left for a trip through France. In London again a few weeks later, he had an interview with the new Colonial Secretary, Sir George Murray. He now requested the services of two paid assistants, who would travel through the extensive tract he had applied for and watch over the progress of the settlers. For himself he asked a salary of £200 per year—which would be in addition to his pension of £400. These requests were referred to Sir John Colborne, who had succeeded Maitland as Lieutenant-Governor the previous fall.[30]

The Colonel sailed for New York in March, 1829. "We presume," the *Colonial Advocate* of April 30 remarked on reporting his arrival from Liverpool, "the Colonel's last trip to London had for its object in part, the augmentation of his seventeen hundred dollars pension, which he obtained out of the slender means of this colony and without the people's consent, by his prayers and supplications to the British Government. Doctor Strachan's agents in London, Judges Boulton, Campbell and Powell are expected out soon. The united incomes of these old cumberers of the ground, derived from the Canadian people, but against their will, is sixteen thousand dollars a year. It is grants like the above on the part of governments which sow the seeds of what is called sedition in colonies."

Lieutenant-Governor Colborne praised Talbot's success in settling the country and bringing it into cultivation many years earlier than it would have been had he not devoted his life to it. But now that lands under any management were eagerly sought after, he told Murray, he could see no advantage in removing a large number of additional townships from the control of the Commissioner of Crown Lands. Although of the opinion that the Colonel should be permitted to retain control of the townships already under his jurisdiction, he wished to learn more about his Settlement before coming to a final decision.[31] For this reason he set out in October on a tour of the London and Western Districts, stopping for a time at Port Talbot as the guest of the Colonel. His later despatches to Murray contain high praise for Talbot: he had successfully settled an extensive tract and established good roads from Woodhouse to Sandwich, a distance of 130 miles; he had given assistance to many of the immigrants from Ireland and Scotland who had come in without money; his system was despotic, but everyone appeared satisfied with his arrangements and appreciated his labours.[32]

Nevertheless, Colborne had not altered his mind about placing additional townships under the Colonel's jurisdiction. His tour had convinced him that it was possible to make arrangements for settlement, and for the opening of roads, which would bring in greater revenue and "more solid advantages". Persons of influence and education, of whom few had been located by Talbot, could be induced to come in; and roads could be opened with alternate lots reserved for the Crown, which would become valuable as time passed. Colborne noticed that the Colonel's own estate in Dunwich and Aldborough, which he estimated could now be sold for £24,000, had attained this value because he had encircled his lands with industrious settlers, and he thought the government could reap equal benefits by distributing the Crown reserves among the settled lands. What he did not seem to know was that this had been tried for many years, and was one of the chief hindrances to advancement of settlement and road building.

In making these observations to Murray, in support of his contention that no new townships should be joined to the Talbot Settlement, Colborne noted that no more than 737 patents had been issued to settlers there, although the population numbered at least 30,000 souls. The unlimited credit accorded his settlers for the payment of fees brought in very little revenue to the government, and was still more objectionable, Colborne thought, than the new system of auction sales of land under the direction of the Commissioner of Crown Lands, with the purchase money paid in five annual instalments, to which Talbot objected.[33]

In answer to his request for a return on all locations made since his last report, and the amount of land still vacant in each of his townships, Talbot had informed the Lieutenant-Governor that it would take him a year to compile the list of locations, because of the casualties resulting from "fraud, speculation, and failure of settlement duties and actual residence". He did, however, submit a general statement of the amount of land still vacant and grantable, which showed that very few lots remained unlocated except in the townships of Essex County. "As to the payment of Fees," he wrote, in answer to Colborne's question on that head, "there is not any time fixed, as the Settlers in most cases apply to me as soon as they have completed the duties required, for my certificate, to enable them to take out their patents, and I take it for granted, that they are then anxious to secure a title to the Land, but the difficulty of procuring the amount of the Fee, must frequently retard their application at York." He did not recommend a demand for the payment of fees at the time of location, for the reason that most new settlers did not have the money, it would be almost impossible to get back the fees where failures occurred, and "not one in twenty would fulfil the regulations required, as they would naturally think that there would not be any risk of losing the land after the fees were paid." In fact, he concluded, "the lamentable state of the greatest portion of this fine Province, as to actual settlement, I attribute to the issuing of Deeds before the Grantees became residents and improved their Land, which must appear obvious to every person who travels thro' the country."[34]

Colborne was not convinced that the "unlimited credit" accorded Talbot's settlers in the payment of their fees should be continued, and although he did not wish to recommend that the townships in the Talbot Settlement be put under the Commissioner of Crown Lands, this solution to the problem must have received serious consideration in the Colonial Office. It was one of the reasons why the British government in April, 1830, appointed John Richards to examine and report on the whole question of land settlement in the North American provinces. That summer Richards travelled through much of the London District, observing the good roads, the cultivated fields, and the generally prosperous condition of the Talbot Settlement, contrasted with the great blocks of wild land, traversed by bad roads, which the government had granted to non-residents in other parts of the district. Stopping for a time at Port Talbot, as the Colonel's guest, he was told that the Colonel had located 6,000 families. Finding later that only 785 of these had taken out their patents, he reported to the Colonial Secretary, on his return to England early in 1831, that 5,215 of Talbot's settlers had not taken out their patents, and that between £35,000 and £40,000 in fees remained unpaid. He recommended that they be required to pay their fees and take out their patents within some specified time. In addition, he recommended that the Colonel be required to render an account of his "landed concerns". "The instability of human life," Richards concluded, "renders it improper to postpone this settlement to any future time."[35]

Talbot was surprised when he learned from Colborne the details of Richards' report, and that Colonial Secretary Goderich had directed the carrying out of his recommendations. While disclaiming responsibility for the failure of his settlers to take out their patents, or for any "inconvenience and confusion" in the land-granting department, he nevertheless promised to notify the settlers that they must apply for their patents as soon as they had completed their settlement duties. He did not think, however, that any settler, even if he had the money to pay the fees, should be given his deed until he had lived on the land for five years, "in which time the Settler becomes in most cases attached to the spot and considers it his home."[36]

The Colonel sent a copy of this letter to Goderich, with a lengthy explanation of his disinterested motives in undertaking the settlement of so much of the London and Western Districts. "I have not," he stated, "from the commencement of taking the superintendence of this Settlement been allowed the slightest assistance in the way of a Secretary or Clerk, and have myself performed the whole of the arduous duties which must necessarily attend the management of so extensive a portion of new Country, which must unavoidably incur no small expense and diminish my own private resources, by having had to supply with provisions, clothing, etc., numerous destitute Emigrants, until they were able to make their own Land produce sufficient means of support for themselves, for without relief I afforded, many must have starved."[37] But his struggle to expand the boundaries of the Talbot Settlement had been lost; Colborne had advised against permitting him to delegate any part of his authority to assistants; and it seemed that his long reign would soon be ended.

## CHAPTER X

# *The Settlement of the Talbot Country*

Colonel Talbot had undertaken the laborious duties of an unpaid government land agent, in the beginning, to ensure the building of a highway connecting his isolated settlement in Dunwich with the Long Point region. His interest in opening additional roads, and in peopling the waste lands of the southwestern part of Upper Canada, soon developed far beyond any material advantage to himself. He may have been motivated by a lust for power; but there is no reason to disbelieve his often-repeated statement that he sought recompense only in the pleasure of being instrumental in the transformation of the wilderness into a land of prosperous farms. He was driven in the same direction, however, by the increasing pressure from immigrants and others who found their way to Port Talbot in search of land.

Early in 1821, when he asked that the Talbot Road be continued from Mersea to Sandwich, the Colonel recommended that a "Middle Road" be surveyed midway between it and the Thames River and Lake St. Clair, starting at the western boundary of Aldborough and ending at Sandwich; and also new roads along the lines dividing the townships in Kent County, to provide communications with the Thames region; all these roads to be opened by settlers established along them. The government gave its approval, and Mahlon

Burwell began the surveys that spring, but it was several years before all were completed.[1]

In the fall of 1823 Talbot complained to Secretary Hillier that he was "continually harassed by enquiries about land", most of them from people impatient to secure lots in Howard Township, where Burwell had recently completed the survey of the Middle Road, as well as the remaining unreserved parts, comprising more than 38,000 acres of rich land. At his request the government agreed to place Howard under his superintendence, on the same conditions as applied for the townships elsewhere in the Talbot Settlement. The Colonel asked that the plan of Howard be sent to him at once, so that he could begin to make locations and "enable the families, who have been waiting several months in the expectation of obtaining locations in those places, to erect houses before the snow falls too deep".[2] However, it was only when he was in York the following January that he was able to secure the plan. On his return to Port Talbot a few weeks later he found himself almost overwhelmed by the impatient people. "Every hour of the day that I have been at home," he informed Hillier, "I have been beset by Battalions of applicants for land in Howard, certainly not fewer than 1,000, the third day 500 in a body, in consequence of which, and to get rid of the pest, I intend having a Lottery on the 1st of March, so as to give a general chance, but I will not include the Middle or Town Line Roads in it, keeping them for a more select description."[3]

When making his recommendations for these roads in 1821, the Colonel had requested, without success, that he be given the superintendence of the new Longwoods Road, just north of the Thames River, between Delaware and the Moravian village. The whole range of lots on the south side of this road, and the area between it and the river, was reserved for the support of a military hospital; on the north side there was the usual amount of Crown and clergy reserves which, unlike those on the Talbot roads, had not been moved back. The Surveyor-General had begun to give out locations of the available lots on the north in the fall of 1820, many of them to speculators and non-residents who did little or no work on them. The handful of scattered settlers who actually occupied their lots were unable to clear much of the road, and it long remained a mere trail, almost impassable for vehicles, the subject of bitter complaints by all who traversed it.[4]

Although the Longwoods Road was a route rivalling that of the Talbot Road, the Colonel was exasperated by the failure of the government to open it, especially as he was eyeing this region to help him get rid of the "unpleasant visitors" who were besieging him with demands for land. In February, 1824, he renewed his request that the road be placed under his superintendence, and that the reserves on both sides be removed, so that it might be settled throughout; he also asked to be allowed to locate any other vacant lots in the Longwoods townships of Lobo, Caradoc, Ekfrid, and Mosa.[5] Its hand forced by the rising clamour for the improvement of the road, the government gave in. The reserves were removed from the road and it was placed under Talbot's superintendence, with the provision, however, that the lots on the south side must be sold to pay the costs of the Indian purchase and the survey. He was also permitted to locate all vacant lots in the four Longwoods townships, except the broken lots of less than one hundred acres which Maitland had put under special reserve.[6]

The Colonel was not happy to learn that he could grant only the vacant lots along the north side of the road, where much of the land was already held by non-residents. At his insistence, on April 1 it was decreed that the settlement duties on lots held for two years or more must be completed within three months, or the lots would be declared vacant.[7] But finding that he could not sell the lots on the south side, because of the prevailing scarcity of money, Talbot informed Lieutenant-Governor Maitland on May 7 that he would not accept the superintendence of the road unless these were opened to grant.[8] The government delayed coming to a decision until the following fall, when the rains had made the Longwoods Road a sticky morass. "It was at the Risque of my life," Chief Justice Powell complained bitterly to Maitland on October 9, "and destruction of my carriage that, bearing the King's Commission and limited to a day, I was drugged through the mud, by oxen, for a space of twenty-four miles." In all that distance he found but six actual settlers.[9] Unable to wait longer, the government now gave Talbot authority to locate freely the lots on both sides of the road.[10] So quickly did he act that by November 24 he was able to report the location of all except eight or ten that were undesirable for settlement. Having heard nothing further about the forfeiture of the unimproved grants on the north, he suspected, he said, "that the Yankey Eagle has spread its baleful Shadow, to screen the Delinquents."[11] A few days later, however, the Surveyor-General reported that these lots were open for re-location, except for seven on which the settlement duties had been completed previous to July 1.[12]

The government was more lenient with the delinquents in the rear concessions. In the fall of 1830, when Talbot had but few lots left to locate in his settlement, he informed Lieutenant-Governor Colborne that this was the unhappy result of "the odious system that was heretofore pursued by the Executive Government of locating land to non-residents, which is painfully the case in the Longwood townships". At the time he took charge, he declared, the principal part of these townships had been "culled and located to God knows who, at York . . . and of course that Tract presents scarcely anything better than a wilderness. . . . In all my labours, nothing mortifies me more than impediments that so frequently occur, by land remaining waste and not available."[13] Stirred by this complaint, the Council on May 10, 1831, decreed that no more deeds should issue for the Longwoods lots that had been located at York, until an inspection had been made with a view to forfeiting those found to be unimproved.[14] The following October Deputy Surveyor Peter Carroll was instructed to make the inspection. His report showed that the settlement duties had not been performed on one hundred and ten lots in Caradoc, Ekfrid, and Mosa, although the time limit had long since expired.[15] Nevertheless, no further steps appear to have been taken, and ten years later Talbot stated that he did not think there was a single settler on the lots in these townships which had been located at York, and he believed there were still many of them for which patents had not yet been issued.[16]

In the meantime, in August, 1824, the Colonel had offered to superintend the settlement of the newly-surveyed northern part of Zone (now Euphemia), the next township to the west of the Longwoods; but he refused to take "fag ends", and the Surveyor-General must be given to understand that no lots in this township were to be located at York. The usual practice there, he wrote, was "to select from the field notes the essence of the land for the best customers, who do not become actual settlers."[17] Maitland agreed, and Talbot took charge of locations in Zone, to the chagrin of some of the government officials who had hoped to obtain land there.[18] But despite this extension, the pressure of applications increased rather than diminished. On November 24, not long after his return from a trip to Niagara, Talbot wrote to Secretary Hillier: "I have been more pestered than I have ever been, or you can imagine, about land, since my return. I have sent a large force of southern Irish to Sandwich, which I expect will be followed by vast numbers next year, which must cheer the old inhabitants of that insulated part of the Province."[19]

For those applicants who had money, and wished to obtain more desirable locations, Talbot had school lands to sell at fixed prices, for which he received a commission of three per cent on all sales. These lands, comprising about 91,000 acres, and situated in the townships of Blandford, Houghton, Middleton, Southwold, Yarmouth, and Westminster, had been put under his control in 1823, but it was several years before all of them were surveyed and made available.[20] In the summer of 1824 the Wharncliffe Road was surveyed through the school reserves in Westminster and the Crown reserves west of the Forks in London, to connect the settled concessions in the northern part of London with the Commissioners Road through Westminster.[21] On August 6, just after the completion of the survey, Talbot reported that he had sold three lots on the new road at twelve and a half shillings per acre.[22] The following spring he was also given charge of the hospital lands between the Longwoods Road and the river.[23]

During the early months of 1825 Mahlon Burwell finished the survey of the Middle and Talbot Roads through Essex County to Sandwich on the Detroit River, and the following summer he began work in Orford Township on the eastern end of the Middle Road. Writing to Secretary Hillier on July 1, Talbot said that he had many applicants wishing to settle in the Essex townships, but he was unable to do anything for them until he received the plans. Two Kentish families had recently arrived from Pennsylvania, whence thirty more were expected before winter, as well as a number of English and Scottish families from West Virginia. These the Colonel wished to place on the Middle Road in Orford, and he warned that the officials at York should be on their guard against "a gang of speculators, who have been following the Surveyor and choosing lots, which they say, that they will go to York and get grants of, in spite of *Old* Talbot."[24] In September, when Burwell finished the survey of the Middle Road and adjacent lands in the southern part of Orford, Talbot asked for permission to locate settlers there at once, without waiting for the plans, so that houses might be erected before the arrival of winter. He also begged again for the plans of the townships in Essex County. These did not come, and in December he told Surveyor-General Ridout that it would be "mortifying and cruel in the extreme", if the families that had been waiting at Port Talbot for so many months to go to that region should be disappointed.[25] Ridout did not reply, and the exasperated Colonel turned to Hillier, who explained that the delay had been occasioned by the new system about to go into effect, for the sale of Crown lands at public auction, in place of the old system of grant on the payment of fees. Until it could be decided whether or not the Talbot Settlement would be affected by this change, the Colonel was to make no new locations, except to those persons already promised.[26]

This ban was soon lifted, and Talbot continued to make locations as before. A temporary halt occurred during 1828 and the early part of 1829, when he was in England, but by the end of the latter year he was able to report that the Middle Road was completely settled through Orford, Howard, and Raleigh, and that the Talbot Road was being opened by settlers from Gosfield to the town of Sandwich. Burwell had surveyed parts of the townships of Romney, Mersea, and Colchester, back from these roads, during 1829, but although these lots were put under Talbot's superintendence, many of them were too wet to be desirable. Throughout the rest of the Talbot Settlement there were scarcely any lots left for location. In the fall of 1830, when immigrants were coming to the province in unprecedented numbers, Talbot informed the Lieutenant-Governor that he felt "much mortified" at not being able to satisfy those who came every day to his house seeking land.[27]

The Colonel had not been able to open the Middle Road across the Township of Harwich, because it crossed the reserves and the lands held for many years by non-residents,[28] but he did not give up hope that something might yet be done to remove these impediments. In the spring of 1830 he suggested to the Commissioner of Crown Lands that a range of lots on each side of the road be surveyed through the clergy and Canada Company's blocks of reserves, which he was convinced would readily sell for twelve shillings sixpence per acre.[29] Some years later this plan was adopted, lots on the road in Harwich were sold by the Commissioner at fixed prices, and the Middle Road was finally opened from Aldborough to Sandwich.

Most of the lands now disposed of by the Colonel were also by sale. In September, 1831, he received the plan of the school lands in the southern part of Southwold, which Burwell had surveyed the previous spring.[30] A month later he was selling school lands in Yarmouth to immigrants at twelve and a half shillings per acre. "Every vessel," he wrote at this time, "brings lots of Highland Scotch, many of whom possess the means of purchasing."[31] But he disliked the Scots, and two years later, when John Elmsley wished to purchase 5,000 acres in Westminster, he insisted that he dispose of his land only to English immigrants, and not to Highlanders. He also insisted that Elmsley sell his land as soon as possible to actual settlers only.[32]

In the summer of 1831 there had been a movement on foot to take from Talbot the sale of the school lands, and to place them under the direction of the Board of Education in each district. As soon as he heard of it the Colonel wrote to Strachan in protest. No one, he declared, could sell these lands to as good advantage as himself, and the district boards "would do nothing but job". Nearly all the lands were situated in the London District, and even if a division could be effected it would be difficult for the boards in other districts to supervise the sale of their portions.[33] At his suggestion it was decided to let him continue selling the lands, and the proceeds were divided among the various district boards. Writing to William Allan two years later, he stated that he was selling school lands every day. Those in Blandford were most in demand, principally by retired naval and army officers, but he had others for sale in the townships of Mosa, Ekfrid, Westminster, Middleton, and Houghton. He sold none for less than twelve and a half shillings per acre, and some for as much as three or four pounds.[34] "I have had an addition of several respectable English families lately," he informed Colborne in November, 1833, "who have purchased near St. Thomas, and they expect that many of their friends will join them next year, as they are delighted with the country."[35] But immigration had declined since the peak year of 1832, and sales became slow. "This is a bad year for selling land," Talbot wrote in August, 1835, "in consequence of the very few Emigrants that have come to my part of the Province."[36]

By this time the only free land still available for location in the Talbot Settlement was in the townships of Zone, Raleigh, Tilbury, Rochester, and Malden. These lots became valuable in later years when the land was drained, but at this time few persons were willing to perform the settlement duties on them and pay the heavy fees.[37] In the spring of 1834 a young Scot named John Robertson applied to the Colonel for land. Talbot said that he had a few scattered lots yet to dispose of, but the best had all been taken up. "He gave me my choice of three lots," Robertson wrote to his father, "and I went to see them, but as they lay out of the way of market, with bad roads, and the discouraging accounts the settlers around gave of the place, being so level that in spring it would be almost all covered with water, which prevented them getting their crops down in time, and in summer it dried up so that there was great difficulty in getting water—some who had dug wells could not use the water and the oxen could not drink it—these, and the general complaint of the early frosts in Autumn destroying their Indian corn and other green crops, made me give up the intention of settling in Canada. . . ."[38] Nevertheless Talbot guarded these lots jealously, keeping them for actual settlers. When a member of the Baby family applied to him at this time for land under a militia right, he said that he did not locate military grants, "and what land I have left at my disposal in the Western District is only for actual settlers, which is absolutely required in that part of the Province, where so injurious and extensive a monopoly was made by persons who have kept the country in a state of wilderness."[39]

Although he had but few lots left to dispose of, Talbot's work was far from done. Until the settlement duties were completed, the fees paid, and the patent taken out, his control over each located lot remained as firm as ever. In the fall of 1835 Deputy Surveyor Wilkinson published a notice in the Sandwich *Canadian Emigrant*, stating that he had been authorized by Colonel Talbot "to prohibit his settlers on Talbot Street West, and Maidstone Centre Road, from disposing of their lots or improvements, as in the event of any settler leaving his lot he will re-locate it to another individual."[40]

The Colonel also had considerable work to do yet in the town of London, the settlement of which had been entrusted to him in the spring of 1827. On January 30, 1826, a Provincial Act had provided for the transfer of the London District seat of government from Vittoria to the Forks of the River Thames in London Township, where Simcoe had planned a town which was to be the capital of the province. Colonel Talbot, Mahlon Burwell, James Hamilton, Charles Ingersoll, and Captain John Matthews of Lobo were named commissioners for the construction of the new jail and courthouse. At their first meeting, held on March 6, the commissioners arranged to advertise for plans and estimates for a brick and stone building not to exceed £4,000 in cost. As chairman of the commission Talbot recommended that the new town of London be situated on the high ground in the northeast triangle formed by the union of the two branches of the river.[41] This advice was accepted, and Burwell surveyed the town plot the following June.

The site for the court-house, chosen by Talbot and Burwell after a visit to the spot, was not approved for some months, so that it was not until April, 1827, that the contract for the construction of the building could be awarded.[42] In the belief that the Colonel had charge of locations within the town plot, many people had been coming to Port Talbot to obtain lots. To avoid what he termed the "speculation, imposition, and delay" that would result if locations were made at York, Talbot now offered to undertake the superintendence of settlement within the town. "Now that the Courts of Justice are regularly held in the Plot," he wrote to Secretary Hillier, "it is most desirable that there should be Houses of accommodation."[43] The nearest inn was several miles away on the Commissioners Road in Westminster. Temporary offices for the local government were in a two-storey frame structure which had been built on the court-house grounds during the winter, and which was intended for the use of the district school.

The government was unable to decide whether the lots in the town of London should be located by Talbot, under the old system of free grants on the payment of fees, or sold under the direction of the Commissioner of Crown Lands at public auction. As the weeks went by the people and the Colonel became increasingly impatient. Finally, on June 28, the latter wrote to Hillier: "By the delay in not arranging any system about the Town Lots in the Town plot of London, I can assure you, that there will be much mischief—as vagabonds are now taking possession of the best lots, and putting up little Log Huts on 3 or 4 lots and fancy that they are to hold them in consequence. I am astonished that you folks at York are not quicker."[44] Two weeks later an order-in-council placed the town under Talbot's superintendence under the old terms as to fees and settlement duties.[45] So rapidly did it develop that by November, as reported by a visitor: "A considerable tract of country has been cleared—roads laid out—bridges built—and between 20 and 30 buildings, about half of Frame, have been erected—including a temporary jail and Court House—a very respectable Tavern—a Blacksmith's Shop—a Brewery (erecting)—one or two small Merchant's Shops and some very good Dwelling Houses. . . . The Court House, which will be one of the most magnificent buildings of its kind in Upper Canada, is commenced, under the superintendence of a most respectable architect (Mr. Ewart) a great proportion of the bricks having already been made, the foundation dug, and preparations for actively carrying on the work are in a forward state."[46]

An anonymous correspondent of the Sandwich *Canadian Emigrant*, writing in January, 1834, contrasted the remarkable progress of London with that of Chatham, where auction sales of lots were held only at infrequent intervals under the direction of the Commissioner of Crown Lands, and where the sale of the lots fronting on the river and creek had been suspended until they could command a higher price. The writer advised applicants for lands not to apply to the Commissioner or to the local land agents, "but to make application to Colonel Talbot, who will locate them without trouble, ceremony or delay."[47] In July, 1835, this or another writer wrote to the Toronto *Patriot* to protest against the evils resulting from the non-resident grants in Chatham. "Colonel Talbot who obtained the management of the Town of London adopted a different principle," he declared. "He granted the lots to individuals on condition of their building and becoming immediate settlers, and if they did not comply in a reasonable time they forfeited their lot, and another person obtained it; by these steps London gradually rose and held out to the council an example of what might be accomplished by an energetic and vigorous policy. . . ."[48]

The settlement of the town plot of London went forward rapidly during 1827, and the growth of the village does not seem to have suffered from the Colonel's absence in the United Kingdom during the next year and a half. After his return in 1829 his advice was frequently sought by the Executive Council whenever it had to make decisions concerning special grants to churches or district officers, or the grant or sale of mill sites in or adjoining the village. He continued to supervise the performance of the settlement duties; and when portions of the reserves adjoining the town plot were sub-divided, as in 1835, he directed the surveys and sold the lots.[49] His connection with the early history of London was much closer than has been generally recognized; and there are no grounds for the charge which has sometimes been made, that he neglected London because it threatened the position of St. Thomas as the capital of the Talbot Settlement.

By the mid-1830's the Colonel's work was slowly drawing towards its close, but more than a decade would pass before it was finally ended. In July, 1837, Mrs. Jameson noticed while staying at Port Talbot that each morning there were "groups of strange figures lounging round the door, ragged, black-bearded, gaunt, travel-worn and toil-worn emigrants, come to offer themselves as settlers."[50] But there were few free lands now left for them; probably some came to buy school lots, or to see the Colonel on other business.

CHAPTER XI

# The Great Migration

DURING his stay in London in 1822 Talbot had become acquainted with Colonial Under-secretary Robert Wilmot, who assumed the additional name of Horton a year later. Horton was a zealous advocate of assisted emigration of paupers to the colonies, believing this to be the remedy for the burden of poor-relief that lay so heavily on the English parishes, and for the low wages and unemployment that resulted from a surplus population. At the same time, he was convinced, these emigrants would become successful farmers on the Crown lands, helping to produce wealth and strength for the colonies and for the Empire as a whole.[1]

A year after his return to Canada Talbot informed Stuart-Wortley that he had just received a letter from Horton, "transmitting his plan of emigration to Upper Canada, which I like exceedingly, and trust it may be carried thro' Parliament, but I am so much vexed with the Bourbons for disturbing the world with their hazardous game, that I would not be sorry if they were all driven to Russia." Having made some observations on the plan, he sent them to Stuart-Wortley with the request that he give them to the Under-secretary.[2] Some time later he received from Horton a copy of his committee's report on the "State of the Poor of Ireland". It made him shudder, he told Horton, to find that the people of the South of Ireland were in such straits, but he trusted that the report and Horton's efforts would "have the effect that they deserve and prove a relief to many thousands of these distressed peoples". In a letter to Stuart-Wortley he said that even the worst of his neighbours, the Indians, were "infinitely better off than the poor of the South of Ireland, and this country could provide comfortably for some hundreds of thousands of them".[3]

Horton had investigated the situation in Ireland because the English labour market was depressed by the influx of workers from that country. The British government decided to test his ideas by sending a number of Irish poor to Upper Canada in the spring of 1823. Under the direction of Peter Robinson, brother of Attorney-General John B. Robinson, 568 persons were conveyed free to Packenham Township west of the Ottawa River. Each head of a family received a grant of seventy acres of land, on condition of settlement and the usual quit rent at the end of five years, with the right to buy the remaining thirty acres of the lot for £10 within ten years. In addition the settlers were given seed, implements, and provisions for twenty-one months. The total cost to the government was £12,593. Two years later £43,000 was spent in settling 2,024 Irish paupers in the Peterborough area north of Rice Lake, under the same conditions.[4]

Interested in the experiment, Talbot visited Peterborough in February, 1826. Some weeks later he reported to Horton: "I accompanied Sir Peregrine Maitland last winter on a tour of inspection to the new Irish emigrant settlements, about 100 miles from York. I was anxious to see how they were getting on, and whether the scheme of transporting the poor of Ireland to this country was likely to prove beneficial or not, and was happy to find them doing admirably. These people were sent out last summer, about 2,000 souls, and did not get on their land until late in November; all of them that

I saw had snug log huts, and had chopped each between three and four acres, and I have every reason to think that they will realize a comfortable independence in the course of this year, and be of no further cost to the government; and it was satisfactory to hear them express their gratitude for what was done for them."[5]

The mortality rate, however, was high the first year, and many of the emigrants* became discouraged and removed to the United States.[6] Horton's Emigration Committee was finally forced to admit that as a land settlement scheme the experiment was a costly failure. It advised, therefore, the termination of gratuitous government aid to emigrants, and the substitution of voluntary emigration of able-bodied Irish and English paupers under fifty years of age, who would be assisted by the Irish landowners and the English parish rates. In April, 1827, Horton introduced a bill in Parliament "to enable parishes to mortgage their poor rates for the purpose of providing for their able-bodied paupers by colonisation in the British Colonies", such emigrants to receive free passage to Canada, one hundred acres of land, agricultural implements, and food rations for one year, to be repaid by a small quit rent on the land. This bill failed to pass, but the government took steps to assist the flow of emigration by appointing A. C. Buchanan as resident superintendent and emigrant agent at Quebec. He arrived in July, 1828, and for many years did much to help the new-comers with information and advice.[7]

Approximately 12,000 emigrants landed at Quebec in 1827, and as many more in 1828, but a large proportion

* The words "emigrant" and "emigration" are used in place of "immigrant" and "immigration" throughout this chapter, to follow the practice of the time, as well as to avoid frequent shifts and confusion where quotations from the records are used.

moved on to the United States. In 1829 nearly 16,000 arrived, of whom three-quarters were estimated to have remained in the Canadas. But the great migration to the British provinces really began in 1830, after the United States put restrictions on the "dumping" of paupers, and fares to that country were raised; before the close of navigation 28,000 emigrants had come to Quebec during the year.[8] Many English parishes assisted the emigration of their poor. Letters written by people who had been sent out by Wiltshire parishes were published in pamphlet form and acted as a strong inducement to others to follow.[9]

In February, 1831, Lord Howick introduced into Parliament an emigration bill which embodied Horton's ideas of co-operation between the government, the parishes, and private individuals who might be interested in assisting the emigration of pauper families. The bill provided, among other things, that the parishes might borrow on their rates, and that the colonies might employ the destitute on various public works. Talbot had previously received letters from England predicting, as he informed Stuart-Wortley, now the Baron Wharncliffe of Wortley, "a triumph to Wilmot Horton's plan of Emigration, to which people are beginning to look as a practicable and promising measure of relief in the present distress of the United Kingdom." He was quite satisfied, he said, "that England could not adopt any measure that could more successfully relieve her of the burden of the poor labouring class, than by sending such as may be willing to Upper Canada, where want is not known, but the reverse, for many Emigrants who came out a few years ago, have now more than they can find sale for, particularly Horned Cattle, but Wheat, Pork and Potash are articles in demand and command money payments, which is a new event, for 2 or 3 years back nothing but barter was in use."

The Colonel offered a few suggestions of his own, which he believed would not only insure success for the emigrants but would eventually repay the government for the inevitable expense involved. He thought that each adult settler should be given no more than twenty-five acres of land; but the remaining seventy-five acres of his lot should be reserved for him to buy within four or five years, at a price of thirteen and a half shillings sterling per acre, payable with interest in four annual instalments. The patent should not be given until the settler had lived on the land for five years and had completely cleared, fenced, and cultivated ten acres in front, and cleared one-half the width of the concession road. Talbot also recommended that the rations of flour and meat supplied during the first year should be only half the size of those allowed Horton's Irish settlers, because men who received too much made little effort to clear their land to provide for themselves, and often sold the surplus rations to buy liquor. The only other government assistance needed, he said, was an axe and hoe for each man, corn and potatoes for seed, and perhaps a cow, in addition to a supply of blankets for those who arrived destitute.

Under these conditions, Talbot believed, the plan would succeed, provided care was taken to see that it did not follow the usual pattern, by which "all Government undertakings are made jobs of". "By adhering to such a system," he declared, "I am positive that two material objects might be realized, relieving the United Kingdom of its increasing burden, and promoting the value of the Colonies, for the more a Colony is peopled, the greater quantity of the manufactures from the Mother Country will be in demand." If

Wharncliffe found his ideas worthy of notice, and if a bill should be brought before Parliament, Talbot suggested he make use of them. "Perhaps," he concluded, "you might consult with Lords Lansdown and Grey on the prospect, but should any suspect that I am desirous of acting in any shape in execution of the scheme, you may assure them that I am not, being already worn out by the labours attending the superintendence of settling a new Country."[10]

It was not until the summer of 1831 that news came to Upper Canada of the defeat of the emigration bill. In the meantime, acting under directions from the Colonial Office, Lieutenant-Governor Colborne prepared a number of townships in the Newcastle, Home, and Western Districts for the reception of the expected influx of emigrants. In each of the selected townships a superintendent was stationed, with orders to erect at the entrance a building where the new settlers could be sheltered until they were located on the land, which was for sale at prices set by the Commissioner of Crown Lands. The government also undertook to open a road through each township. A. C. Buchanan, at Quebec, and the agents at Montreal and Prescott, were requested to give all necessary information to enable the emigrants to proceed to their destinations. Those going to the Newcastle District would disembark at Cobourg; those wishing to settle in the Home or Western Districts would proceed to York.[11]

One of the regions selected for settlement was that lying east of Lake Huron, between the townships near the mouth of the River Thames and the Canada Company's Huron Tract. Peter Robinson, now Commissioner of Crown Lands, informed Talbot in March, 1831, that he planned to lay out a road from the northeast corner of Caradoc Township to the mouth of the River aux Perche on Lake Huron. The Colonel replied that he decidedly approved of the plan, as the land was excellent, the River Sable on the north and Big Bear Creek on the south could furnish the settlers with fish to feed them during most of the year, and the distance from Lake Huron to York was no greater than that from Sandwich. He advised Robinson to employ a good surveyor "to explore minutely the Tract, commencing at the N. E. corner of Carradoc, not to take a Westerly course until he had crossed the Bear Creek, for it is evident that there must be an elevation or Ridge separating the waters that run into these Rivers, and when he finds such Ridge to follow it faithfully until he gets to Lake Huron." He also recommended that no more than two ranges of lots be surveyed on each side of the road until they were completely settled, and that no deed issue until the settlement duties had been completed and the settler had resided on his lot for five years.[12]

On July 4 Talbot reported that Deputy Surveyor Peter Carroll and James Nevills, whom Robinson had employed at his suggestion, had found an excellent line for the road, which would be surveyed within six weeks. "A magnificent settlement may be accomplished in the Extent," he wrote, "and it now remains with you, to do it, but I must caution you, in Yankee style, to be wide awake in guarding against imposition and speculation, and to have a proper person to watch over the Settlers being actual residents and that they faithfully perform the duties that may be required of them. . . . I shall take constant interest in the road, and should like it to be called William the Fourth's Road, and my advice is that you should, as much as possible, avoid placing Highland Scotch on it, as of all descriptions they make the worst settlers for new Roads. English are the best."[13]

During this year great numbers of the British poor were sent to Canada by the landowners and the parishes; and many other emigrants had sufficient wealth to pay their own way. By September 10 more than 11,000 had disembarked at York or the Head of Lake Ontario, while 4,700 had gone to the Newcastle District to the east of York. A total of 50,000 arrived at Quebec during the season. Of these some remained in Lower Canada or in the more eastern sections of Upper Canada, while uncounted numbers went to the United States. Colborne settled 3,000 indigent emigrants from Wiltshire and Yorkshire in the townships of Oro, Douro and Dummer.[14] On July 23 he informed Talbot that he had opened the townships of Adelaide and Warwick, on the road to Lake Huron, for location, and "should the Emigrant Bill pass, I shall forward 2 or 300 families to the westward, if we can collect them before the end of October."[15] But the bill did not pass, largely because of opposition from the parishes, and the belief that the emigration movement would succeed without government assistance. However, an emigration commission was set up for the purpose of giving out information, and administering any funds provided by individual parishes.

In December the government of Upper Canada announced that indigent settlers, unable to buy lands at the regular auction sales, would be assigned lots in certain townships at fixed prices, the first payment to be made without interest at the end of three years, and the remainder in three annual instalments bearing interest.[16] In May, 1832, following the receipt of instructions from Lord Goderich, notice was given that the townships already prepared were Ross, Pembroke, and Westmeath on the Ottawa River in the Bathurst District, and Sunnindale, Oro, Medonte, and Orillia in the Home District. Each head of an indigent family was promised fifty acres of land, for which he would eventually pay five shillings per acre. The local superintendents were charged with building a small log house for each family. Some assistance would also be given by opening roads leading to the lands to be settled; but the government would not provide any provisions or implements, or help in bringing the lands into cultivation.[17] A month later it was announced that employment and locations could also be obtained on a road being opened from Kempenfelt Bay on Lake Simcoe to the Township of Sunnindale, and in Adelaide and Warwick on the new road to Lake Huron.[18]

A. C. Buchanan was appointed chief superintendent for the Emigrant Department for both Upper and Lower Canada, with charge of the local agents at Montreal, Prescott, Kingston, Cobourg, and York, in February, 1832. For some reason Colonel Talbot had taken a violent dislike to him. "To be sure," he told Robinson, "Lord Goderich is most provoking in all his arrangements, and that of appointing that Beast, Buchanan, to the charge of the Emigrants in both Provinces, is not the least of His Lordship's mistakes." He was hardly more pleased with Colborne's arrangements in the Western District. "I have not any faith in Sir John's plans for the new Surveyed Tract," he declared.[19]

At the request of the Lieutenant-Governor an emigrant society was established in nearly every county in the province, with funds supplied by public subscriptions. An Emigrants' Asylum had been built at York in the fall of 1830, and the Society for the Relief of the Sick and Destitute was in existence some time before then. The York Emigrant Society was formed in the spring of 1832 when Colborne appointed a president and a committee of nine. It provided an office where emigrants could obtain information concerning lands, employment and public boarding-houses; and it urged tavern-keepers to prepare sheds in their yards for the accommodation of the poorer emigrants at moderate rates.[20] Similar services were performed by the Cobourg branch of the Newcastle Emigrant Relief Society, which also provided shelter, took care of the destitute sick, and arranged for the conveyance of the emigrants to their destinations at fixed prices.[21] Colborne informed Goderich that he had encouraged the societies established at Prescott, Kingston, and York, as well as the local settlers who were interested in improvements, to open much-needed roads, and had promised that part of the expense would be borne by the government.[22] It was expected that many of the indigent emigrants would be able to earn enough by their labour on these roads to take them to their destinations, after which they might obtain employment for a time on local government roads.

A great wave of migration had already begun to form in the British Isles. During the last week in March, 1832, nearly one hundred ships of the first class were being fitted out in the London docks alone, to carry passengers and their baggage to the colonies. Large numbers of people were moving to London, Liverpool, Bristol, Southampton, and other ports to embark for Canada.[23] The Earl of Egremont had already sent out 1,000 paupers from Sussex, largely at his own expense, during the earlier part of March.[24] By the middle of May more than 3,000 persons had landed at Quebec, and thousands more were on the way. The advancing flood moved inland up the St. Lawrence—by steamboat to Montreal, and from there by small boat to Prescott above the rapids, where other steamboats could transport them to ports on Lake Ontario. On its second trip from Prescott the steamer *Great*

*Britain*, overloaded with 1,200 emigrants, was unable to get close to any wharf at Kingston and was forced to proceed up the Lake.[25]

By no means all the emigrants were paupers. The *Caroline*, which left London in May, was reported to have among its passengers some fifty or sixty who possessed among them from £15,000 to £20,000, as well as breeding stock, agricultural implements, grass seeds, and other products. The editor of the Kingston *Standard* commented on June 2: "Among the multitude of Emigrants who have stopped, *in transitu*, for a few hours at our wharves, we observed many of the most respectable and better orders of society."[26] A large number of these appear to have purchased lands from the Canada Company.

The coming of the emigrants also brought uneasiness to the inhabitants, as rumours spread that there had been deaths on the ships or in the quarantine station below Quebec from the dread Asiatic cholera, which was then raging in several parts of the British Isles and Europe. The health officers at Quebec continued to deny the stories until June 11, when they announced that thirty persons had died in the city from the sickness during the previous three days. Nine days later the scourge reached Montreal; and within two weeks many hundreds had died of it at Quebec and Montreal, with lesser numbers at Prescott, Kingston, York, and other places.[27] On July 2 Talbot informed Peter Robinson that he had talked that morning to a Dr. Rolls, just arrived from England, and that his account "of the sufferings of the Emigrants, between Montreal and Prescott, is dreadful by the desertion of the Boatmen and the cruelty of the Inhabitants, who will not admit any of the Emigrants into their houses or furnish them

GRAND MILITARY STEEPLECHASE, LONDON, CANADA WEST, 1843

From John Ross Robertson Collection, Toronto Public Libraries

with provisions, so that in fact the poor creatures are dying on the banks of the St. Lawrence by starvation."[28]

A group of Lord Egremont's settlers from Sussex had landed at Port Stanley just a few days before the Colonel wrote to Robinson. One of them, a boy, died of what was believed to be cholera several hours after landing. The rest went on to Delaware and Caradoc. Deputy Surveyor Roswell Mount of Caradoc had been appointed superintendent for Adelaide and Warwick and the new road to Lake Huron, which was soon to be called the Egremont Road in honour of the philanthropic earl. Mount and his assistant, Bela Brewster Brigham of Delaware, settled the emigrants in Adelaide, and looked after their interests. On July 8 Colonel Talbot reported to Robinson that this first group were said to be "a very healthy, well looking people", but that several inhabitants of his own settlement had recently died after a brief illness, "which the Quacks pronounce to be cholera". Two weeks later he admitted that this disease had taken the lives of several persons at London, Port Stanley, St. Thomas and elsewhere. On August 12 he wrote to William Allan that "cholera, that dreadful scourge, has for some weeks been stalking thro the Talbot Settlement, upwards of 100 cases half of whom have been fatal. My house has escaped and I flatter myself the disease is taking itself away." A month later he was able to report that his people's health was very much improved.[29]

The original group of settlers on the Egremont Road was augmented in August by the arrival of 114 others from Sussex and Wiltshire.[30] In October the editor of the London *Sun* visited Adelaide and found that there were about 1,600 persons there, "all of whom will, before the winter, be settled in their own cottages, with good roads to their door, employment without seeking for it and provisions provided for them at the lowest price possible."[31] About a month later Roswell Mount reported that he had spent £1,844 in the settlement of 3,500 persons in the two townships of Adelaide and Warwick. This sum included wages paid for work on the local roads, but not the expense of bringing the emigrants from York to Port Stanley by schooner. The total cost to the government of Upper Canada in locating 30,000 emigrants in various townships was about £10,000. Colborne explained to Goderich that many of the expenditures were occasioned by "the embarrassing circumstances" under which the movement took place. The government had been forced to give speedy relief by removing the emigrants from the ports on the St. Lawrence and Lake Ontario, where thousands had collected, and conveying them to their destinations; and it had employed many destitute families on various roads along the way, so that they could support themselves.[32]

Although the lands under his own superintendence were nearly all settled, Talbot profited from the great migration by being able to sell beef cattle for the use of Mount's settlers. In the spring of 1831, when it seemed probable that the emigrant bill would pass and that the British government would send out paupers, he asked the Commissioner of Crown Lands to keep his stocks in view if cattle were required for their use. He was at a loss how to dispose of them, he wrote, and to winter as many as he had would be a great expense.[33] In September he offered them for sale to a York butcher, who promised to buy them after Christmas if the Colonel would keep them until then. This was impossible, Talbot told the Commissioner, because to keep the thirty head of cattle in beef order would consume all his hay, and the rest of his stock would die before spring.[34] As soon as the first settlers landed at Port Talbot the following summer he again asked the Commissioner to remind Mount that he had several head of cattle for sale. In September, Mount purchased from him 13,416 pounds of beef for £131. Talbot was then engaged in building a new house. This sum, he told a friend, made him "feel very comfortable, and will prove much assistance in paying my carpenters and masons".[35]

The winter that followed was an "aggravating" one for the ageing Colonel, because of the alternate snows and thaws that made travelling difficult. It was also a period of hardship for the settlers in Adelaide and Warwick. Late in January, 1833, two gentlemen from Adelaide came on foot to Port Talbot, giving "a dreadful account of the Roads, and the great want of provisions and the consequent sufferings of the Emigrants."[36] Two months later Talbot was astonished to learn that Mount had already spent a total of £4,000 in his two townships. He thought that the government should have let the settlers build their own huts and thus spared itself this cost. On the other hand, he approved of it supplying them with provisions, and he feared that the recent stoppage would make it difficult for most of them to live until their first crops of potatoes and corn could be harvested. He informed Commissioner Robinson that he had heard rumours of a plan to break into the government stores at Adelaide and seize the food. However, the weather was now showing some signs of spring, which would "be more encouraging to the poor creatures".[37]

Emigration to Canada fell off sharply in 1833, when the Quebec arrivals numbered about 22,000, as against 52,000 the previous year. The Quebec *Gazette* attributed this decline in part to the poll tax levied by Lower Canada, which bore heavily on the poor emigrants, but much more to the "dreadful mortality" occasioned by the Asiatic cholera of 1832.[38] But despite the decline, the limited assistance given to the emigrants continued to be very costly for the government of Upper Canada. When the accounts were audited in September, 1833, it was found that nearly £32,000 had been expended under the direction of the Commissioner of Crown Lands during the previous fifteen months. Mount's expenses for Adelaide and Warwick now stood at £7,558.[39]

New impetus was given to the emigrant trade in 1834 with the ending of the poll tax, the subsidence of cholera, and the passage of a British Act permitting parish rates to be mortgaged to defray the cost of transporting indigents to Canada. A. C. Buchanan announced on September 7 of that year that 30,306 emigrants had arrived at Quebec during the season, an increase of nearly fifty per cent over the corresponding period of 1833, but still far below that of 1832.[40] Some of these people went to the western townships of Inniskillen, Brooke, Plympton, Sarnia, and Moore (in the present County of Lambton), where Crown lands could be bought at auction at the upset price of ten shillings per acre.[41] Paupers sent out by the English parishes and large landowners continued to be settled under the old terms for a short time. But the great migration to Canada was temporarily halted by the political disturbances that followed, and it was not until the next decade that it began again in greatly increased volume.

## CHAPTER XII

# *The Audience Window*

In his earlier and happier years the Colonel's treatment of his settlers was kind, although often brusque. He was a type of "benevolent despot", who liked to speak of the people as his children, and himself as the father of the settlement. "It is highly interesting," remarked a visitor to Port Talbot in 1817, "to see the father of a family just arrived from England, calling on Colonel Talbot to solicit a lot of land. Refreshments are given him, and a kind welcome. On seeing that he has a recommendation from home, he gets two hundred acres of land, on which he settles himself and family."[1] One year later some Scottish immigrants experienced the Colonel's kindness, as described by George Munro:[2] "In the autumn of 1818, two or three of the Highland emigrants, arrived at the Sixteen in Aldboro', came to the Colonel for land, which he at once gave, and by way of sealing the contract, treated each of them to a good horn of whiskey; and while at dinner, the Colonel paced the room, instructing his guests how to build houses, clear land, plant corn and potatoes, with other useful directions; beseeching them to be industrious, sober and peaceable. At bed time, the Colonel produced a pile of blankets, and requested his guests to make their own bed. One of the party said, 'We never made a bed!' The Colonel took the mattress, placed it on the floor, before the fire, brought the backs of three chairs to the subservient position of pillows, spread one blanket, then turned round, and said,

'Spread the rest of the blankets fairly on the top of that, and learn to help yourselves in Canada.' The men commenced, but the Colonel getting out of patience with their awkwardness, took the rest of the blankets and spread them, at the same time remarking, 'I have often made my bed of hemlock boughs, and considered it no hard work.' "

Young immigrants were frequently given employment on the Colonel's farm until they were ready to take up land. When they fell sick he took care of them. "I saw him," Munro wrote, "piling blankets over his shaking patients, and instead of charging for board and attendance, as many would have done, he paid them full wages for all the time they were sick, which few or none would have done. No one ever served him who did not love him sincerely and devotedly." Talbot often spoke of the expenses involved in caring for his new settlers; and many of the early ones, whom he helped in time of distress, remained his lifelong friends.

About the year 1822 a young man named Joseph Elson came to ask the Colonel for a location on a U. E. Loyalist right that he had acquired from his employer. "I happened to find him in good humor," Elson wrote,[3] "and after his first salute of 'What do you want', and looking at me for an instant, invited me into his room and kept asken me questions and chating [*sic*] and taking snuff and drinking whiskey until I began to think that he had forgotten what I wanted; but all of an instant he calls 'Jeffrey bring me the map of London', telling me at the same time I would have to think it a great favour for him to allow a U. E. right to be laid on his settlement." He then gave the youth the numbers of several vacant lots to choose from in the northeast part of the township, and abruptly dismissed him.

Finding that the lots were far removed from any road or settlement, Elson returned to the ninth concession, where his friend Joseph Fowler lived, and obtained the numbers of some lots in the vicinity that the local settlers said were vacant, but which he heard later belonged to the Colonel. When he returned with these numbers, Elson recalled later, Talbot "looked at them half a minute, his blue eyes shining like two forks of lightning, threw down the paper and said the settlers knew nothing about it. 'There is 19 and 20 in the 9th concession. If there is nothing done on them you can have one of them, but I think it is strange you could not suit yourself out of all the number I gave you. There is McConnel living on the 16th concession and he is much older than you, and I tell you that the back part of London will be the front by and by. Now you can be off.'" A few days later Elson was back once more to say he would take Lot 20. The Colonel replied: "I said you could have one if there was nothing done on them." Elson said there had been no improvements made on either, and that nothing would ever be done on Lot 19 because it was all swamp. "I aint afraid of that, said he. By that time my name was on the map, and the farewell salute You can be off."

It was probably about this time that Talbot began to interview prospective settlers through the window of his sitting-room, which opened on the verandah. "He admits no applicants for land into his house," Sir Francis Bond Head wrote in 1837, "but when he feels disposed to listen to them, he opens a small compartment of his window which he closes and secures the instant he has delivered his reply. If the answer be favorable, and if the application be granted, the petitioner waits untill [*sic*] thro' the window he has seen his name inscribed in pencil on a plan and upon the identical lot which he has solicited–this is all the title which exists of his location."[4]

The use of the audience window is said to have resulted from the Colonel's encounter with a stalwart Highlander named Duncan Patterson, who threw him to the ground and held him there until promised the desired location. It was, no doubt, a precaution taken at the time the people of Dunwich and Aldborough were demanding their deeds and additional grants at the lowest fees, when feeling against him ran so high that he feared for his safety. If rejected applicants or other visitors proved obstreperous, Jeffrey Hunter, the Colonel's personal servant, would be ordered to set on the dogs. Talbot explained to William Baby and his brother in 1841, that he was "so pestered with these land grabbers who squirt their vile tobacco juice in every direction, that I find it impossible to endure it, and I have adopted this plan of transacting all my business through this open window."[5]

It being well known that the Colonel did not like to transact business in the afternoon, applicants from a distance usually arranged, if they arrived too late, to remain over night at a nearby inn, to be on hand at the proper time in the morning. Those coming from the west found it convenient to stop at Henry Coyne's inn on the Talbot Road in Dunwich. Robert Alexander has left the following account of his father's experience when he stayed there in 1830: "That grand, benevolent, patriotic lady, Mrs. Coyne, administered to his wants. Not only that, but she gave him good advice how to manage the old Colonel. She was an angel of mercy to many a footsore traveler asking for land. She told him not to approach the Colonel until after he had broken his fast in the morning. The Colonel received him kindly, gave him a grant, Lot no. 10 on the town line between Howard and Harwich, and there he squatted in the year 1830."[6]

The Rev. William Proudfoot was not so fortunate when he and some friends came to Port Talbot seeking land in Tilbury in 1834. Although "well aware that it would not be safe to call for him after dinner, it being his constant practice to take too much brandy", they disregarded Jeffrey's hint to that effect and approached the window of the room where Talbot was sitting. The minister did not like his politics, and disliked even more his sharp salutation—"What do you want?"—and his lack of courtesy. "He was evidently in a half drunken state," Proudfoot noted in his diary, "and his manner was exceedingly rude and insulting. I have seldom seen a man more contemptible in his appearance; short, and ill made, his face fiery and stormy, and his manner the very antipodes of what is to be found amongst all who have the smallest pretensions to the name of a gentleman."[7]

There were many others, especially among the Reformers, who had come to hate the Colonel with intensity. "However high a man's station," an anonymous writer declared in the spring of 1833, in a letter published in the St. Thomas *Liberal,* "however superior his talents or attainments, however inexhaustible his wealth, his fellow creatures however low, however ignorant, however indigent, have a right to expect and demand from him gentlemanly, civil and respectful treatment when it becomes necessary for them, in the ordinary affairs and transactions of life, to come in contact with him." But Talbot had tried to eradicate these amiable qualities from his character, filling their places "with vulgar impertinence, and tyrannical impudence," the writer charged. Many of the King's loyal subjects were deterred from seeking his bounty, knowing that they would have to "submit to a flood of vulgar abuse before they can even be heard, or their claims taken under consideration". The poor emigrant, who had experienced many privations in reaching the promised land, found himself "assailed with the most abusive and insulting language", for no other reason than "the power of the strongest is over him, and he must bear it". The Colonel called himself "The Father of the Talbot Settlement", but he was neither disinterested nor impartial in his dealings with his children. The settlement of the surrounding country enhanced the value of his huge landholdings in Dunwich and Aldborough. Ignorant immigrants were forced to take inferior land, while he reserved good land for those not so easily duped; and an applicant's chance of being located depended less on the justness of his claim than on finding the Colonel in a good humour. "Do not men often apply to you," the writer asked, "to be located on the waste lands of the Crown, and receive a flat insulting denial, that would drive any *spirited* man from your office, and afterwards return at some more happy hour to obtain his rights without difficulty?"[8]

There is some truth in these allegations, although the writer painted Talbot in colours that were much too dark. In later years the Colonel did display a great deal of capriciousness, and bad manners, in his treatment of his settlers and applicants for land. But on the whole he gave rough justice, and to those whom he believed to be honest, and who were not "radicals", he gave consideration and even mercy. Some of the stories told about him during his lifetime and after his death may be apocryphal, but they serve to illustrate the attitude of many of his people toward him, as well as something of his character.[9] He was said to have disliked "Yankees" or "sharp fellows", who acquired their property "by whittling chips and barter"—which he explained as meaning that they "began by giving a shingle for a blind pup, which they swopped for a goose and then turned into a sheep". Such people met with short shrift from him, as did anyone whom he suspected of attempting to deceive him. His patience was soon exhausted when dealing with pompous individuals who used big words and did not come directly to the point. One of this type was told to come down to the level of Talbot's understanding, so that he might learn what he wanted; and finding that the man wanted to have a poor family ousted so that he could get their land, the Colonel dismissed him abruptly.

Taking great pride in his own homespun clothes, the Colonel insisted on his settlers dressing in the same way. "I will grant no land to any who can afford to dress in the rotten refuse of the Manchester warehouses," he is reported to have told an applicant who came dressed in fine broadcloth, with the general appearance of a dandy. Not until a year later, when the man applied again in home-made clothes, did he receive a location. There is also the story of the well-dressed American who "guessed" he wanted a lot of land, who was told by the Colonel that he "guessed" he had none for him. The man then changed clothes with an Englishman and tried the second time, endeavouring to hide his American accent. Talbot merely looked at him, turned his head, and called out in his hoarse voice: "Jeffrey, Jeffrey, set on the dogs, here's a wolf in sheep's clothing."

Talbot's overbearing nature rarely brooked opposition of any kind, but there is the account of the proud Scot who won his respect. When his application was rejected the Scot swore he would get land by going to the Colonel's "betters" in York. On his return he had to admit that he had found neither land nor the "betters" he had been seeking; whereupon the Colonel invited him in, supplied him with whiskey and something to eat, and gave him a lot of land. Occasionally a bold approach proved successful, as in the case of an American named Thurston, who received a location after declaring that his only certificate of character was from God, and that God had told him to take care of himself and get as much land as possible. But those who counted on such methods were usually disappointed. "My dogs don't understand heraldry," the Colonel retorted when a fellow Irishman stated that his family was as ancient and honourable as the Talbots of Malahide, "and if you don't take yourself off, they will not leave a coat to your back."

Most of Talbot's difficulties with his settlers arose from his enforcement of the settlement duties and his own regulations for the transfer of locations. He admitted to Secretary Hillier in 1820 that in some instances he had located five or six individuals in succession to the same lot, before he was able to obtain "a faithful settler". He sometimes permitted exchanges of locations to be made; but if his consent had not previously been obtained such exchanges were void. In the same way, sales of "rights" without his permission were regarded by him as evidence that the settlers had never intended to fulfil their obligations. "My practice with them," he told Hillier, "is short—on proof of fraud I erase the name; and then the lot is again vacant."[10] Sir Francis Head described this procedure in 1837: "If he deserts his lot—if he attempts to sell it, assign it, or if he neglects to perform his settlement duties, Colonel Talbot takes up a piece of india-rubber which is attached to his pencil and as he very justly expresses it 'just rubs him out' from which moment the man becomes as much a nonentity as the flame of a candle which has been blown out. By the pencil and India rubber Colonel Talbot thus governs in solitude—by the one implement he rewards or attracts, by the other he punishes or repells his subjects, and as he is judge jury and executioner of his own law, I need scarcely add that there exists in no country on the surface of the globe an authority more despotic than the power which Colonel Talbot possesses."[11]

Although Talbot had "rubbed out" many settlers before 1819, it was not until late in that year that one of them appealed to the Lieutenant-Governor and Council against his action. This was John Peer, who, with the Colonel's permission, had built a sawmill on the North Branch of the Talbot Road in Westminster before the survey was completed. After the survey it was discovered that part of the dam was on a lot adjacent to Peer's lot, belonging to Peter Myers. Talbot agreed that Peer might purchase that portion of Myers' lot occupied by the dam. In 1819, two years later, Talbot learned that Myers had sold his entire lot to Peer. Regarding this as a breach of Myers' agreement made at the time of location, the Colonel rubbed his name off his map and gave the lot to Calvin Burch, with the stipulation that Burch pay Myers for the improvements. Learning later that most of the improvements had been made by Peer after he bought the "rights" from Myers, Talbot agreed that Burch should pay Peer according to a valuation set by three arbitrators. Peer then used this as an acknowledgment of his right to make the improvements, and appealed to Lieutenant-Governor Maitland against the Colonel's action in depriving him of the lot.

Talbot had always made it a rule to have the person last located on a lot pay the previous occupant the value of whatever labour he had performed, but this did not imply any right on the part of the latter. The Council was in some doubt, however, about Talbot's power to dispossess Myers or any settler once located. This had always been a prerogative of the government which Talbot had assumed, and now exercised as a kind of prescriptive right. No action was taken on Peer's petition, although the case came up again in 1822 when Burch applied for his patent. At that time it was rumoured that Peer was attempting to sell his own lot as well as whatever claim he had to the one in dispute. The Colonel reported to Secretary Hillier, later in the year, that Peer had taken his family to Michigan, and had "written to his former neighbors in this settlement, stating that he is at length *fixed* under a Government that suits him, and that none but Fools and Rogues will remain in Canada. I have only to regret that the fellow has had one acre of this country, to assist his speculations in Yankee Land."[12] Peer had had trouble with some of his neighbours at the time the case came to Talbot's attention in 1819, and in view of the latter's leniency in enforcing his rules in other instances, it is apparent that he dealt strictly with Peer because he considered him a trouble-maker.

The right of the Colonel to dispossess one occupant in favour of another, for breach of the regulations, was not again seriously questioned by the Council, although occasionally a settler resisted. When Talbot undertook the superintendence of the Longwoods Road he took vigorous action against those who attempted to sell their rights to locations. In 1825 he wrote to Hillier: "The Longwoods Road is in fair progress, but it will require another year before I can report decisively, as it requires all my vigilance to check the fraud and speculation of the people. I have had to turn out several already, one for having sold a lot without ever going on it, to a Yankey for two watches, and another for selling another lot under the same circumstances for a U. E. right and 70 dollars. I trust these examples prove beneficial."[13]

The next year Talbot met with considerable difficulty from George Bateman of Caradoc, who claimed a lot on the Longwoods Road as a gift from Samuel Alcock, although the lot had been declared vacant by the government after Alcock had returned to Ireland without doing any work on it. The Colonel re-located the lot to Edward Jennings, who attempted to take possession but was driven off by Bateman and his four sons. During the altercation Jennings' brother was struck on the head with an axe. Talbot then turned to Hillier for advice as to how he should proceed against Bateman. He said that, having turned out some of the defaulters on the road, most of the others had taken the alarm and gone to work on their lots; but if such a flagrant imposition as Bateman's were overlooked he would be unable to enforce further improvement. The Attorney-General advised Hillier that a letter from him or the Surveyor-General might convince the Batemans that they were wasting their labour on the lot, "and make them desist from chopping the trees at all events, though they may continue to hack at Mr. Jennings". He also suggested that Jennings go to a magistrate and have the Batemans bound over to keep the peace, and to answer at the next quarter sessions court for the assault. This advice was followed and Jennings secured the lot. Bateman was tried for assault but was acquitted when he was able, as Talbot put it, to make "the stupid jury believe that the land was his, and of course had a right to defend his property".[14]

In dealing with young men the Colonel was often extremely indulgent in the enforcement of the settlement duties. This is illustrated by the case of a youth named Nahum Thayer, which began in the fall of 1825 when he applied for a deed for a lot on the Talbot Road in Orford Township. The Council was surprised to find that the performance of his settlement duties had not been certified by Talbot but by a number of Thayer's neighbours, and also that a Robert Hindman had been returned by Talbot for the same lot in 1817. When this was brought to the Colonel's attention he stated that "every correct petition" from his settlers had his recommendation and signature on it, and he gave a lengthy explanation of his troubles with Thayer. In 1819, he said, he had dispossessed Hindman for failure to live or work on the lot, and had given it to Thayer, who had in turn abandoned the lot after doing a small amount of work on it. During the next five years the other settlers made loud complaints about the uncleared road in front of Thayer's land, but although the Colonel warned the youth more than once to go on it, he took no further steps until 1825, when the settlers stated that they would have to leave their farms if this and two other lots were not located to men who would clear the road in front. Talbot then removed Thayer's name from his map and gave the lot to Hoaxhead Manifold.

Thayer then came to see him, Talbot said, and in the course of a long argument defied him to remove him from the lot. A few days later Manifold appeared to complain that Thayer and several of his men had threatened to kill him if he did not get off the lot, and had then begun work on it and the road in front. Talbot immediately wrote to Thayer that he was wasting his time and labour, which soon brought him to Port Talbot to demand payment for his work. Talbot said Manifold would pay him according to a valuation made by two men, one chosen by each party; but Thayer insisted on naming both, and when the appraisal was made he objected that it was too low. After further argument he seemed to agree, and asked Talbot for another lot. Despite all that had occurred the Colonel offered him one in Malahide. After looking at it Thayer said he did not like it, and he asked for one in the rear of the Talbot Road in Orford. Talbot said he would give him this lot, if it were not reserved, as soon as he received the plan of survey. He heard nothing more from Thayer until he attempted to secure a deed for his original lot.[15]

Because of the leniency shown in this and many other cases, the settlers who were strictly dealt with felt that they had been discriminated against. In 1833 Edward Allen Talbot, a magistrate of London Township, argued that the Colonel was not justified in dispossessing John Ardill, although he had occupied a lot for ten years without completing the settlement duties, because it was not customary for the Colonel to insist upon the work being done within any specified time.[16] The Council rejected this reasoning, but it must have appealed strongly to other settlers who had been shown no indulgence. On his part Talbot seemed to feel that the trouble arose from his strictness, rather than his laxity in enforcing the rules. This was so even in the case of Nahum Thayer. "I cannot conclude," he wrote after describing the events, "without observing that if I had not adopted, and pursued, an energetic system of enforcing settlement duties, that it would have been impossible for myself, or any other person, to have accomplished what I have—viz: good roads and a consolidated settlement. . . ."

As he grew older the Colonel became more arbitrary in his decisions. Behind the safety of the audience window men's lives were deeply affected by the use of the pencil and the indiarubber eraser. On one occasion, however, he was defeated by one of his settlers, whom he had dispossessed.

One day in the summer of 1836 this man appeared before the window, after fortifying himself at the nearest tavern, to demand the return of his land. Meeting with an angry refusal and an order to be gone, he departed shouting threats of vengeance. The next day as Talbot was leaving the house with George Munro and Hercules Burwell, he saw the man approaching from the road. "The Colonel," Munro recounted later, "shaking his fist said, 'Clear yourself you d — Heilan rascal; did you not yesterday threaten to break every bone in my skin?' He then turned quickly and went into his room. In about a week after I met Col. Burwell (Colonel Talbot's nearest and dearest friend), who smilingly said, 'Our mutual friend, the Port Talbot chief, at long last met his match in the person of the Scotchman, who was there when you and Hercules were getting the deeds signed.' The Highland hero, instead of taking himself off, went into the kitchen and sat down with the Colonel's men to dinner. He did the same at supper and, following the men to their long bedroom, jumped into bed. The morning following he was first at breakfast; the same at dinner and supper. This he kept up for two days. When Jeffrey complained to the Colonel he ordered him to the window, and asked him what did he mean. 'I mean to live and die with you, you old devil if you do not give me back my land.' 'Take your land and go to hell with it, and never let me see your face again,' was the conquered Colonel's reply."[17]

## CHAPTER XIII

# *Rolph and Matthews*

At the summons of Robert Gourlay, a radical Scot who had recently come to Upper Canada, a convention assembled at York in July, 1818, for the purpose of discussing the advisability of sending representatives to England "to call attention to the affairs of the Province". The discontent that was prevalent at this time was largely economic, resulting from the depression following the war, the delay in military land grants, the obstruction to settlement occasioned by the Crown and clergy reserves, and the restrictions placed on immigrants from the United States. The London District contained, in Gourlay's words, "some of the most spirited people in the province", and discontent was as strong there as in any part of Upper Canada, but it sent only one representative to the convention. Gourlay blamed this poor showing on the "efforts made against the cause by Colonel Talbot and his surveyor, Colonel Burwell", who was a member of the Legislative Assembly.[1]

Gourlay was banished the following year, but in time more moderate leaders arose who worked out a policy of constitutional reform. In the meantime, Talbot's angry settlers in Dunwich and Aldborough were forming, within the very heart of his "principality", the nucleus of opposition to him and to the government that he represented. In the election of 1820 they refused to vote for the government candidates, Mahlon Burwell and John Bostwick. The Highlanders of Aldborough were excluded from the polls on the technical ground, not previously enforced, that they had not yet received their deeds; but they firmly believed that it was because of their opposition to Burwell and Bostwick.

During his stay in the Talbot Settlement in 1820 the English traveller John Howison noticed that the Scots were extremely clannish, and that they were suspicious of their neighbours. Nevertheless, they had already begun to acquire some of the democratic ideas common to the New World. Speaking only their Gaelic language, and clinging together in the midst of a strange and apparently hostile environment, they were at first unable to believe that in certain respects they were considered the equals of any man. When at last they learned that it was true, they were even more inclined to resent the arbitrary actions of those in power.[2] This feeling was by no means confined to the Scots. The very success that Talbot achieved in the peopling of the wilderness doomed his paternal and sometimes despotic rule, as well as the rule of the clique at York known as the Family Compact.

There were other settlers in the Colonel's own township of Dunwich, principally Irish and Americans, who bore a deep resentment towards him and all that he stood for. Except for the Pattersons, Backuses, Storeys, Pearces, and a few others who had come in before the war and were well treated by him, nearly all the rest were dissatisfied with their land grants, and had joined in signing the petitions against the Colonel. Among the leaders were Henry Coyne and his brother-in-law Singleton Gardiner, who had lived in the United States for a fcw years after emigrating from Ireland, and who now operated inns on the Talbot Road in Dunwich. Gardiner's dispute with Mahlon Burwell and Leslie Patterson, the local magistrates, aroused such indignation locally that it contributed to the defeat of Burwell in the election of 1824. Many believed that Gardiner was being persecuted because of his liberal views, and because he had been considered as a candidate for the provincial Assembly in opposition to Burwell.

Gardiner's trouble originated in a misunderstanding on his part, which resulted in his failure to perform a certain portion of his statute labour on the roads. For this some of his personal possessions were seized by the constable and sold at auction to satisfy a judgment against him. His saddle, which was also seized, was ordered returned to him; but when he went to the constable's house and took away the saddle in the constable's absence he was arrested for larceny. When brought before the magistrates he struck Burwell, and was held for trial at the next court of quarter sessions on a charge of assault and battery. In April, 1823, he was convicted and sentenced to serve three months in prison, pay a fine of one hundred dollars and court costs of eighty dollars, and to remain in prison until the fine and costs were paid.

Earlier in the year seventy-three inhabitants of Dunwich and Southwold addressed a petition to the Lieutenant-Governor on Gardiner's behalf. Gardiner informed Secretary Hillier that the people of his neighbourhood were "obliged to suffer the most absolute tyranny and oppression that was ever thought of since the dayes of Christ", and that he and a number of others were determined to leave a settlement where Colonel Talbot allowed them to be thus treated.[3] After his conviction he again appealed to Lieutenant-Governor Maitland, who was advised by the Attorney-General that the magistrates in quarter sessions were not competent to imprison for costs.[4] On October 6, having served his term of three months and nearly as much more for failure to pay the fine and costs, Gardiner was released on orders from Maitland.[5] A civil suit that he had started against Burwell and Patterson was later dismissed on technical grounds. On October 6, 1824, the anniversary of his release, Gardiner and forty of his friends celebrated the defeat of Burwell in the recent elections, with a dinner at which there were "appropriate toasts and songs, with plenty of good cheer".

In the northern townships of the county a man had already come to the front as the champion of the people against the rule of the magistrates. This was the fiery but erratic Captain John Matthews of Lobo, a retired officer of the Royal Artillery, and a former Roman Catholic who had adhered for a time to the Anglican faith before finding his spiritual home among the Unitarians. Coming to Quebec in 1819 as aide-de-camp to the Duke of Richmond, he found on his arrival that the Governor had died, and he moved on with his family to Upper Canada. For a time he lived on a farm on the Niagara River, where a traveller met him and wrote that he was "quite a polished gentleman", who none the less spent a good deal of time working on his farm.[6] A few months later, after weeks of travelling through the London District looking for a place to settle, he moved to the banks of the River Thames in Lobo, not far from the village of Delaware, where he had secured a grant of eight hundred acres of land.[7] He was far from content, however, with what he described as an inconvenient situation where the soil was stony and not worth over one dollar per acre; the choice lands, he found, were already spoken for. "I have been in this country now nearly eighteen months," he wrote Hillier in November 1820, "which have been all spent in this unceasing, anxious, tantalizing, vain, pursuit. Hope following hope, and disappointment as regularly following in the footsteps of disappointment, and a situation is ultimately chosen for me, opposed to all my views, and which had been previously selected and culled over, under circumstances also, neither flattering or gratifying to my feelings."[8]

Matthews soon came into conflict with Daniel Springer, a magistrate living in Delaware, who had managed to secure for himself some of the most desirable lands in the region. Springer had property on both sides of Matthews', and they quarrelled over their boundary lines. They also quarrelled over a farm which Matthews bought at auction, but which Springer claimed under an old licence of occupation. Matthews believed that brush fires on his property were set by Springer's agents.[9] His letters to the government officials were filled with charges against Springer and others in his neighbourhood, which he referred to as "a corner notorious for its regardlessness of law and regulation".[10] It was not long before he became noted as a radical, who placed the ultimate blame for the people's troubles on the local magistrates and their superiors in the provincial government. "I have heard," he told Maitland in the fall of 1820, "complaints and murmurs and continued expressions of dissatisfaction (if not disaffection) from one end of [the London District] to the other." He urged the Lieutenant-Governor to take action to remove abuses. In the spring of 1823 he declared that the many traitors from the district in the last war had been driven to the enemy by the bad administration of the laws by Springer and his fellow-magistrates. "And in acts like these," he warned, "I forsee the ground work of at some future period more hangings, more confiscations, and possibly even the loss of the colony."[11]

Matthews now began to think of becoming a candidate for the provincial Assembly, where his views would carry more weight. This became known during the course of a controversy with some of his opponents, which was carried on through the columns of the York *Weekly Register*. He accused one of his anonymous enemies, thought to be Burwell, of supporting for personal gain the separation of Middlesex from the London District and the establishment of St. Thomas as its capital. Matthews appeared as the leader of those who wished the capital to be placed in the vicinity of Delaware or London.[12] His nomination occurred in February, 1824, when a group of Reformers met at the home of Archibald MacMillan in Westminster. "We want an Honest Independent man to represent us in Parliament," they resolved, "one who, while he sincerely regards the rights of the Crown, will never consent to vote away the Rights of the Subjects nor tax the Poor to add increased wealth to the already opulent office-holder, or sinecure; and such a man, from our personal acquaintance we believe to be CAPTAIN JOHN MATTHEWS."[13]

Another Reform candidate, for the two seats to which Middlesex was entitled, was found in the person of Dr. John Rolph, a younger man than Matthews and very different in character. Unlike the hot-tempered Captain, who lashed out at his opponents in bitter terms at the slightest provocation, Rolph was pleasant and ingratiating, and had considerable popularity amongst all classes. He had come from England in 1812, and for a time lived with his parents at Charlotteville. Talbot knew the family well, and in 1811, when his brother William was visiting him, there was even talk of William marrying into "the Honourable family of the Rolphs".[14] John Rolph later took up land in Southwold and was a frequent visitor at Port Talbot. A brilliant lawyer and physician, he appears to have had political ambitions for some years before 1824. He was chiefly responsible for the inauguration of the Talbot Anniversary in 1817, which Burwell opposed. At the celebration in 1824, which took place a few weeks before the election, he was chosen to make the reply to the Colonel's address. About the same time he undertook to start a medical school at St. Thomas, and requested that the Colonel be its patron. "Everything that is good and useful," he told Talbot, "should begin in the Talbot Settlement under your auspices." His suggestion that the approaching election would be an opportune time to give public introductory lectures and to appeal for subscriptions, indicates that the project was not without political implications.[15]

Talbot's friendship with Rolph, and his appreciation of the honour done him, did not blind him to the fact that Rolph had liberal tendencies, which in the Colonel's eyes made him a most unsuitable candidate for the Assembly. He was even less inclined to favour the troublesome Captain Matthews, who not only openly abused the magistrates, but was the leader of those who opposed St. Thomas as the seat of the courts for the projected District of Middlesex. Matthews had been careful never to attack the Colonel himself, and in a letter to Secretary Hillier had spoken of his "cultivated, generous, and manly" mind and his character that stood "high above all suspicion of wrong doing".[16] But William Lyon Mackenzie, editor of the new and radical newspaper, the Queenston *Colonial Advocate*, was under no illusions concerning Talbot's position in the election. The influence of the Colonel was immense, he wrote, and he would "throw it all into Burwell's scale".[17] Burwell had been a member of the Assembly since 1812, when he defeated the notorious Benajah Mallory of Oxford to become the representative for the electoral district of Oxford and Middlesex. Writing twenty years after the event, the editor of the St. Thomas *Liberal* stated that this election was held at Captain Secord's in Yarmouth, "so that Mallory and his friends were obliged to travel nearly 60 miles through the woods to the poll. There they found the 'Father of the Settlement' providing votes for his favourite, with as much expedition as the Yankees manufacture their cut-nails—by furnishing all who were willing to support the claims of the Young Aspirant to office, and who were not already qualified, with LOCATION TICKETS. At the next election there was no opposition whatever. And at the succeeding one, it was ascertained that the Scotch Settlers would not comply with the wishes of the *Talbot Monarchy*, and their votes were refused on the plea of their not having obtained their deeds!"[18] Burwell had now been in office for twelve years, during which he had been an unwavering supporter of the government, the result, Mackenzie suggested, of his favourable surveying contracts, which in 1823 alone amounted to nearly one million acres of land. His "considerable budget of bonds, mortgages, book debts, etc., etc.," could be used as a weapon against those who dared to vote against him.

It was this formidable opponent that the Reformers hoped to defeat; and they were aided by all the local animosities, which were now directed against Burwell. In Aldborough the Highlanders had just apologized for the language used in their memorial three years before. "Enclosed you will receive the submission of my Highlanders," Talbot wrote to Hillier on March 19, "which I trust the Lieut. Governor will have the goodness to accept as a sufficient acknowledgement. I am particularly anxious that His Excellency should forgive these people, in order to prevent worst consequences. They are a stupid, ignorant, obstinate, and vindictive race, and I am persuaded that should they continue in disgrace, the end will be, that they will become most inveterate Rebels."[19] Maitland accepted the apology, but the Highlanders remained sullenly angry, and they were in no mood to vote for the government candidate.

On nomination day, July 16, 1824, the little village of St. Thomas, named in honour of the Colonel seven years before, was crowded with five or six hundred people from all parts of the county.[20] Some of them wore oak leaves and ribbons on their hats inscribed with the words "Matthews and Liberty", or "Rolph and Matthews". About ten o'clock in the morning Colonel John Warren, the returning officer, dressed in blue and with his sword at his side, mounted the hustings that had been constructed on the high ground near the church. He was accompanied by Colonel Talbot and the three candidates, Rolph, Matthews, and Burwell, who were about to contest the two seats. As soon as Warren read the writ Talbot left the platform, and mounting his horse remained among the crowd of people to listen to the speeches.

William Lyon Mackenzie, who had come to St. Thomas to observe the election and to aid the Reform candidates, was favourably impressed by his first view of the noted Colonel. Talbot was dressed in a plain blue surtout coat and trousers, and carried an Indian blanket folded like a horseman's cloak and fastened behind his horse's saddle. "His air is that of a military officer of distinction," Mackenzie wrote, "insomuch that had he not been pointed out to me, I should have set him down in my own mind as a person of some consequence. In youth he must have possessed a handsome person and well formed features; for even now, and he is nearly sixty years of age, his features have nothing harsh, and his appearance is prepossessing. I have seen him, I like him, and I hope his children, for so may he call the settlers in Middlesex, will teach their little ones to revere him as a Pater Patriae, the father of his country." Mackenzie was to regret this last sentence, and he omitted it when, a few years later, he published the remainder of the account in his book on Upper Canada.

Mahlon Burwell spoke first, defending his past conduct in the Assembly, and attacking "a jolly good-looking" farmer who was present, whom he suspected to be the author of a "political squib or cracker" directed against himself. "This ebullition of resentment," Mackenzie wrote, "in so inappropriate a place, lost him many friends; and a poor man of the name of Gardiner, with whom he had a law-suit concerning the value of an old house, and who complained of foul play, lost him a good many more." The next speaker was Captain Matthews, whose "manly athletic form and courteous demeanour, added to the independent English principles he professed to espouse, secured to him a distinguished place in the good graces of many a worthy yeoman". Rolph, the last speaker, promised to act with independence and defend the people's rights. He concluded by complimenting Colonel Talbot as the founder and father of the country, its friend and benefactor. Mackenzie thought the Colonel must have been "highly gratified with the delicate compliments paid him", and that he was in general "well beloved by his people".

At the conclusion of the speeches Mackenzie addressed the people from his wagon; and during the remainder of the week, while the voting was in progress, he worked for Rolph and Matthews. But it was unnecessary, he found, for "the Talbot settlement would have elected the opposition candidates, if twice the influence the local government and Colonel Talbot possessed had been exercised against them." During the election more than one hundred people rode in from Long Point, and the newly-elected members for Oxford came with their bands of yeomen, to vote for "the men of the people's choice". "Happy groups of horsemen from every quarter ride up to the hustings, shouting blithely 'Rolph and Mathews!'—'Mathews and Liberty!'."

"The triumph of independence in Middlesex is complete," a resident of St. Thomas wrote at the close of the polls. Rolph and Matthews were returned by a large majority. Matthews was so popular in the northern townships that his majority would have been even greater "if location tickets had been permitted to vote, as they have hitherto done".[21] Mackenzie noticed "the usual quantity of quarrelling, fighting, brawling, scolding, fiddling and dancing, talking and drinking" at the election, but he was happy with the results. "This is a settlement of a few years old," he wrote, "which has risen against the influence of the executive, and the natural disadvantages of so dense a wilderness. Good words will increase their love of liberty, and fill their minds with a more ardent desire for internal improvement. . . . The ardent desire for rational freedom which obtains in this district was to me very pleasing."[22]

Colonel Talbot was far from pleased. "It is with much pain that I inform you," he wrote to Hillier, "that the Middlesex Election closed yesterday and that Matthews and Rolph are returned, the former was supported by all the *Old* country and Yankee Radicals, who were most industrious in haranguing the *People*, amongst the most forward was that Vagabond McKenzie and as you may suppose 'said the thing that was not', with respect to Burwell's conduct in the House of Assembly. I greatly fear that Government will have a very troublesome set to manage. . . . If the Scotch had been faithful to their promise to Burwell he would have succeeded, but Matthews' party persuaded them not to vote."[23]

The election of Matthews greatly enhanced his influence in the community, and gave him hopes that he might be able to develop the region along the Thames River at the expense of that on Lake Erie. "It may be," the Colonel told Hillier after describing his plans for his settlement, "that all my schemes are visionary, as I am told that the bold Captain Matthews has swore, since he has been elected a member, that he will reduce the Talbot Road to a simple footpath!"[24] When Matthews' continued charges against Magistrate Daniel Springer induced the Lieutenant-Governor to order an investigation, Talbot interceded in Springer's behalf, although he did not wish, he said, to appear personally in "any of these dirty works". In a private letter to Hillier he suggested that Francis Walsh, member for Norfolk, George Salmon, chairman of the London District court of quarter sessions, and Colonel John Bostwick of Kettle Creek, be named as commissioners to meet at Westminster to examine the evidence against Springer. His object, he said, was "to prevent the appointment of any that are devoted to Matthews, such as Askin, the clerk of the Peace, old Backhouse and several others". An investigation by all the magistrates of the district, which Maitland had in mind, "would not be conducted fairly or impartially, as the majority of that Body will lean to Matthews, who has contrived to insnare Scofield into his ranks".[25] These arguments appear to have prevailed, and Matthews was defeated in his efforts to have Springer deprived of his powers as a magistrate.

John Rolph was not long in establishing himself as the leading Reformer in the new Assembly. But even Mackenzie could not but feel some sympathy for the Attorney-General, John Beverley Robinson, who as the spokesman for the administration was the particular object of Rolph's attacks. Writing after Parliament was prorogued on April 13, 1825, Mackenzie declared that Robinson had been "literally overwhelmed—his measures, whether good or bad, whether the fruit of an enlightened mind, or of an arbitrary and tyrannical disposition, shared one common fate".[26] About the same time, unaware that the session had ended, Talbot wrote to Hillier that he was impatient to learn how the "August Assembly" was getting on, and if it had any intention of retiring for the season. "The Country talk is that Rolph is the man," he said, "and such a man, as has never been in the House before him, and that the Attorney General has no chance with him."[27]

During their stay in the Assembly Rolph and Matthews were persistent in their attacks on the rule of the "ignorant and corrupt" magistrates. An opposition member asserted that Matthews "never rose on this floor, without throwing out some invective against the magistrates."[28] The administration regarded him as a special nuisance. In what appeared to be an attempt to get rid of him, in the fall of 1827 he was ordered home to England as a pensioned officer to answer charges that while at the York Theatre, nearly two years before, he had called for "Yankee Doodle" in honour of the American players, and had urged the audience to remove their hats during the singing. Matthews was completely exonerated of any suspicion of disloyalty, both by a special committee of the Assembly and the authorities in England, but the temporary suspension of his pension, and the cost of the trip, caused him severe financial distress.[29]

Matthews and Talbot came to know each other more intimately during 1826 and 1827, when they were forced to work together as commissioners for building the court-house at London. After the first meeting of the commission at St. Thomas, in April, 1827, the Colonel wrote to Hillier: "I dined and remained the night at the *head* Inn, a large party to dinner, Matthews, Rolph and about twenty others. Matthews behaved better than I ever knew him to, and took all my Billingsgate good naturedly, but Rolph was sulky."[30] The following January Matthews expressed his opinion of Talbot and Burwell in a letter to Secretary Mudge. "Colonel Talbot's high and honourable general character," he declared, "can derive no advantage from any eulogy of mine; but perfection is not the lot of any son of Adam. . . . Colonel Talbot has two principal faults. The first is occasional unbridled passion, by which he has inflicted many a severe and unnecessary wound, where the spirit was already sufficiently subdued. The other is, that he does not offer even the shadow of defence to the most open attacks of servility and flattery. Truth of necessity often avoids him."

Matthews then went on to speak of Mahlon Burwell, a man of "prepossessing appearance and manners, and unfortunately possessing too much talent for the benefit of his poor and ignorant neighbours". Under "the all powerful influence of Col. Talbot", Burwell's recommendations had for years "commanded all the appointments military as well as civil throughout the County, and good care he has taken to recommend none that would not bend their knee, and bow their heads to him. Himself also he has not neglected. He is registrar of the County. He is Commissioner in Banco Regis. He is Post Master. He is colonel of militia. He is a magistrate. He is a deputy surveyor, and also a

Surveyor of Highways, and by his supreme authority is always elected chairman of the Court of Quarter Sessions, where under the pretence of justice he administers injustice. Foreman also of the Grand Juries at Assize times, where his dictum is of course received as superior to the Law. It becomes necessary therefore to be a sattelite [*sic*] of this man, or to suffer the persecution and punishment which he assumes the power to inflict; and to submit without a possibility of redress to the injuries, falsehoods and insults of himself and his friends."[31]

Soon after this, having discovered that he was "never cut out for a legislator", Matthews announced that he would not be a candidate in the coming election. But a few days later, when he and Rolph were nominated at a meeting held in London, both accepted.[32] In July they were successful against Burwell and James Hamilton, the government candidates. During the 1829 session Matthews was absent most of the time, apparently because of ill health. He was present, however, just before the close, when he rose to complain of injustice inflicted on his son by the local magistrates, who "punished him for the political conduct of his father".[33] On this personal note the political career of the "Bold Captain Matthews" ended. His name does not appear in the report of the debates during the next session, he having apparently returned to England before that time. It was fortunate for him that he was not present in Upper Canada during the next few years, when cooler heads than his were turned towards rebellion as the only avenue of reform.

## CHAPTER XIV

# *St. George's Day, 1832*

THE development of the Reform movement in Upper Canada was temporarily halted by Sir John Colborne, who arrived in the fall of 1828 to succeed Maitland as Lieutenant-Governor. In the elections of 1830, which followed the death of George IV, the people showed their approval of Colborne's conciliatory policy by returning a majority of the government candidates to the Legislative Assembly. The Middlesex electors returned Mahlon Burwell and Roswell Mount, both deputy surveyors, whose contracts with the government had brought them wealth and influence.[1]

Talbot's pleasure at these events was tempered by news of the progress of Reform in England. Writing to Lord Wharncliffe on May 1, 1831, in reply to his letter of January 29, the Colonel said that "the picture you have drawn of the state of my beloved Engd grieves one to the very quick, but God grant that the result may not prove so terrible as you prophesy. . . ." He was convinced "that it would be madness on my side to weigh anchor, from Lake Erie, in these unsettled times, and give up a certainty for an uncertainty. It is quite true, that this Country affords me but little enjoyment, yet I am independent, and have the satisfaction of witnessing daily, this New World increasing and improving in every particular, more rapidly than I believe to be the case in any other portion of the Globe, and landed property is becoming more valuable, and available, every year, and at all events, worst come to the worst, by retaining it I shall possess the means of affording an asylum, in case of necessity, to those Friends I most value. I said as much in my last letter to Ly Wharncliffe, and that I had immortalised you in this hemisphere, by naming some of my roads after you and your family. I have Wharncliffe Highway, Wortley Road, Caroline Row, a beautiful line of Lots along the banks of our Thames and a short road between Wharncliffe Highway and Wortley Road, I have called Stuart Place."[2]

Stuart-Wortley had repeatedly declared himself opposed to the principle of parliamentary reform while a member of the House of Commons. After taking his seat in the House of Lords as Baron Wharncliffe of Wortley he continued to take the same stand. In the spring of 1831, when the Grey ministry introduced in the Commons a bill to redistribute parliamentary seats on a more equal basis, and to extend the right of voting, Wharncliffe initiated a discussion of the question in the Lords, and gave a hostile analysis of the government Bill, which was soon after defeated in the committee stage. Grey then persuaded King William to dissolve Parliament and appeal to the people in a general election, which resulted in a triumph for the Reformers. The second Bill passed the Commons on September 21 by a large majority; but two weeks later, with Wharncliffe active among the leaders of the opposition, it was defeated in the Lords on the second reading. The ministry prorogued Parliament and prepared a third Bill, in which certain concessions were made. Agitation for reform throughout the country now became violent; rioting occurred in London, Bristol, and other cities, and the political unions became so aggressive that some of them were suppressed by proclamation.

At this point Wharncliffe took a step that must have surprised and dismayed Colonel Talbot when he heard of it. Losing confidence in the possibility of successfully blocking the measure, and convinced of the dangers which would follow another rejection of the Reform Bill, Wharncliffe broke with the Duke of Wellington and the Tories and agreed to support the Bill, which passed the second reading on April 9, 1832. But in committee he and other lords insisted upon certain amendments that the ministry refused to accept. Earl Grey advised the King to create a sufficient number of new peers to carry the Bill, but William refused, and the Cabinet resigned. Wellington tried unsuccessfully to form a ministry, and Grey was recalled. King William now went so far as to consent to the creation of new peers, but he was able to avoid this step by using his influence with the Tory lords, part of whom, including Wharncliffe and Wellington, abstained from voting, thus permitting the Bill to pass. It received the royal assent on July 7, 1832.[3]

If Talbot wrote to Wharncliffe during this period his letters have not survived. But his opinion of the events transpiring in England was expressed in letters to others. On July 2, 1832, he wrote to tell Peter Robinson that he had just heard "that Lord Grey is again Premier, and that there have been alarming meetings in the large towns of England addressing the king in favor of Reform, 100,000 in London expressing a desire that Willm the 4th would abdicate as he had not resolution to create the Peers required to carry the favourite measure. I am quite in the dismals, and almost dread the arrival of the post which probably will be here in less than an hour." A few days later he wrote again: "I am quite dolesome at the state of things in England, as the consequences may involve us all in misery. William the 4th has much to answer for, for had he been spirited after the first rejection of the Reform Bill and called in the Wellington party, order and security might have been restored, but as matters now are there is no saying the length reform or change may be carried."[4]

It is in the light of his concern for the momentous events transpiring in Great Britain that the Colonel's actions against the Reformers of his own settlement must be considered. The disorders in England were accompanied by the beginning of a more militant phase of the struggle between the Reformers and the Tories of Upper Canada. In the summer of 1831, following his expulsion from the Legislative Assembly on the charge that his newspaper articles had libelled that body, William Lyon Mackenzie called a meeting at York to adopt a petition of grievances, which would be sent to England. A Central Committee was appointed to further the adoption and distribution for signatures of similar petitions in the various townships throughout the province. Opposition meetings of government supporters were held for the purpose of drawing up addresses of loyalty, but eighteen townships adopted the grievance petitions.[5] Among the latter were several in Middlesex County. "The *grievance mongers*," a local resident reported in February 1832, "have endeavoured to get up meetings in this District and to procure signatures to petitions through the agency of *knaves* and *fools*, and in a few townships a sort of meetings have actually been held, at which long speeches have been made by *pedlars* and *strollers*, to persuade us that we ought to be discontented; and the number of signatures to these petitions have been swelled chiefly by the names of runaway negroes, and of people who have neither habitation nor property in the country. The sensible part of the community only laugh at such silly attempts to do mischief, but the faction will no doubt state that these grievance petitions are signed by his Majesty's loyal subjects, etc. etc."[6]

In his celebrated speech on St. George's Day, Talbot declared that the "rebels" had "commenced their work of darkness under the cover of organizing Damned Cold water drinking Societies, where they met at night to communicate their poisonous and seditious schemes to each other and to devise the best mode of circulating the infection, so as to impose upon and delude the simple and unwary. After practising this game they fancied they had acquired strength and assumed a more daring aspect, and appeared openly under the mask of the Grievance Petition . . . a thing of trash and sedition founded on falsehood fabricated for the purpose of creating discontent, and in the end rebellion in this Province. . . . These incendiaries opened their campaign judiciously by having their first field day in Malahide, where their greatest strength prevails. . . . Here the old Schoharie line for a while drove a pretty considerable trade. They next tried their strength in Yarmouth, where, aided by a few Hickory Quakers, they succeeded in organizing a committee of vigilance whose duty I suppose was to sound 'the conchshell of sedition in every valley and on every hill', and where aided by certain characters, who making a cloak of religion to cover their seditious purposes, and who secretly lent them the light of their countenances, they prospered to the present time."[7]

The meeting held in Bayham Township on February 21, 1832, does not seem to have been very seditious. The report, published in the *Colonial Advocate*, begins by asserting "the privilege of British Subjects to assemble and express opinions on the conduct of their representatives in Parliament, and to assert their rights and privileges they have reason to think are invaded." This the members proceeded to do in a series of resolutions. They denounced the expulsion of Mackenzie as a "wanton and flagrant attack on the liberty of the Press and a gross violation of the rights and privileges of the Electors" of his county, a wilful disregard for the opinion of people in other constituencies, and a neglect of the important affairs of the province. Nevertheless, they would "wholly discountenance any measure that may have a tendency to throw the country into confusion, or that shall in any measure disturb the peace; but shall feel it to be our duty to co-operate with all who are desirous of promoting tranquillity, and of resisting tyranny of every description."[8]

Colonel Talbot looked upon such meetings of the people as seditious. He believed that all Reformers were democrats and republicans, and that their principles were destructive of proper government. He despised the Methodist itinerant preachers because of their activity in the temperance societies and the grievance meetings; they were the "saddlebag preachers" or "Ryersonian strollers", who had long been accused of American and radical sympathies. Urged on by Mahlon Burwell, he now decided to forsake his long-standing policy of avoiding politics, and take his place as the leader of those who were opposed to Reform. On March 19 he issued a proclamation to his people, signed "Thomas Talbot, Father of the Talbot Settlement", which reads as follows:[9]

> HAVING SEEN THE PROCEEDINGS of different Meetings held in the Talbot Settlement, on the subject of *imagined* grievances, and finding that it is now necessary to ascertain the real sentiments of the Inhabitants, so as at once to put down the fever (by a few only) manifested, to encourage disaffection to the British Government, I give

this notice, recommending a general meeting of my settlers on St. George's day, the 23d. of April next, at the King's Arms at St. Thomas, at noon, when I shall attend.

The day following the publication of this notice a Reformer of Yarmouth wrote to Mackenzie: "The inhabitants near me are generally in favor of reform, but its opponents are very violent and vicious. I am an old inhabitant, but never saw the Talbot Settlement in such a ferment as at present. The Lion is aroused. The antis have got Colonel Talbot at their head, and a proper head he is for such a body. . . . He is to attend a meeting on the 23rd of April, and altho' unpopular his presence will have great influence on those who have not got their deeds from government. . . . I never was called a disaffected person until now; it seems astonishing. I have always been, as was thought by many, too much the other way; but the conduct of our rulers is now deserving a severe check from the people."[10]

Violence was not long in coming; but it appears to have been precipitated by the Reformers, at a Tory meeting held at St. Thomas late in March. The *Colonial Advocate* reported with satisfaction that "the parties soon proceeded from words to blows; bloody noses were given and received; Lawyer Givens speechified; eyes were gouged out; the faces of the tories were reformed, the chairman, secretary, magistrates, etc., were upset and the object of the meeting defeated."[11] But Joseph Pickering, the Colonel's farm foreman, saw the Reform movement declining before "a general burst of loyal feeling". Loyal addresses, he wrote on March 21, were "general throughout the Province, called forth by the attempt at excitement and disaffection of a few demagogues, to serve their own sinister purposes, and whose aim is to subvert the

British Constitution, by instilling their democratic principles".[12]

The "pedlars of W. L. Mackenzie's grievances" decided to issue their own proclamation in reply to that of the Colonel. On March 27 the Malahide and Yarmouth Committees of Vigilance met at Burbee's Inn in St. Thomas and appointed a committee of three for the purpose. The committee, consisting of Lucius Bigelow, George Lawton, and Asahel B. Lewis issued a circular, signed "A Freeholder", on April 9. They began by comparing the advance of reform and liberal government under the Whigs in England, with the reactionary policies of the government of Upper Canada. The Colonel's Tory zeal, they charged, was the result of the thousands of acres of land, and the pension, which he received from the government. His meeting had been called for the purpose of trying "to overawe and brow-beat [the people] into a public expression of sentiments different from their real political feelings." "Col. Talbot may be the father of the Talbot settlement," they concluded, "but he will find on the 23rd April that he has many sons who are of age and think and act for themselves, and who are not afraid to tell grey beards the truth."[13]

The Tories answered in a barrage of circulars, and letters to the St. Thomas *Journal.* One writer charged that most of the "disaffected" were recent immigrants from the United States, and that all had been peaceful until the Vigilant Committees began to disseminate "the doctrines of a designing demagogue [Mackenzie] who aims at engrafting Republicanism on a British Constitution". The loyal men of the settlement must put down with their voices the disaffected, the republicans, the revolutionists, the "rebellious faction that infest our land". Talbot wrote to Peter Robinson, about a week before the event, that he expected "some hot work at my Benefit on the 23rd, Squibs flying in all directions".

It was not without reason that the Colonel chose St. George's Day for his attack on the dragon of Reform. When the morning arrived he rode forth from Port Talbot on horseback, accompanied only by his faithful servant Jeffrey Hunter, and armed only with the cutting phrases of a prepared speech. St. Thomas was already crowded with bands of men who had come from every part of the Talbot Country—from Long Point to the Detroit River. They arrived on foot, in carriages, and on horseback, with flags flying and bands playing, eager, it seemed, to show their loyalty to the Lieutenant-Governor and the Constitution. It was nearly noon when word came that the Colonel was close at hand, and a group of some two hundred horsemen led by a bugler rode out to meet him. As they escorted him up Sterling Hill, on which hundreds of people waited, Talbot removed his hat to the cheers of the crowd, while a band struck up "The British Grenadiers", and the skirl of bagpipes was heard. On he rode, erect and proud in the saddle, past the house of Colonel Warren where a party of gentlemen and another band saluted him. Removing his hat with regal dignity he looked about, "and with a look of conscious victory eyed every individual as if to ascertain if an enemy of Britain could be found in such a company".

Arriving at last at the King's Arms Hotel within the village, the Colonel was escorted to a platform that stood in front, on which waved British flags and a great scarlet banner emblazoned with a crown and the words "Sir John Colborne and the British Constitution". In front of the inn and along the adjacent streets more than 2,000 persons gave voice to cheers. The white-maned old Colonel raised his hat and looked for a moment at the sea of faces, drinking in the unfamiliar and heady tonic of acclaim. Then, stepping to the front of the platform, he began his speech in "the same original, eccentric, and peculiar strain" which he was accustomed to use in his own home. The paper that he had prepared beforehand begins with the military command: "Silence and Attention!", but, speaking as though it were extemporaneous, he appears to have omitted this. He began by stating that he felt it necessary "to refute a base, slanderous and unprincipled calumny which has been circulated about me, by a set of infamous and worthless ruffians, who from motives of disaffection and rebellion have labored to convince you that I called this meeting for the purpose of overawing and browbeating my settlers into the adoption of such sentiments as I might think proper to propose to them." His only purpose, he said, was to give every man an "opportunity of publicly declaring what he is, in order that I may know who to trust in the hour of danger, in order that you may well know who you may safely esteem as friends or regard as enemies to your peace and happiness."

When the cheering had subsided, Talbot went on to speak of his efforts during the past thirty years to form "a truly British Colony"; but despite all his care a few black sheep, some afflicted with "the rot", had crept into his flock. Cheers and laughter interrupting him, he calmly took his snuff-box from his pocket, gave it a tap, raised the lid, and took a pinch of snuff, completing the manoeuvre by shaking his fingers in front of his nose. He then began to describe the formation of the "subversive" temperance societies, and the Reform meetings in Malahide and Yarmouth. In Malahide, he had heard, "the old Schoharie line turned out in full force, having a Yankey deserter for their drill sergeant, and a long sprout from a U. E. for their flag staff." He attacked the "Hickory Quakers" of Yarmouth, and the Methodist itinerant preachers, and he praised the Constitution, Great Britain, and Sir John Colborne. Annoyed by some talking among certain persons in the crowd, he stopped to take another pinch of snuff, shook his fingers in front of his face as before, and said: "I am an old man, gentlemen, but tough!"

After speaking for some time longer, he announced that Edward Ermatinger would read a prepared loyalty address, which all those who approved would sign, so that he would be able "to separate the tares from the wheat, the sheep from the goats, the true Briton from the rebel who would lay waste and desolate your happy homes". But first he asked those who were in favour of the King and Constitution to hold up their right hands. All did so, to the accompaniment of prolonged cheers. The Colonel then asked all those who were in favour of a republic to hold up their hands, which met with no response except from one young man who held his up by mistake. Then came the reading of the address of loyalty to the King, after which Talbot announced that copies would be placed at various places for signatures. When the usual round of cheers had subsided, he closed the meeting with a benediction: "Now God of his infinite goodness and mercy bless and preserve all you that are true British subjects and keep your hearts and minds untainted by sedition or corruption."

That evening the Colonel was the guest of honour at a dinner at the King's Arms Hotel, where "the utmost hilarity prevailed—Loyal Toasts were drunk, and St. George's Day passed off in a style unprecedented in this part of His Majesty's dominions." A week later Talbot wrote to Sir John Colborne: "I had a splendid *turn out* on St. George's day, when the Rebels were all silent and quiet, and I gave my children some wholesome advice." The province was now well revived, he believed, and it was gratifying to find "that the disaffected are but few, considering all the noise that has been made".[14]

The fame of the Colonel's St. George's Day speech spread across the province. The editor of the York *Canadian Freeman* rejoiced that he had struck a finishing blow at the power of "the saddlebag faction".[15] The York *Courier* commented: "The Ryersonian strolling demagogues, and their secret and somewhat influential co-adjutors in the village of St. Thomas, who indirectly encouraged and promoted the 'hole and corner meetings', had not, one of them, the courage to come forth in the open light of day, and meet the 'father of the settlement' and the other advocates of the British principles, face to face, at the great meeting: but when they witnessed the proud and triumphant display of patriotism and true loyalty which was exhibited at the meeting, they shrunk into their native nothingness—alike, as it would appear, ashamed of their cause and afraid to advocate it: and the friends of 'Sir John Colborne and the constitution', in consequence, carried every thing before them, unopposed and uninterrupted."[16]

The liberal papers, however, such as the Brockville *Recorder*, thought it a little strange that a no-grievance address should have been carried unanimously "in a district where such men as McCall, Captain Matthews, and John Rolph have been frequently returned". The secret was solved, the *Recorder* declared, when it learned that the people were only asked whether they favoured the British or a republican form of government. The address was then pronounced carried, although many of the people present were opposed to it.[17] No opportunity was given for the expression of grievances, only the opportunity to express loyalty or disloyalty. Talbot might, the St. Thomas *Liberal* stated the following December, "with as much propriety have asked professors of the Christian religion to vote for the faith of Mahomet as to have insulted the people of the London District by calling a vote for a republic, when not one of them had ever expressed a wish to that effect. Such chicanery of the creatures of the executive, to draw the public gaze from their own conduct, they have left no measures untried to engage the people in strife and civil war, they have without the least shadow of reason construed opposition to their monopolizing, illegal measures, into rebellion against the British Crown."

The exaggerated language used elsewhere in the same editorial reveals the bitterness engendered by Talbot's speech. Instead of the "fatherly language which was expected, the ears of his auditors were shocked by the coarsest, lowest and most vulgar bursts of blacguardism [*sic*] that have ever been witnessed by any body of people in this province. Vollies [*sic*] of curses were profusely showered upon a respectable body of Christians and upon the philanthropic cause of Temperance. . . . If it was too late for the Colonel to *practice himself the rules of Temperance Societies*; if he realy [*sic*] regarded the interests of his children he would not have pronounced the most reckless curses upon those who were disposed to do so. If to retain his extravagant salaries untouched, it was natural to oppose reform, it was most abusive, insulting and disgraceful in him to bestow such ungentlemanly epithets upon all who were not willing to pin their faith upon his sleeve, such as black sheep, rotten sheep, etc. etc."[18]

The Reformers charged that coercion was used after St. George's Day to obtain signatures to the "loyal address".

At a militia meeting in Mosa, it was reported, the chief business seemed to be to get subscribers to it. Some were induced by threats to sign the document. The major refused to make one man a sergeant because he would not support it; and for the same reason he refused to issue a certificate that a farmer had completed his settlement duties.[19] "A Highlander of Aldborough" declared that the same type of coercion was used in his township, and that many of the signatures were duplicated. "During the time that the pretended Father of his Settlement was pushing his petitions to the King (God defend his sacred Majesty from the pretended loyalty of such petitioners) about for signatures," he wrote, several were deposited throughout Aldborough. Many people signed all the copies. The writer concluded by asking his fellow Scots if they or their children could ever forgive "him who arrogates to himself the venerable title of Father of the settlement, for the irreparable wrong done fourteen years since, when arrived in this Province, by being placed as they were on fifty acres of miserable sandy land, instead of receiving as they then ought 200 acres of good land in good locations."[20]

CHAPTER XV

# *The Road to Rebellion*

Having taken the field to win what appeared to be a decisive victory against the Reformers, Talbot and his Tory forces remained in a state of readiness to guard against further outbreaks. A visitor to Port Talbot, about the middle of June, 1832, met the Colonel "returning in high spirits from attending a grievance meeting in the neighbourhood, which he and his friends had, by a series of counter resolutions, converted into a loyal and constitutional one."[1]

However, the Reformers were far from being crushed. The following December they announced they would hold a meeting on January 17, 1833, for the purpose of forming a political union. The Tories replied by distributing copies of the following broadside:

NOTICE

The Ripstavers, Gallbursters, etc., with their friends, are requested to meet at St. Thomas, on the 17th of January, at 12 o'clock, as there will be more work for them on that day. The Doctors are requested to be in readiness to heal the sick and cure the broken headed. Let no rotten eggs be wanting. As the Unionists are all Yankees, a few pieces of pumkin will not be amiss.

Whatever Unions may be in *England*, it must be remembered that in *this country* with Republicans at their head, they are the next step to Rebellion. The *object* of the nasty Republican Trio, that is to say of the Hypocrite, the Atheist, and the Deist, in their intended meeting is to wheedle weak and simple mortals so far into the paths of Rebellion, that they cannot afterwards retreat, even if they wish to do so. Therefore, most noble Ripstavers, check the evil in the beginning, that is, hoe them out—sugar them off—in short sow them up. The Dastards may think to screen themselves from the public fury by holding their meeting at a private house: but public or private put yourselves in the midst of them. You have a right to be there. It is a *public* meeting.

Asahel Lewis, editor of the St. Thomas *Liberal*, reprinted this in his newspaper, and pleaded with his fellow Reformers to act as peacefully as possible, reminding them that violence could never be productive of any good, nor could anyone be forced into a belief that was in opposition to his own senses. "Is there any one," he asked, "foul enough to suppose that all the threats, bullying, brow-beating and blackguardism, made use of on 23rd of April last to over-awe the people, and quench the rising spirit of liberty, availed the party who had recourse to such methods to support their fallen fortunes? On the contrary many of their own followers left them in disgust."[2]

Colonel Talbot had no doubts about the efficacy of violent measures to suppress the hated Reformers. A few days after the meeting he wrote to Peter Robinson: "My *Rebels* endeavored to hold a meeting at St. Thomas on the 17th, Dr. Franklin's birthday, as I am informed, but in which they were frustrated by my Loyal Guards, who routed the rascals at all points and drove them out of the village like sheep, numbers with broken heads leaving their hats behind them—the glorious work of old Colonel Hickery. In short it was a most splendid victory."[3]

The *Liberal* had a somewhat different story. It reported that 400 signatures to the Union's constitution had been obtained before the meeting began; and that finding their opponents in possession of the rostrum in the Seminary, where they had planned to meet, the Reformers assembled outside to elect their officers. When the Tories discovered this they emerged and attempted to attack Dr. Goodhue, a leading Reformer and temperance advocate. Foiled in this, they armed themselves with clubs and roamed the streets looking for Reformers, many of whom were beaten. Most of the mob of about fifty persons were Irish Orangemen from the vicinity of Port Talbot, the *Liberal* stated, led by an Irish magistrate and his sons.[4]

The Colonel happily predicted that the "rebels" would not venture to call another meeting, "at least not in St. Thomas"; but one was held at the Seminary in South Yarmouth on February 5. Again the "knights of the Cudgel from Port Talbot", led by a number of St. Thomas lawyers, merchants, and other gentlemen, advanced to the scene; but learning that about two hundred of the Reformers had armed themselves with oak staves, they remained at a discreet distance. They later retired to St. Thomas to roam the streets, shouting and brandishing their clubs, late into the night.[5]

On St. George's Day Colonel Talbot had projected himself openly into the struggle between the Tories and the Reformers. Before that day few except the disgruntled inhabitants of Aldborough and Dunwich had dared openly to say anything against him. But at a time when many were beginning to think of him as the benevolent patriarch of his settlement, he had violently dispelled the illusion. Having forsaken the sanctuary of the throne to mix with common men in the public arena, he was no longer shielded from blame by his ministers. As the personal leader of the reactionary element he was exposed to the most virulent attacks by all who hated the old regime. An open letter addressed to him, published in the *Liberal* in the spring of 1833, called attention to this changed position in the following words:[6]

> The high official stations you hold—your long residence in the county—and the venerable title of Father of the Settlement, which you have of late assumed, has naturally drawn public attention towards you.
>
> Had you continued to exercise only a secret political influence, and only presumed to domineer and brow-beat as a Land-Agent, your conduct might have passed unnoticed—you might have gone on to the end of your days, *snapping, snarling and cursing* every one who was so unfortunate as to have business to transact with you. You might have gone down to the grave, and never have heard the murmur of execration which so generally pervades the Settlement, and which must carry to your ears the truth, that you and your curses are equally unheeded and despised.
>
> But Sir, when you presumed to call a public meeting for political purposes, and there to mount a rostrum, and in the most public manner, and with the most cruel vituperations, attempt to blast the characters of every honest man in the country, whose political creed did not exactly correspond with your own,—you cast aside the protecting mantle that age and station had thrown around you, and ever since have stood forth in your naked deformity, a legitimate object of public scrutiny and public censure. After such a public and shameful exhibition of your feelings and motives, you cannot reasonably expect to be allowed to draw your head within your shell, and quietly retire from public view.

The writer then proceeded to excoriate the Colonel for his personal habits, and his treatment of his settlers. It was generally known, he said, even before the Colonel's speech, that he sneered at and ridiculed the temperance societies; he would never countenance any scheme, however worth while, which did not originate with himself or his sycophants; least of all would he support any movement towards moral reform, "which might lead to unfavorable comparisons of [his] own habits with those of others". His insulting and unfair treatment of applicants for the Crown lands had aroused loud complaint against him. "If the duties of your office have become troublesome to you," his critic declared, "if your habits unfit you for their performance, then resign the office; but if then these things are true, and who doubts it? and you still continue to hold the office only to neglect its duties, it then becomes a grievance, and you should be reformed into private life."

Talbot did not deign to answer these public assaults upon him, but he never again called himself "The Father of the Talbot Settlement", and henceforth his only public appearances were before his loyal followers during the Anniversary celebrations. The editor of the *Liberal* reported scornfully on May 23, 1833: "The Anniversary of the day when King Talbot commenced his reign in this District was celebrated at Miller's Hotel on the 21st inst., with the customary pomp and parade. His Majesty attended the Grand Celebration—so that a fair view of this *precious specimen of humanity* could be obtained at better advantage than through the windows of his Castle."

The elections of 1834 gave striking proof that the Reform movement was still strong throughout Upper Canada, although several of its moderate leaders had defected. In Middlesex the Reformers Thomas Parke of London, and Elias Moore, a Quaker of South Yarmouth, won by a wide margin over Joseph Clench and Mahlon Burwell, despite determined efforts on the part of the latter, who denounced a county convention that had nominated Parke and Moore as illegal, and the Reformers as "all but rebels".[7] Two years before, a writer had remarked that "with the powerful aid of Col. Talbot (a Legislative Councillor) the *Burwell Dynasty* has been almost absolute."[8] The editor of the *Liberal* commented in the issue of July 25, 1833: "The County of Middlesex, from its first settlement up to this moment, has been controlled by two distinguished individuals, as absolutely and despotically as is the petty sovereignty of a German despot. This they have been enabled to do through the immense influence their high official stations give them. Magistrates, officers of the excise, surveyors, and militia officers, commissioners to carry the appropriations of public money into effect, all are appointed through the recommendations and influences of these sages of the District—thus forming a host of worthies who are ever at the beck of their Patrons." The Reformers regarded the result of the Middlesex election of 1834 not merely as a victory over Burwell and Talbot, "but as a triumph over the principles he and those he co-operated with have acted upon, in managing the affairs of the province."

The provincial Assembly, now dominated by a Reform majority, asserted its right to control all the Crown revenues in the province. The most important of its measures during the session of 1835 were lost in the oligarchic Legislative Council, but Mackenzie's Committee on Grievances produced the notable Seventh Report, which gave a vivid picture of the extent of Crown patronage. Alarmed at this, and by the exaggerated accounts of disaffection that reached him, Lord Glenelg decided to relieve Colborne and send out a new lieutenant-governor more in sympathy with the policy of the Whig ministry in England. Colborne resigned without waiting to be relieved, and was succeeded by Sir Francis Bond Head.

In the mistaken belief that he was a "tried Reformer", the liberal elements in Upper Canada greeted with enthusiasm Head's arrival at Toronto on January 15, 1836. When Head appointed three liberals to the Executive Council their hopes seemed justified. In St. Thomas and throughout the whole London District there were expressions of satisfaction, and some professed to believe that party strife would now cease, and the government would be purified of its "chronic disease".[9] An address of thanks to the new Lieutenant-Governor was adopted at a London meeting: it was resolved that he had, "so far, merited the gratitude and confidence of the people of the Province".[10] Colonel Talbot also had a favourable opinion of Head, but for a different reason. He believed he would take "a fair, honest and firm course"; but he also feared that "the majority of the people of Upper Canada are too far gone to be reclaimed." He was so discouraged, he told a friend, that he wished he "was possessed of a sufficiency to enable me to remove to the *Moon* or some other more wholesome place of residence, but time will effect all things."[11]

Head's true character was revealed to all early in March, when the Executive Council was forced to resign as a body after asserting its right to be consulted on every item of public business. Sir Francis announced that it existed merely for his convenience, and "to confer dignity upon his proceedings". His new Council consisted only of Conservatives.[12] The disappointment of the Reformers was violently expressed. In the St. Thomas *Liberal*, now under the editorship of John Talbot, there was much talk of betrayal, of tyranny, of efforts to deprive the people of their "properties, liberty, and all that is near and dear to freemen". The Reform representatives in the Assembly were told that the only recourse was to refuse to grant any of the monies under their control, until the government complied with the reasonable demands of the country.[13] The Assembly was well aware of the weapon at its command; on April 18 it adopted an address withholding the supplies. The Lieutenant-Governor retaliated by refusing to grant the contingencies, and by reserving all the money bills passed during the session. The resulting financial difficulties, and the paralysing effect on public works, he blamed on the Assembly; and he appealed to the people for support in the approaching elections, against a party that he called an enemy of the Constitution and the British connection.[14]

The people of the London District were not deceived by Head, a writer declared, and they applauded the action of the Assembly in withholding the supplies.[15] John Talbot in the *Liberal* exhorted them to stand firm, promising if they did so they would, in the next session, procure the recall of Head and the introduction of responsible government. "Up, men of Canada, to the fight," he urged. "Another Reform House and toryism is dead. Another Tory House and Reform is thrown back for half a century! The British Constitution and nothing but the Constitution, down with Head's despotism!"[16] On his part the Lieutenant-Governor employed every device and argument to discredit his opponents. In reply to a "loyal address" from many residents of the London District, he said that the Reformers were scheming demagogues, "a few dark designing men", who hoped to rule the country in their own interests. Critics of the government were branded as Yankee rebels and traitors. The Assembly was held responsible for all the financial troubles. A return to prosperity, and an end to threatened rebellion, could only be gained if the Tories won the election.[17]

Among the most active supporters of the government were the Presbyterian and Anglican ministers. In Aldborough Township the Rev. Alexander Ross, the Presbyterian minister, communicated regularly with Head's private secretary on the political situation in his neighbourhood. Late in June he wrote that Middlesex had been "extremely fertile in producing the weeds of radicalism", and that the Reformers were trying by every means "to wile our simple minded Yeomanry into the gulph of treason and destruction". They were secretly led, Ross declared, by Bela Shaw, an American storekeeper and postmaster in St. Thomas, but "the visible instruments are Kent and Talbot, editors of the Liberal newspaper—Kent is a Scotch, Talbot an Irish adventurer." Ross was by no means certain that the Tory candidates would win in the Middlesex election, but he was confident that radicalism could be greatly reduced if active measures were taken. He had already succeeded in forming a Constitutional Society among the loyal inhabitants of Dunwich, Aldborough, Orford and Howard; and a meeting had been held at St. Thomas in support of the Constitutional candidates. In addition, his assistant, the Rev. Donald McKenzie, was about to visit his fellow Scots in London, Lobo, and Williams townships, for the same purpose. "I think," Ross concluded, "that I can see distinctly radicalism writhing in the throes of death, and I cannot but believe that the name of Sir Francis Bond Head will long, long, be remembered for having transfixed the monster."[18]

The Anglican ministers, led by Dr. Strachan, were equally active in political affairs. "The Rev. Mr. Cronyn," the *Liberal* declared, "is rendering himself as obnoxious to the farmers of this country as he was once to the people of Ireland. He is here as he was there, a busy meddler in the affairs of State; and a violent stickler for the domination of his church, and the exclusive privileges of his order. He went along with the Tory candidates throughout the Township of London soliciting votes. . . ."[19] Dr. Strachan was the Colonel's guest during the Anniversary celebration on May 21. Politics and religion had been carefully avoided at past meetings, but on this occasion Talbot remarked, in the course of his customary after-dinner speech, that he hoped Sir Francis Head would long remain in the province to keep the people in order. He then proposed the health of Dr. Strachan and "the Clergy of Upper Canada". In his reply Strachan referred to the Anglican Church as the established church of the province, which angered many people who were members of other churches.[20]

The Middlesex elections began at London on June 27, 1836, and continued throughout the week. The Reformers Parke and Moore were re-elected for the county, but Mahlon Burwell won in the town of London, which had just secured the right to have a representative. The voting was attended with more than the usual amount of fighting and riotous behaviour.[21] The *Liberal* reported that on the final day the Tory leaders brought in the Orangemen from the back concessions of London, who attacked the hustings with stones and clubs just as the polls were about to be closed. Parke and Moore escaped to a neighbouring house, while their agents, John Talbot and Hugh O'Beirne, took refuge in the court-house. Some time later, while John Talbot was in the house of his brother, Edward, the mob attacked again. Escaping through the back window he fled to the home of John

Wilson, the returning officer, who escorted him out of the village.[22] Moore and O'Beirne, in fear of their lives, escaped on horseback.

The *Liberal* charged that government officials had issued deeds to lands, free of the usual fees, which were handed out by the Tory magistrates at the hustings as bribes.[23] Similar charges were made by Reformers in various other counties.[24] Dr. Duncombe repeated them in his memorial to the British government. Thousands of patents, he said, had been issued by the Lieutenant-Governor after the dissolution of Parliament in May, and some after the elections began, to enable his supporters to vote, although by law no freeholder could vote unless he had held his deed at least three months.[25] The select committee of the Assembly, appointed to investigate these charges, found that nearly 1,500 patents had been issued during the three months' period from the dissolution of Parliament until the close of the elections, but all except 233 of these had been issued under warrants made prior to Head's arrival in the province.[26] The committee assumed that people holding such warrants had rushed to secure their deeds so they might vote, and that Head and the government officials had done nothing illegal. It apparently made no effort to investigate other charges of irregularity, on the part of local officials, in giving out certificates of completion of settlement duties, nor did it say anything about the minimum time limit for holding a deed before voting.

The Reformers were now in a minority in the Assembly, and they found themselves savagely attacked by Head and the governing group as republicans and rebels, who wished to break with England and join the United States. The moderate Reformers began to desert the party, leaving a hard core of radicals. A few weeks after the elections the *Liberal* called on all Reformers throughout the province to organize into one great association, for the purpose of laying before the public the general principles of Reform, rather than petty grievances. These principles included the right of Canadians to all the privileges of the British constitution, a responsible government, and full control of the revenues. At the same time, "every intention of Revolution, every wish for Republicanism should be disclaimed".[27] But before another month had passed the same paper was praising "the free and flourishing United States", where "industry is amply rewarded—where land is cheap—where no dominant Church is by law established to shame the lowly chapel of the dissenters—where Orangemen dare not congregate and howl together for the blood of men; and where Tories and tyrants are deprived of their sting".[28] During the early part of 1837 it published a number of letters from former residents of Upper Canada, praising the American system of government.[29] The following summer it went so far as to publish a letter written by a congressman of the United States, in which it was suggested that the people of Canada were eager to enter the Union.[30]

One of the most radical centres in Middlesex was the village of Sparta in South Yarmouth, inhabited by the Hicksite or Hickory Quakers, who had long been suspected of disloyalty because of their American origin and their opposition to military service. Not far from Sparta lived an Englishman named George Lawton, who taught school for a time at the Seminary on the Sparta Road, and whose intelligence and skill in oratory made him a natural leader of the local radicals. During 1837 there also appeared in the settlement a Dr. John Wilson, whom the Tories referred to as "an American quack". Mounted on a cream-coloured horse, and wearing dark green spectacles, the doctor's tall thin figure could be seen making his calls along the Yarmouth roads; and everywhere he went there arose "a silent commotion", and more recruits were added to the cause of rebellion.

The Yarmouth Reformers held a meeting at Sparta early in September, 1837. Two weeks later sixty men, armed with clubs, and led by George Lawton bearing a long stick with a sharpened file in the end, rode from Sparta to Richmond to attend a great meeting of their friends in Bayham and Malahide. A crowd of Tories, also armed, seized the intended meeting-place and formed a loyal association, which expressed its confidence in the government, and its thanks to Colonel Talbot "for his fatherly protection of this settlement". A clash was avoided when the Reformers withdrew a short distance and held their own meeting.[31] That they stood on the brink of rebellion is shown by a resolution passed at a Reform rally held at St. Thomas on October 6, which reads as follows: "That, time after time, both in this province and in Great Britain, most loyally, nay most servily [*sic*], have we petitioned for a redress of the long and frightful catalogue of the wrongs of Canada. Our prayers have been spurned, and our feelings have been deeply wounded by the insults that have accompanied the contemptuous disregard of our most humble supplications for justice; that we have too long hawked our wrongs, as the beggar doth his sores, at the fastidious threshold of haughty oppression, when, derided and mocked, we have been sent empty away. That, since our iron-hearted rulers have turned a deaf ear to the voice of our complaints, we, confiding in the goodness of our cause, resting as it wholly does on reason, truth and equity for its support, will call upon the God of Justice to aid us in our holy struggle as Britons and as men."[32]

There could be no longer any doubt that the radicals were preparing for battle. Throughout the province Mackenzie and his followers had become increasingly militant and even openly seditious, while the Tories were determined to suppress them by force. Disturbed by the meetings in the southern part of the county, the loyal inhabitants of Middlesex held a great meeting of their own at London on October 21. Deep concern was expressed at the news that on several occasions persons from Yarmouth and vicinity had "attended public meetings unlawfully armed with loaded fire arms and other dangerous weapons, for the avowed purpose of carrying their measures at such meetings by force, and preventing a free expression of public opinion." It was the belief of the loyal inhabitants, "that if this organized and armed body who follow the sattelites [*sic*] of Mackenzie from meeting to meeting be not suppressed by Her Majesty's Government, either the people of this District and of the Province generally must submit to the arrogant and insolent assumption of its name by a mob, for the purposes held in scorn and execration by the vast majority, or bloodshed must ensue."[33]

On December 4 Mackenzie and his followers began to assemble in arms near Toronto. Three days later they were dispersed by the militia and loyal volunteers, and Mackenzie fled to the United States. The rebels of the London District, under the leadership of Dr. Duncombe, gathered at the village of Scotland in Brant County, but only a handful stayed to meet Colonel Allan MacNab's force when it arrived on the 14th. With the exchange of a few shots the rebellion in Upper Canada was over, although not the hunting down of the fleeing rebels by MacNab's Indians, the persecution of loyal Reformers, and the raids of the "Patriot" bands from across the American border.

Many of those who fled to the United States conspired there to overthrow the government of Upper Canada, and some met death in battle or on the gallows during the next two years. But John Talbot, the last editor of the St. Thomas *Liberal*, was quickly disillusioned. Writing from Detroit to Hugh O'Beirne on January 14, 1838, he said he hoped soon to be out of sight of Canada, and out of hearing of Canadian politics. "Lawton and other Canadians have been very active here," he wrote, "the Citizens have been persuaded by them that they could do wonders—I have taken no part whatever in their proceedings nor shall I. They tell me I have turned traitor to them. . . . The schemes of madness ever ends in disgrace—recollect what I told you in Clovis' about McKenzie's attack. Has not my anticipations been realized?"[34]

## CHAPTER XVI

# *Rubbed Out*

THE events of 1837, in Colonel Talbot's view, had followed inevitably from the government's failure to use the strongest measures against the Reformers. Within his own settlement, immediately after his St. George's Day speech in 1832, he had used his authority as superintendent to dispossess three settlers of London Township, named John Nixon, William Jackson, and Levi Lewis, who were reported to have signed the grievance petition. These settlers, with John Ardill who had been dispossessed two years before, appealed to the Lieutenant-Governor, thus beginning a *cause célèbre* that five years later ended in a partial reversal of the Colonel's actions, and an order for the termination of his jurisdiction in the Talbot Settlement.

In the case of John Nixon the Colonel admitted that he had nothing against the man except his political views. "He is a most decided Yanky in principle," he explained to the Lieutenant-Governor, "and made every exertion to influence and induce the simple and ignorant men to sign the Grievance petition, and consequently [I] would not bestow His Majesty's bounty on such a character." Nixon had told him that a "reform in the Government was necessary, and would take place, but for his part he would live independent either in London or the United States as suited his pleasure, etc., which I consider as a sufficient avowal to prevent me granting him land, so long as we enjoy the present British Constitution."[1] But Talbot neglected to explain that he had actually located Nixon on a lot after giving his consent to the purchase of the improvements from the first occupant. Some time later Talbot's agent sent Nixon a letter informing him that the Colonel had "altered his mind with respect to your having the lot, on which he had entered your name. He has rubbed your name off the map and entered another upon it."[2]

Although politics played a part in the dispossession of William Jackson and Levi Lewis, Talbot based his defence on other factors. He insisted that he had deprived Jackson of his lot because of failure to complete the settlement duties during the nine years since he was located. Jackson countered by pointing to the fact that the Colonel had not enforced the requirements in many other instances. The real reason why he was proceeded against, Jackson believed, was that Talbot heard a rumour that he and his father had signed the grievance petition. When he came to Port Talbot with a sworn statement that this was not true, the Colonel had refused to look at it, or to give him "a patient hearing in defence of his conduct and loyalty". Talbot had called him a "Methodist rebel", and declared that neither he nor any of his family would ever get an acre of land in the province.[3] Levi Lewis, the Colonel explained, had been located by him in 1824 as the son of a Loyalist, entitled to two hundred acres of land rather than the one hundred given to ordinary settlers. After his St. George's Day speech he took one hundred acres away from Lewis, on the ground that he was not the son of a Loyalist and besides was so lazy he had cleared less than ten acres of land. Lewis contended that he had cleared and fenced twelve acres, and that he had never claimed to be the son of a Loyalist; the two hundred acres

COLONEL THE HON. THOMAS TALBOT

From a portrait in the Library of the University of Western Ontario

given him had been the usual amount for settlers at that time. He suspected that the Colonel had acted on the basis of false reports concerning his radical views.[4]

In the case of John Ardill, also of London Township, there was no question of politics. He was dispossessed in 1830 for non-performance of the settlement duties after eleven years of occupation. Talbot stated that he discovered this dereliction on Ardill's part when a number of immigrants arrived and applied for locations near their friends in that township, and he began an investigation to see if any lots could be declared open for re-location. Learning from some of Ardill's neighbours that he had left the township four years before, after doing only a small amount of work on the lot, Talbot erased his name from the map and assigned the lot to William Armitage, one of the immigrants. Upon hearing of this Ardill came to Port Talbot to explain that he had gone to work on the Welland Canal to earn money for his family, and had been forced by sickness to remain away longer than he intended. Talbot agreed that he might have his lot back if he could come to an agreement with Armitage; which Ardill did with the help of a constable, several of his friends, and Magistrate Edward Allen Talbot. Some time later Armitage came to Port Talbot to complain that he had been forcibly ejected by a mob of men, who had then burned down his house. Ardill also appeared to present his side of the case, but Talbot refused to listen to him, giving the lot once more to Armitage.[5]

On being shown the petitions of the four settlers, in the fall of 1832, Talbot declared that they were the product of Edward Allen Talbot, "one of the most troublesome and mischievous characters in the Province". No person was less inclined to be harsh or oppressive than himself, he said, but he was determined to adhere rigidly to the system he had adopted from the beginning, of enforcing settlement duties and residence. He suggested that a proper answer for the Lieutenant-Governor to give to such petitions was this: "That His Majesty's Government having placed the Townships forming the Talbot Settlement under the control of the Honorable Thomas Talbot, that the provincial government does not interfere with his plans or Regulations."[6] Colborne replied that he was loath to suspend any of the Colonel's arrangements, but it was his prerogative to investigate any complaints made to him, and to take whatever action he deemed necessary, regardless of whether the lands were under the superintendence of Talbot or the Commissioner of Crown Lands.[7]

"It is scarcely necessary to say," Under-secretary Hay informed Colborne, who had referred the whole matter to the Colonial Office, "that Mr. Secretary Stanley could not for a moment contemplate investing any individual with an unlimited and arbitrary power of this kind. He is fully aware of the great public benefit which has arisen to the Province from Colonel Talbot's exertions in the settlement of Emigrants to Upper Canada, and it is with reluctance that he finds himself compelled to question the propriety of any of the proceedings of a gentleman to whom one large part of the Colony is so much indebted for its prosperity; but he feels imperatively the necessity of at once repudiating decisions concerning grants of land, grounded upon political motives."[8] The conflicting statements of the Colonel and the petitioners, however, prevented Lord Stanley from making a final decision. He therefore directed Colborne to investigate further, and to restore to their lands those who were found to have properly performed their settlement duties.

Colborne's investigation consisted of a request that Talbot give him a more detailed report. Still insisting that Ardill, Jackson, and Lewis had been deprived of their lands for failure to complete the settlement duties, the Colonel had to admit defeat in the case of Nixon. He explained that in 1832 Nixon had become "one of a wicked and seditious faction, and exerted himself much in endeavouring to assemble Public meetings with a view to overthrow our Monarchical and substitute a Republican form of Government in the Province. Such a character I considered it my duty to keep in check by giving him to understand that if he persisted in being an agitator and a disturber of the Peace of a Settlement to which I had devoted so many of the best years of my life in forming, that I should not allow of his obtaining land under me. Happily the preponderancy of Loyal feeling manifested by the Upper Canadians, frustrated their diabolical designs, and tranquillity being restored, I did not dispossess Nixon of the land, which continues located to him."[9] Acting on this new information the Council in April 1834 decided that Ardill, Jackson, and Lewis had been deprived of their lands justly.

The affair did not end there, however. During the session of 1835, when the Reformers were in a majority in the Assembly, Thomas Parke of London was appointed chairman of a committee of the House to investigate and report on the grievances of the three unsuccessful petitioners.[10] The Assembly at the same time evinced an embarrassing interest in the whole question of Talbot's jurisdiction, requesting from the Lieutenant-Governor not only complete information on the Talbot Settlement, but on the granting of his pension. It was not until after the arrival of Sir Francis Bond Head to replace Sir John Colborne, in January, 1836, that the Assembly was supplied with most of the information that it had requested.[11] This was handed over to the committee, which issued its report the following April.[12]

It is not surprising that the committee, headed by one of Talbot's political opponents from London Township, should have decided that Ardill, Jackson, and Lewis were "honest, loyal, and industrious" settlers who had fulfilled every condition of settlement. Instead of securing their deeds they had been "in an instant deprived forcibly and violently of [their lots] with the colour of authority, without even the least reward for their labour or the possibility of redress, and this too under British Laws and British usage, as the fruit of the hard toils of so long a period of residence in the Province, to which they came to seek an asylum under the protection and fostering care of the British Crown". After listening to the Colonel's "most extraordinary testimony as to the proof upon which he founded his conduct", which was unsupported by any documents or witnesses, the committee came to the conclusion that he had "removed the one set of Locatees and put in possession the others, with as much concern as if he had been moving figures on a chessboard".

The committee was not content to recommend the return to the petitioners of the lands that had been taken from them; it suggested that the Colonel's long rule be terminated. "When your Committee takes into consideration the irresponsible nature of our Government," the report concluded, "which defies control either by the people or their representatives, they must admit such occurrences cannot be rare, and they think they are only further proof of the necessity of such reform in our institutions as will cause the just rights of the subject to be respected, and his complaints redressed, and not leave one quarter of the Province (said to be one of the richest, most fertile and flourishing with a population of 33,000) in rights and property, at the sole disposal of one individual, uncontrolled either by the Executive Government of this Province or its Legislature, and acting under a verbal authority, without any specific instructions or limits to his power, or apparently only (as in these cases) on his mere caprice; and when appeals are made against these decisions by those aggrieved, his unfounded statements are sufficient authority for his oppression."

In an attempt to counteract this report before it should be transmitted to the British government, Talbot drew up a memorial to the Colonial Secretary. "After having located many thousands of persons," he wrote, "and forced more rigid superintendence than the Government either would or could have carried into effect, if your Memorialist is to be exposed to be harassed by the Assembly taking up the idle tale of every mischievous or dissatisfied person, then the very means by which alone your Memorialist was enabled to accomplish great public good, will be made the occasion of endless trouble and annoyance to himself." He had been forced to assume and exercise a great deal of power and discretion in order to insure settlement and prevent imposition; if now, after twenty-five years, any sudden interruption or change in this system should take place, only confusion would result. Within three years, he expected, the few remaining lots in his settlement would be occupied. He would then begin to draw its affairs to a close. In cases of conflicting claims he would have to be guided by his own knowledge of persons and facts, which he could not transfer to others without the risk of injustice resulting.[13]

Like his predecessors at the Colonial Office, Lord Glenelg found it impossible, because of the many conflicting statements, to come to an immediate decision in the matter. He therefore asked Lieutenant-Governor Head to take steps to have still another investigation made, and in the meantime to assure Talbot that he did not intend to interfere with his system of management.[14] Following the precedent set by Colborne, Head turned the investigation over to the Council, which one year later, on August 10, 1837, issued a lengthy report. It came to the conclusion that Jackson and Ardill, having failed to perform the settlement duties within two years, had been rightfully dispossessed. However, to obviate any chance that Ardill might have suffered from a mistake or harsh proceedings on Talbot's part, it recommended that he be given one hundred acres of land in some other place. The case of Levi Lewis turned on a question of fact. The Council was inclined to believe Talbot's testimony, although he could not produce any documents to substantiate it, that he had given Lewis an extra one hundred acres of land, believing he was the son of a Loyalist. Again wishing to avoid any chance of injustice, the Council recommended that Lewis be given two hundred acres of land elsewhere.

In concluding its report the Council noted that it had experienced a great deal of difficulty in trying to arrive at the truth, because of the system employed by the Colonel, which had long been countenanced by the government. It did not wish to express an opinion as to the wisdom of entrusting such an undefined authority to any individual; but now that his work was so nearly done, it did not consider it advisable to make any change in the system which he had so long and so successfully employed.[15]

Lieutenant-Governor Head was in complete agreement with all except the final recommendation. He thought that the absolute power wielded by Talbot had been justified while the settlement was in its infancy; but now that it was nearing maturity a different system was necessary. The only records he kept were names written in pencil on township maps, and these were often illegible except to himself, because of many erasures. These "frail words" were all that protected the rights of many settlers who had long ago completed their settlement duties, but had neglected to apply for their deeds. In the event of Talbot's death, or of fire destroying his house and records, before he had wound up his land affairs and turned control over to the Commissioner of Crown Lands, the greatest confusion would ensue.

In recommending that the Colonel be required to give up his agency, Head wished to make it clear that he had only the friendliest feelings toward him. "I have always found him ready," he told Glenelg, "to attend to any suggestions I have offered him. I have always found him quite above being influenced by any desire to maintain an Imperium in Imperio; and I believe on his part he feels that the political change I have effected in this Province has secured to him his immense property, which he is perfectly sensible would in case of a revolution have been the very first sacrifice on the altar of Democracy."[16]

The Colonial Secretary agreed with Head, and in his despatch of November 10, 1837, directed him to carry out the Council's recommendations regarding Ardill, Jackson, and Lewis, and to see that Talbot wound up his affairs as promptly as possible and handed over the management of his settlement to the provincial government. This was to be done in such a manner as to "relieve him from pain, which, I fear, cannot entirely be separated from the renunciation of the great, but most anomalous authority with which he has so long been invested."[17] The Lieutenant-Governor carried out these commands on February 17, 1838. An official letter notified the Colonel of Glenelg's decision, and gave him authority to employ the necessary clerks to carry it out. A private letter, written the same day, was intended to assuage the pain. "I have (to use your own phrase) 'rubbed you out'," Head wrote, "but I feel confident you will see that I have done so not only for the public interest but for your own. I know perhaps more of your enemies than you know yourself, and I am certain that if they could have succeeded in throwing this Province into a Revolution, your property would have been the first thing plundered, and you yourself would have been one of the first persons whose life would have been 'rubbed out'."[18]

The old Colonel gave no hint of the shock that this news must have given him. "I can assure your Excellency," he wrote in answer to Head's official communication, "that I do not feel in the slightest degree annoyed at being displaced. . . ." In a private letter he wrote: "10,000 thanks for your very friendly, flattering and highly satisfactory note of the 17th Instant, accompanying your despatch notifying my being placed on the shelf, and I do assure you that I shall retire from public service with the grateful consolation of having been a faithful and honest servant to the Government."[19] To this the Lieutenant-Governor replied: "Your despatch and letter has given me very great pleasure, and I only do you as well as myself justice when I tell you that they are exactly what I expected from you. A republican would never have forgiven me, but for that very reason a *gentleman* would. I quite approve of your getting the assistance of a Deputy Surveyor and hope some of these days to meet you in England with nothing between us but a bottle of good Port Wine. I suppose you have heard that General Sutherland is on his way to Toronto! The other General from the East has not yet come to rub me out—but he will!"[20] A few weeks later, with the arrival of Sir George Arthur, Head departed for England.

In his memorial to the Colonial Secretary in 1836 Colonel Talbot had recited the long roll of townships, exclusive of Dunwich and Aldborough, forming the Talbot Settlement—Middleton, Houghton, Bayham, Malahide, Yarmouth, Southwold, Orford, Howard, Harwich, Raleigh, East Tilbury, West Tilbury, Romney, Rochester, Mersea, Gosfield, Colchester, Maidstone, Sandwich, Zone, Mosa, Ekfrid, Caradoc, Lobo, London, Westminster and Blandford—twenty-seven townships extending more than 130 miles from Long Point to the Detroit River, and north to the boundary of the Huron Tract. Under his supervision half a million acres of land were reclaimed from forest and swamp and brought under cultivation; and thousands of people were settled without the evils of non-residence and speculation that plagued the regions under the control of the government. Now that his work was nearly ended, he could view this great settlement as the monument of thirty-five years of privation, struggle, and toil. Others might disagree with his statement that it had cost the government "not one farthing of expense", for there was his pension; but his broad lands in Dunwich and Aldborough would have been his, at least in part, if he had never been superintendent of the Talbot Settlement, and whatever he gained for himself in pension and land was not too great a return for his services.

The Colonel had accomplished his work by means of a personal authority almost unhampered by any control by the provincial government. In no other way, perhaps, could it have been done so well, and with such little cost to government and settler alike. There were, inevitably in such an autocratic system, instances of faulty judgment or personal prejudice on his part which resulted in hardship and even injustice, but taking his administration as a whole, as John Rolph remarked just before the Colonel's death, complaints against him had been "of the rarest possible occurrence". It is only in Dunwich and Aldborough, where his arrangement with the government was not in the best interests of the settlers, that his work might be adversely criticized. There his own lands presented many of the evils of non-residence and speculation that he fought against in other townships.

The Colonel had warned Head in 1838 that it would be some months before he could make out a final return of locations in his settlement, so that he could wind up his land affairs. He intended to have the surveyor Peter Carroll visit each township and report on every lot, to determine what casualties had occurred through the death of the original occupants. In relinquishing his control of the Settlement he felt the most concern about the Western District, where the low, wet land was discouraging to farmers. "I have made it my business," he told Head, "to persuade and *propel* the settlers to drain their respective pieces of land, which eventually will make their Farms not only productive but highly valuable, and secure the Talbot Middle Road to be the greatest thoroughfare to Sandwich, as the other Roads leading to the Detroit Frontier have become nearly impracticable owing to the rising of the waters of Lakes Erie and St. Clair—and I much fear that the Executive Government will not bestow the steady interest and vigilance that I have done in accomplishing the grand and necessary work."[21]

During the next two years the government received no indication that Talbot was ready to give up control, except for the unusually large numbers of certificates of completion of settlement duties that he sent in. Finally, in February, 1840, the Governor's secretary wrote to ask "in what state the matter now stands".[22] Talbot replied that Carroll had not yet been able to make the survey of the lots, because of the disturbances following the rebellion in 1837. An inspection now, he said, before quiet had been completely restored, would be attended by "much mischief and confusion", because many settlers had been forced to leave their lots to live near their friends in the older settlements or to serve in the militia.

Surveyor-General Robert B. Sullivan, to whom the Colonel's letter was referred, was not greatly impressed by these arguments. He did not see why Talbot could not make a return of locations at once, and then the government could give indulgence where it appeared warranted.[23] However, Governor Sydenham did not press Talbot further, and he was left alone to complete his work. It was a long and difficult task to unravel the tangled skeins of transfers of locations, or of divergent claims, when his records were primitive or non-existent. It was also difficult to induce all the settlers to take out their deeds, which meant paying heavy fees. Some of them had occupied their lots for twenty years or more, with no other title than their names pencilled on a map, and a certificate from Talbot stating that they had performed the settlement duties. With his consent, and the simple process of rubbing out one name and substituting another, farms could be bought and sold or otherwise transferred. To many, Talbot's sitting-room was the only registry office, and his certificate the only deed that was necessary.

In the spring of 1846 the government attempted to hasten the process by ordering all settlers to take out their patents within a stated period. Talbot sent the notice of this to his agents in the various townships, asking them to circulate it among the settlers so they would not lose their lots.[24] By this time he was old and often ill, and eager to get his business completed as soon as possible. Where there were conflicting claims he was willing to accept any arrangement that would satisfy the parties concerned. In September, 1847, George Macbeth, his assistant, wrote to James Price, the agent in Raleigh: "There has been so much changing about that John Edwards in Romney, that the Colonel does not know what to do about it. . . . You must let them know that they must positively make their final arrangements and let the Colonel know who is to have the lot—so that there will be no more changing."[25]

Certificates were still being sent in by Talbot's agents[26] up to the time he departed on a trip to England in May, 1848, but his work was so nearly completed that he was able, the previous March, to write: "The most of my land labours are at an end and I have to abdicate like other Sovereigns."[27] It was now ten years since Sir Francis Bond Head informed him that he had been "rubbed out", but at last he could rest from his labours. He had not yet abdicated as lord of the manor at Port Talbot, and perhaps not even as superintendent of the Talbot Country, for he could not bring himself to relinquish the township maps on which he had recorded the locations of his settlers. Until his death in 1853 he held these records, which were necessary for tying up the last few threads of the fabric he had woven during half a century.

CHAPTER XVII

# *The Lord of the Manor*

ONE summer day in 1839 an English traveller named James Brown turned off the main road near Burwell's Corners in Southwold and, passing through an ornate gateway, found himself "in a spacious noble-looking avenue" leading to Port Talbot. Before him, for two or three miles, stretched "the wide road with its grassy margin, and overhanging and shady recesses of the tall, deep, old forest" known as the Colonel's Wood. "Having reached a winding of the avenue," Brown recalled, "I was led by a gentle ascent and crescent-sweep to a view of the open grounds, where sheep and horned cattle were grazing in numbers. Descending into a flat grassy vale through which a stream flowed, I crossed a bridge; and on gaining the top of the opposite bank, a range of fine park presented itself, and at its extremity, overlooking the lake, I perceived the dwelling of the old Colonel."[1]

Like an eagle's eyrie the house stood on a cliff more than one hundred feet in height, at whose base the restless waters of Lake Erie gnawed steadily, from time to time dislodging huge trees and masses of earth. On both sides of the little harbour at the mouth of the creek the high clay ramparts of the shore swept in an immense curve to the blue horizon. Behind the house, as Mrs. Jameson observed in 1837, was "an open tract of land, prettily broken and varied, where large flocks of sheep were feeding—the whole enclosed by beautiful and luxuriant woods, through which runs the little creek . . ."

On the east the land fell away sharply into "a wild woody ravine", at the bottom of which wound the Colonel's Creek, till it stole quietly into the lake.[2] In flood times this stream became a raging torrent, sweeping away the sand-bar at its mouth. In the spring of 1827 a violent hurricane damaged the trees and fences, and Talbot wrote of his creek rising so high "that my superb canoe was carried away into the lake, a most serious loss at this my best fishing season."[3]

The magnificent situation contrasted strongly with the untidy appearance of the buildings. The rough log house, erected in 1804, remained the Colonel's home until 1833, when it was succeeded by a larger one of squared logs. Surrounding it was a haphazard collection of shabby log buildings which served as blacksmith and cooper shops, poultry houses for swarms of geese, turkeys, ducks, and chickens, and storehouses of various kinds. The old house was cold and draughty in winter, even though it was caulked each fall with clay; and the huge fireplaces, and woollen blankets hung on the bedroom walls, did not suffice to make it comfortable. But Talbot liked to convey the impression that it was something more than a pioneer dwelling, referring to it fancifully as his castle. "He has now a very comfortable house," Mrs. Stewart wrote after meeting him at Peterborough in 1826, "or palace I should say, for he is not only lord of all he surveys, but virtually king."[4]

In this place the Colonel entertained visitors of high estate. Lieutenant-Governors and other officials of the government, as well as many distinguished travellers from the British Isles, were happy to accept his hospitality. Each year, before the Anniversary celebrations, he sent out pressing invitations to his friends, as in 1827 when he urged Secretary Hillier to get on his horse and accompany Perry Maitland, the Lieutenant-Governor's son, "and be here some days before and prepare yourself with my cool drink for the service of the day." But Hillier could not come, and Talbot wrote again, some time after the great event: "If you have seen Perry since he left the gay scenes of this happy Palatinate, and that he has given you a faithful report of the anniversary, I am persuaded you have cause to repent not having attended it. The only check to our frolick was Coffin's gout. I can assure you that there was not any lack of cool drink, and we unanimously voted to reverse Port Talbot to Talbot Port."[5]

Cool drink was the Colonel's remedy for many ills. The following September he wrote of the "sickly state" of his household. "I am the only soul in it," he declared, "who can be said to be on his legs. Ague, Ague, Ague—cool drink has preserved me." During the cholera scourge of 1832 Dr. Goodhue of St. Thomas called on him and remarked on his good health. "Damn your calomel, pills, opium and blisters!" Talbot replied to the Reformer and temperance lecturer. "There is my morning doctor [pointing to a cold bath in the corner of the room], and there [glancing at a bottle of whiskey] is my afternoon physician. At night I sleep soundly, owing to a clear conscience, for I throw politics and Temperance lectures to the devil."[7] But a man who drank in the morning, he was convinced, would die a drunkard. "Damn it, Burwell," he told his friend, "if you continue to drink liquor before dinner, you'll be a drunkard before you're forty years of age." Tradition says that he had a mark placed on a building to act as a primitive sun-dial, which he could watch from his sitting-room window and thus determine when it was safe to begin drinking for the rest of the day.[8]

The Colonel recommended the salubrious spring climate of Port Talbot to such of his friends as were in need of a rest, or were recovering from illnesses, after the strenuous winter season in York. Early in 1832 he invited the ailing Commissioner of Crown Lands to come and remain at least a month, suggesting that he travel in "a strong one-horse waggon" rather than on horseback, and that he plan to arrive a week after the Anniversary in May, when he himself would be "recovered from the pains and penalties of that meeting". He promised Robinson that he should live "as quietly and regularly" as he pleased, and he would not be given "the *Blue Pill,* simply my fine Southern air will do the needful by sending back another man".[9] A year later he wrote again: "Another visit to Port Talbot next spring will complete the business in full, besides I have a very comfortable bedroom in my new house, which will not require to be lined with blankets." Despite two months of "unmerciful weather" he had visitors nearly every day.[10]

The old house had finally become unbearable. At the beginning of December, 1831, a severe cold spell set in before he got around to caulking the walls, and his house was "more open than a barn". What concerned him most was that fifty barrels of cider and ten of perry (pear juice) had frozen in his cellar. A few months later he hired a number of carpenters and masons, who began work on the new house. The sale of his beef cattle to Roswell Mount in September, 1832, for the use of the settlers of Adelaide, enabled him to pay the workmen.[12] The house was completed by the spring of 1833, in time for a new influx of visitors. The interest on some money invested for him at that time by William Allan would, he wrote, "help to keep the pot boiling, which is very necessary under the great increase of visitors to Port

Talbot of all descriptions, and I sincerely wish I could see you amongst the number." He was expecting a visit from the bishop soon, and "now that the Steamer Adelaide passes by me twice a week, it is probable that I shall not have any cause to complain of the want of Society during the Summer."[13]

In June Talbot received a visit from Lieutenant-Governor Colborne. It was quite unexpected, he told Allan, which pleased him because it "prevented fuss". The next day the Lieutenant-Governor departed "in the same quiet manner that he came". Visitors were now so frequent and numerous that Talbot had to struggle to keep himself "from sinking"; to increase his income he asked Allan to invest an additional £200 for him in the stock of the Bank of Upper Canada.[14] The following October he wrote to Peter Robinson: "I have had constant visitors since the summer commenced to this time and have acquired numerous valuable settlers; amongst my distinguished visitors Lord Aylmer, who spent 3 days with me. . . ." A few weeks later he was visited by a Mr. Jones of Plympton, "a discontented Bore"; and he had "a large party of Shore's to dinner".[15]

Built of squared logs, the Colonel's new home was a much more pretentious building than the former one. Along the south side, facing the lake, was a long Dutch verandah on the level of the ground. Visitors approached the west end of the house through a gate in a rail fence, at the end of the hedge-lined road which circled the ravine. The front door was at the south-east end of the house, and opened into a large storeroom or vestibule crowded with piles of homespun blankets and bolts of cloth, sacks of grain, sheepskins, and barrels of flour, with an occasional hen hatching her eggs in an empty barrel. Here Talbot kept his saddle, bridle, and martingales, and his famed sheepskin coat and cap; and from it he carried feed to the poultry that swarmed about the yard or roosted on the verandah among the dogs. From the rafters of the verandah hung various farm implements, and even, on occasion, a dead wildcat.

Entering quickly to avoid letting in the hungry poultry that darted for the door as soon as it was opened, the visitor was ushered into the Colonel's sitting-room, from whose window he interviewed the "land pirates" on the verandah. In the summer, as he sat by the window, the Colonel could look out over the blue waters of the lake and watch the white sails of the passing schooners, and the sea-gulls circling above them. In stormy weather the room was filled with the insistent sound of the surf crashing against the base of the cliff, and the trees of the forest bending and creaking in the wind. This was Talbot's "library and hall of audience", where he transacted business, read the newspapers, wrote letters, and entertained visitors. Its walls were the "naked logs", unadorned, and its only furniture was a long table and two home-made wooden chairs set in front of the wide fireplace, a large desk, and some book shelves.

Next to the sitting-room, at the west end of the house facing the lake, was a large kitchen, with a huge fireplace for cooking and a long table where the workmen and servants ate. The dining-room, overlooking the ravine to the north of the house, was handsomely decorated with red wall-paper and gold moulding. There were also two or three bedrooms on this side; in the fall of 1833 Talbot papered his own bedroom with what he called the "all-over pattern", and another with "the blue ground with the sprig". When William Baby and his brother paid a visit to Port Talbot in 1841, the Colonel showed them an "elegantly furnished apartment" off the storeroom, "hung with crimson velvet paper, Turkey carpet and furniture to match. 'This,' he remarked, 'is my sanctum sanctorum. When my lady friends visit me this is their room'—and nothing could exceed as a rural scene the view from its open window—perched upon a hill of some 100 feet in height, and overlooking a meadow of twenty or thirty acres, with its flock of snow white sheep quietly grazing, and girt with a belt of forest trees still untouched by the ruthless axe." Mrs. Jameson slept in this room during her visit in 1837. She rejoiced, after her long and tiresome trip in an open wagon, to find it very comfortable, "where a fire blazed cheerfully, where female hands had evidently presided to arrange my toilet, and where female aid awaited me."[16]

Underneath the north part of the house a long, narrow cellar provided space for the storage of milk and vegetables, and for the wines and other liquors so essential to the Colonel's comfort. The attic, lighted only by two small windows in each end, was divided into four rooms for the servants and farm labourers. An adjacent log building, perhaps the original house built in 1803, is said to have been used as guest house when necessary.[17] "Around the house," wrote Mrs. Jameson, "stands a vast variety of outbuildings, of all imaginable shapes and sizes, and disposed without the slightest regard to order or symmetry. One of these is the very log-hut which the Colonel erected for shelter when he first 'sat down in the bush', four-and-thirty years ago, and which he is naturally unwilling to remove. Many of these outbuildings are to shelter the geese and poultry, of which he rears an innumerable quantity." Not far away was a large garden, "very neatly laid out and enclosed, and in which he evidently took exceeding pride and pleasure; it was the first thing he showed me after my arrival. It abounds in roses of different kinds, the cuttings of which he had brought himself from England in the few visits he had made there. Of these he gathered the most beautiful buds, and presented them to me with such an air as might have become Dick Talbot presenting a bouquet to Miss Jennings. We then sat down on a pretty seat under a tree, where he told me he often came to meditate."[18]

Mrs. Jameson had always heard her host referred to as "the eccentric Colonel Talbot", but she was struck by "his benevolence, his invincible courage, his enthusiasm, his perseverance". He had accomplished what he set out to do, he told her, "but I would not, if any one was to offer me the universe, go through again the *horrors* I have undergone in forming this settlement. But do not imagine I repent it: I like my retirement." His listener felt that he had paid a heavy price for his success. "He has passed his life in worse than solitude," she wrote. "He will admit of no equal in his vicinity. His only intercourse has been with inferiors and dependents, whose servility he despised, and whose resistance enraged him—men whose interests rested on his favour—on his will, from whom there was no appeal. Hence despotic habits, and contempt even for those whom he benefitted; hence, with much natural benevolence and generosity, a total disregard, or rather total ignorance, of the feelings of others. . . . He is alone—a lonely man. . . . His sympathies have had no natural outlet, his affections have wanted their natural food."

During her five days at Port Talbot Mrs. Jameson admired the Colonel's sixteen-acre orchard of apple, pear, plum and cherry trees, but she noticed that the management of his six-hundred-acre farm, much of it under pasture, tended to be "slovenly", now that he was old and did not employ an overseer. She also noticed his dependence on his servant, Jeffrey

Hunter, whom he had brought back with him in 1818 after a visit to Malahide Castle. Early in 1827 Jeffrey returned to Ireland, much to the distress of his master. "I feel a most lamentable loss and want in Jeffrey and no materials to replace him," Talbot wrote.[19] Many years later he told a visitor that he and Jeffrey had quarrelled, and that Jeffrey had left without notice. In 1828, when he arrived at Malahide Castle, Talbot was assisted from his carriage by his former servant, who took up his trunk without speaking. Nothing was ever said about Jeffrey's abrupt departure from Port Talbot, but when the Colonel returned to Upper Canada the following year he brought Jeffrey with him.[20] Lady Emmeline Stuart-Wortley heard a somewhat fanciful version of the story while at Port Talbot in 1849.[21]

After his return to Canada Jeffrey decided to get married. "So one morning," Mrs. Jameson relates, "he went and took unto himself the woman nearest at hand—one, of whom we must needs suppose that he chose her for her virtues, for most certainly it was not for her attractions. The Colonel swore at him for a fool; but after a while, Jeffrey, who is a favourite, smuggled his wife into the house, and the Colonel, whose increasing age renders him rather more dependent on household help, seems to endure very patiently this addition to his family, and even the presence of a white-headed chubby little thing, which I found running about without let or hindrance."[22]

A year later, while George Munro and Commissary-General Routh were at Port Talbot, they noticed how indulgent the Colonel was towards the Hunters' daughter. "One day after dinner," Munro recalled, "Talbot proposed a walk in the garden. On our way we heard a little girl, about six years old, a daughter of one of the servants, loudly command the Colonel to stop for her. 'Gentlemen,' said he, 'I must wait for the little torment.' He offered her his hand. 'No! No!' said she. 'You must carry me.' He proposed to take her in arms. 'No, no, you must carry me on your back as you always do.' He sat down to let her get on his back: 'No, no, you must go on all fours,' which he positively did, and carried her to the garden and back to his own room. She soon desired to go out. The Colonel opened the door leading to the kitchen, where her mother was. Through this door she refused to go. He then opened another door. 'No, no, you must lift me out through your window.' He opened a leaf of the window . . . and raised the spoiled child, gently placing her on the outside. He was hardly seated in his own home-made, slat-bottomed arm chair, when he had to rise and through said window raise her in, calling her a little pest. 'It is your own fault,' said the general. 'I cannot help it, for she sticks to me like a burr,' said the good and kind old man."[23]

Talbot's fondness for children is shown frequently in his correspondence. He never failed to enquire about those of his friends, and he sent them presents and little messages. Joseph Elson told of seeing him and Jeffrey Hunter at Zavitz's mill in Southwold, about the year 1820: while waiting for the grain to be ground the Colonel would go up to the house and play with a baby there. Elson himself, still a boy, was treated kindly by Talbot. One day while he was skinning a deer that the miller had shot, Talbot asked if he would sell it to him. Elson replied that he could not do so because his employer was not at home. "Then do not you ever sell anything without your master's consent," Talbot said. Elson told him that he did not. "That is a good boy," the Colonel said approvingly, "always mind your master, but I want you to tell Mr. Zavitz that I want him to send me two good fat saddles of venison."[24]

Women, as well as children, were usually the Colonel's friends, for he was courteous and attentive, especially to those of the upper classes. While visiting at Wortley Hall in 1822, he promised to have moccasins made for Lady Caroline and her small daughter. After his return home he wrote to tell them that he was having the moccasins made by Chief Joseph Brant's sister, who made "prettier ones than any other Squaw that I could employ".[25] Each year at the Anniversary Ball he danced with the prettiest and most respectable of the ladies of his settlement. "Many a time," wrote Kearney, "have I heard a good old matron exclaim with conscious pride, that she danced with Colonel Talbot at one of those happy gatherings."[26] For many years it was the one great social event in the Talbot Settlement, when the people dressed in all their finery, to re-enact in some small measure the scenes of the Colonel's youth. "The ladies made a gay appearance," it was reported of the Anniversary in 1828, "some of them were decked with wreaths and garlands of native flowers, exhibiting a most charming display of sylvan innocence."[27]

Occasionally one of the settlers' wives treated the Colonel with scant respect. He told George Munro of his encounter with Mrs. Crane, when he was forced to admit defeat. "She is a country woman of yours," he said, "and a real Scotch virago she is. One day, when at dinner, she came in here and said she came for a horse to take provisions from the block house. I told her to take old Bob, a quiet, strong horse. She said she would not have old Bob, but must have Jane. I said she could not have Jane. She seized that large carving knife and threatened to run it through me, so that I had to holloa to Jeffrey to give the Scotch devil the mare."[28]

Contrary to some of the stories that were told about him, Talbot not only liked women but usually employed several of them about the house. In later days Mrs. Jeffrey Hunter, assisted by a housemaid and cook, acted as general housekeeper. During the early part of 1835 an event occurred that occasioned much gossip throughout the district, and embarrassment to the Colonel. A physician of St. Thomas, who was called to attend a young servant girl in the house, found that she had given birth to a child. After the doctor left, another servant girl found the dead child in a chest filled with feathers. The child was buried secretly and an attempt was made to "hush up" the whole thing; but one of Talbot's enemies heard about it and published the details in the St. Thomas *Liberal*.[29] Talbot's influence with the Attorney-General, to whose attention the matter was brought, was sufficient to prevent any further action being taken. No doubt he wished to avoid scandal, but it is likely that Talbot also wished to protect the unfortunate servant girl.

Travellers who stopped to pay the Colonel a social call found a welcome as soon as he learned that they were not "land pirates" or American sightseers. When Sir James Alexander called on him in 1842, Talbot told him, with obvious satisfaction, about the rather distinguished-looking American who had arrived on horseback only a few days before. Seeing him peering in his window, Talbot demanded to know what he wanted. Taken aback at this rude salutation, the man replied slowly that he would explain, but in his own way. "I hope it will be a short way, then," the Colonel retorted. The stranger then said that he had been in the settlement four days, and was curious to see its founder. "Well, you have seen him," was the reply, "now go away!"

William and Charles Baby were startled by the Colonel's sharp "What do you want?", but after they had introduced themselves he invited them into the sitting-room, provided them with port wine and brandy, and invited them to stay for a dinner of ham and eggs and poultry. William Pope was served a good dinner, including "a capital bottle of port and some excellent cider of his own making". Sir James Alexander and his companion enjoyed a dinner of roast meat and mashed potatoes, with a bottle of port, but they offended the old man when they declined the third glass of wine, and he ordered their wagon brought to the door. Sheriff Parkins, another Englishman, met with similar treatment when he spoke in a disrespectful manner about one of the Colonel's friends. Talbot said he would not permit such language to be used at his table. "Do you call this a table?" Parkins asked, lifting the edge of the cloth and exposing the pine board. Talbot immediately directed Jeffrey to have his visitor's horse brought to the door.[30]

When Talbot returned from Ireland in 1829 he was followed, about three weeks later, by his brother Sir Richard, who had waited to vote on the Catholic Emancipation Bill. Sir Richard came by way of the Erie Canal through New York State, and at Utica was observed to be "very infirm and greatly advanced in years".[31] The Colonel once related to George Munro the following anecdote concerning his brother: "On my last visit to Castle Malahide the porter refused to admit me, pushing me outside. I entered to where my brother Henry [*sic*] was at breakfast. He angrily asked: 'Where are you from, what is your name, and what do you want?' 'I am from Canada, my name is Thomas

Talbot, and I want my breakfast.' He said, 'Thomas, I fear all I heard of you being a recluse in a log hut, your own bread and cheese maker, and your own cowmilker is too true.' For this lecture I paid him last summer in my log castle Talbot. The first thing he asked me for was a drink of milk. I invited him to the door, handed him a home made pail and pointed to a cow grazing near by on the lake bank and told him to go and help himself, for that I and all my settlers helped themselves."[32]

Among the Colonel's visitors were clergymen of various Churches, although he had little respect for any except the Anglican and Presbyterian. In April, 1820, the Rev. Charles James Stewart, an Anglican missionary, baptized several of the neighbourhood children at Port Talbot, with the Colonel acting as sponsor of one of Samuel Burwell's daughters. Talbot later accompanied his guest to St. Thomas, and promised "a handsome contribution" for the church that was about to be built there.[33] When he returned from England two years later he found the church "in a forward state", and began to make arrangements for building another "at Port Talbot".[34] The latter was eventually built at Tyrconnel, about five miles west of Port Talbot. The Colonel subscribed to the support of the Anglican ministers; and until about two years before his death paid rent on the first two pews in the church at St. Thomas, although he rarely attended services. It is on record that in 1847 he subscribed the sum of twelve and a half pounds to a church collection for the relief of the starving people of Ireland.[35]

With the building of St. Peter's Church at Tyrconnel, the Anglican minister from St. Thomas would hold services there every third Sunday, stopping off at Port Talbot on his return the following day to have dinner with the Colonel.

In later years the Colonel's drinking, and racy stories, often exceeded the bounds of propriety, and the Anglican minister stopped coming. Other clergymen came from time to time, and were sometimes insulted. One of them, finding that Talbot began to eat as soon as the food was on the table, suggested that he wait a minute until he could say grace. "Then be damned quick about it!" said the hungry old man. Another clergyman had the temerity to point out that at his age he should prepare himself for death. Angry at such a suggestion, Talbot retorted that he would live when the minister "was dead and damned".[36]

The Colonel had a reputation as a wit and raconteur, and some of his sayings and stories have been re-told by others. "Aye, my Lord," he replied to Bishop Strachan when the subject of a long-winded young clergyman of Tyrconnel came up, "and I never knew anybody that could bear a long sermon, but a Scotchman when he pays for it." Pointing to the stump of a huge oak tree, he told a guest about a certain "cantankerous cur" who had been struck when the tree was felled, but had escaped unharmed. "Had the vagabond been worth a damn to King or country," Talbot concluded, "he would have been crushed to a jelly." One day while in the town of London he remarked that it was no wonder one resident was very rich, because "out of every shilling that he ever touched at least eleven pence three farthings stuck to his fingers." At Lewis' Hotel in Fingal, one Christmas morning, he noticed an Irish acquaintance passing in his sleigh on his way to church at St. Thomas, and he observed that the man's presence at Mass would "gladden the heart of his priest, but faith I reckon if his Christmas dinner and bowl of punch depend on Tom's generosity, poor Father M— will be compelled to keep Lent from St. Stephen's day to 'the hunting of the wren'* on the following anno Domini."[37]

Taking great pride in his homespun clothes, the Colonel was delighted when his friends also wore them. In 1825 he wrote to Secretary Hillier that he was having a muff made from a skin for Mrs. Hillier. "She must appear in perfect Talbot costume," he told him, "and tell her, with my best regards, that I have ordered 20 yards of cloth to be made for her, so be prepared to be down with the cash."[38] "The best coats," he once declared, "are on the backs of stupid fops, broken down merchants, and clerks with beggarly salaries," and "the heaviest gold chain dangles from the fob of gamblers and blacklegs." Women were like books, he said, "too much gilding makes men suspicious that the binding is the most important part of the being that is destined to render some poor son of Adam miserable or happy in this nether planet." Costly ornaments merely indicated "a silly lover, or a husband on the eve of bankruptcy, whilst a plain neatly dressed woman may be presumed to have fair expectations before her in a sensible lover, and, if married, that her husband can show a balance in her favor."[39]

*A synonym for St. Stephen's Day, December 26, when it was the custom in Ireland for men and boys to hunt and kill the wren. I am indebted to Mr. K. R. E. Dobbs of the Editorial Department, The Macmillan Company of Canada Limited, for the following note: "On that day in Ireland mummers went from house to house asking alms 'to bury the wren'. I believe the 'wren boys' still make their rounds. I attach a version of their song which was sung in County Kilkenny in my own boyhood:

The wran, the wran, the king of all birds
St. Stephen's Day he was caught in the furze,
And though he is little his family is great
Rise up Mr.—— and give us a treat.
Shake, shake, shake of the box,
All silver and no brass—
Up with the kettle and down with the pan
Come give us a tanner to bury the wran."

Talbot had his own measure of personal vanity. Writing to Hillier in the spring of 1825, he said: "The most interesting topick of consideration, at present, in the Talbot Settlement, is the subject of a new Transparency, about to be painted for the approaching Anniversary. I have received several official letters requiring my instructions, and have almost decided on a full length, formidable likeness of the Old Colonel, well bedizined with Roses and Gambage."[40] Three years later he was absent in England at the time of the Anniversary, when a resolution was adopted to raise funds, "to procure to be taken by some respectable artist at home the Portrait of the Hon. Col. Talbot, at half length, to be placed, with the Talbot Arms, immediately below the King's Arms, in the Saint Thomas Church, to remain there *for ever*, as the property of the people of the Talbot Settlement; so that the memory of the person who, in the most disinterested manner, had devoted the prime of his life, with the expenditure of his fortune, and directed the energies of his mind, towards the formation, growth and improvement, of this immense settlement, should not be forgotten in the land. . . ."[41]

The only known surviving picture of the Colonel is a portrait in water-colours, showing him seated in his chair beside a table on which are several books, a candle, and a ink-well. On the other side of the chair is a large waste-paper basket, overflowing with paper. His trousers bear broad vertical stripes of scarlet and black. This portrait, in the words of one of his biographers, "shows a full, florid face, beaming with intelligence and good-nature, features and expression strongly resembling those of King William IV, on the whole a striking and attractive figure."[42]

Frances Stewart, who met Talbot in 1826, was surprised to find nothing remarkable in his manner; but his appearance was most unusual. "He had a greatcoat made of sheepskins with the wool on, either of natural black or dyed, and a pair of boots of the same, which he wears over his other boots; and as he is fat and short, you cannot think what a curious figure he is in this Arctic-dress."[43] To William Pope in 1834, he appeared as a "short, stout, hearty middle-aged man, eccentric in some of his manners".[44] Three years later Mrs. Jameson thought he seemed younger than his years, and that his "good-humoured, jovial, weather-beaten face" must have been very handsome when he was young. Despite his homespun clothes "and the primitive simplicity, not to say rudeness, of his dwelling", she found in his "features, air, and deportment that *something* which stamps him gentleman".[45] When Sir James Alexander met him in 1842 he was a "short and strong built man, with a ruddy face, and acquiline nose", who was dressed in a white jacket and trousers.[46]

John B. Robinson, son of the Chief Justice, in later life recalled Talbot's appearance when he stayed at his father's home during his visits to Toronto. On these occasions he "appeared in ruffled shirt and evening dress, with lacquered pumps, after discarding the sheepskin coat and cap, with dangling tail, in which he was wont to appear in winter. . . . A round of festivities in his honour was entered upon at York, to the delight of even the younger generation at Beverley House, and the other hospitable houses, whose guest he was, and a fortnight's gaiety enlivened the old man ere he returned to his lonely bachelor home."[47] William Baby, then eight years of age, recalled in old age his first glimpse of the Colonel in the winter of 1820, when he was a guest of Lieutenant-Governor Maitland. "So well-known and distinguished a person," Baby wrote, "could not make his appearance in Little York (now Toronto) without notice, and particularly did he attract attention to his extraordinary winter dress. Seated by the side of Lady Sarah Maitland in a sleigh, and driving along King street in his sheepskin coat and cap, with its sheepskin tail of eight or ten feet [!] wound round his neck to serve as a muffler, with the end trailing by the side of the sleigh. But when this garb was thrown off and he made his appearance in parlor or drawing-room, how changed his appearance!—the very type of an aristocrat, a handsome and thoroughbred nobleman."[48]

CHAPTER XVIII

# *The Ordeal of Julius Airey*

In the fall of 1831 Captain Richard Airey, aide to the Governor-General, Lord Aylmer, spent nearly two weeks with his uncle at Port Talbot. The Colonel was then sixty years of age, and a decision as to his prospective heir could not much longer be deferred. Although he had never married, his strong family ties induced him to seek someone of his own blood, who would be his companion during his declining years, and succeed to his position on his death. It is probable that he broached the subject to Airey, who was one of the six sons of his sister Margaret. Airey was not yet ready to give up a promising career in the army, as his uncle had done thirty years before, and retire to the backwoods of Canada; but two years later, when he returned from sick leave in England, he brought with him his youngest brother Julius "on trial", as the Colonel's companion and heir apparent.[1] Talbot looked forward to his arrival with pleasure, and if he read an attack upon him in the *Colonial Advocate* a few weeks before, he must have smiled at the writer's declaration that "all his lands, and all his hoarded wealth, together with the countless thousands of acres he has been enabled to grasp from the country will at his death go to persons who never intended to set foot in the Colony, and who care nothing for its interests."[2]

When the Colonel returned from his usual winter's visit to York, in January, 1834, he reported that he found his

COL. TALBOT'S HOUSE AT PORT TALBOT

From the painting by Hubert Marius Robert © Toronto *Star Weekly*

nephew Julius "quite well, and contented with his first trial of retirement".[3] But it was soon apparent that the boy was not happy with the dull routine of country life, the Spartan existence, and the company of his eccentric old uncle. Still in his early teens, he had been suddenly removed from the society of a refined and aristocratic home, and unlike those who went into the army, he did not have the companionship of others of his own age and station in life. Even the new house that had just been completed—a pioneer log building set in the midst of the wilderness—must have seemed uncomfortable and barren to him. It is possible, however, that he spent portions of the first few years at school in London. He became a close friend of Mrs. John Harris of that place, and his letters to her show that his education was by no means neglected. After his first reference to Julius early in 1834 the Colonel's correspondence during the next four years does not mention him; nor do Mrs. Jameson or other visitors to Port Talbot in that period.

As a member of the St. Thomas cavalry Julius Airey went with his troop to Amherstburg early in January, 1838, to assist in the defence of the frontier, which was threatened by attacks of the "Patriots".[4] "So far," Talbot wrote to Lieutenant-Governor Head the following month, "I have passed a most aggravating winter, as I have been entirely alone since the breaking out of the troubles. My hopeful nephew Airey, fancying that the safety of the Province depends altogether on his prowess, has been constantly doing Soldier, he is now at Amherstburg."[5] Julius remained at Fort Malden during the remainder of the year, part of the time with his brother Richard, who was now in command of the 34th Regiment.

Talbot was forced to spend another long, cold winter alone, cheered only by the visits of military officers from London and St. Thomas, and by the arrival of Sir George Arthur and suite in January, 1839, when they stopped for breakfast on their way to Sandwich. "These dolesome times", as he called them, had a very depressing effect on him, and he had no faith in Lord Durham (Radical Jack) and his mission to Canada, from which he had been recalled the previous fall. "Lord Durham is a sad impostor," the Colonel wrote to William Allan on January 30, "if the amount of his mission was divided between you and myself it would be made better use of, than the way in which it was fooled away." As for the raids of the rebels and their friends from across the border, he "was inclined to think that the *trifling* hanging at Kingston and London will cool the scoundrels' courage and prevent them from any further attempts to disturb us." He thanked Allan for taking care of his "little income", without which he "should be parading the limits somewhere", and he told him that he did not intend "to exhibit my person or *Skins* this winter at Toronto".[6]

Lord Durham submitted his epoch-making *Report on the Affairs of British North America* to the Queen in February. His condemnation of the whole system of government, as he found it functioning in the Canadas, and his recommendations, including that of a grant of complete responsible self-government, filled Colonel Talbot with horror. The following September he wrote to "Missy" (Caroline Jane Stuart-Wortley), now Mrs. John Chetwynd Talbot: "In the present state of Canada, sink or swim, it is impossible to leave my property. The Yankys . . . are endeavouring to excite discontent and form associations under the cloak of Durhamites to commence fresh disturbances. They have actually got vast quantities of . . . Bowie Knives, large Butchers' knives, made to murder us Loyalists. Some of these knives are stamped 'Durham', some 'Reform' knives, and others 'responsible Government knives'. So far are we indebted to that fellow Lord Durham. . . ."[7]

Meanwhile, in the spring of 1839 Julius Airey had returned to Port Talbot, to an existence that seemed even more monotonous after the excitement and pleasures of military duty. He now felt that the best years of his life were being wasted on the farm, and that it was too great a price to pay to become his uncle's heir. The relationship between the two had probably become strained long before Julius went to Amherstburg; it was not long after his return until it almost reached the breaking-point. He could find little enjoyment even in what he termed the "unfortunate anniversary". "Pray do not let us be by ourselves," he pleaded with Mrs. Harris, "for then it is dreadful indeed."[8] When May 21 and the celebrations passed without her presence he scolded her: "It was abominable behaviour! When so many are falling away—'Will ye also go?' The next time we meet, we shall have a dreadful fight on this ground!" His hopes had been strong even on the eve of the event, when he wrote to her: "Tomorrow is the Anniversary—happy day! Consequently, I have been working my fingers to the bone, in sewing on buttons, and preparing my finery for tomorrow. I hope to see several of your household—and many of my good London friends, but have my doubts. Yet if they come not—I cut them for ever! . . . We had expected all the Airey Colony, from the West, and they were to have been here today; but my sister-in-law, having been warned by the pleasant Doctor, that three days travelling in a waggon would just kill her, this gay bubble of hope has burst." His yearning for the society of his friends remained unsatisfied, and in the fall he wrote wistfully that London must be very gay, for he had heard that a number of balls, private theatricals, and other types of entertainment had been planned. "News I can have none, of course," he concluded, "because from my residence I only see the stars."

At length, just before Christmas, the growing tension between uncle and nephew flared into angry words. Julius was stricken with remorse. "I hate ingratitude," he wrote to Mrs. Harris, "I am deeply sensible of all I owe. Received a penniless orphan—housed, clothed, fed—how destitute of all feeling should I be—how base—how vile—were I to forget, or be unthankful! On the contrary, I pray you to believe, that I am not so. . . . The not being able to be sufficiently grateful—and the not having the means of showing it, is perhaps what stings me most. To me it is quite dreadful, the idea that I cause a moment's pain to any one—that I embitter the life of a person to whom I am so much indebted,—that I am a burthen instead of a stay—a stranger instead of a son, a child. . . . Undoubtedly, I might have done much better, but I have always acted with the best intentions, and if I have wrecked—it should be remembered, that it was a perilous sea, beset with rocks and quicksands, and utterly unknown, upon which I launched my frail bark—and without age or experience to guide me. Now, however, I see that there were only two things to do—go or stay—but to be always mute. This is the conduct which honor—gratitude—and every virtuous principle dictate—and such I should have followed. I have though, I am afraid, wandered far from this righteous path, and now I am eating the bitter fruits of my folly and wickedness."

No doubt the tragic role that Julius pictured for himself was somewhat exaggerated, but he realized that already six years of his life had been wasted, that he had reached manhood without preparing himself for a profession, and that he had been on trial and had failed. However much he hated the life at Port Talbot, he dreaded to break the ties that meant security. For another year he remained there, trying, too late, to please his uncle. Obediently he submitted, with the Hunters' little girl, to be vaccinated against the smallpox, because the Colonel said he should. He had long since discovered that he had "little, very little, partiality for manual labor", but the work he disliked least was planting trees, and in the spring of 1840 he obtained thirty small ones from the forest by his "own individual, solitary toil", and planted them on the bare sides of the ravine near the house. The illness of the Colonel soon added to his tribulations. The old man had scarcely recovered from one of his severe colds when he fell prey to other disorders. "This house is a perfect hospital now," Julius wrote on April 21, "Col. Talbot has the gout in both feet. Jeffrey is *laid up*, and Mrs. Jeffrey (as she is called) is about to *lay in* (if we may judge from appearance). The house maid has gone home with the ague—the cook is 'ailing'—some how or another. Patterson is not very well—and one of the men is ill. This is not pleasant. Our weather is delightful, is it not? And we are gardening, and all sorts of things. I sent up for some plants and flowers to Amherstburg, but the very stupid people only sent some melon seed."

Julius watched the approach of another Anniversary with mixed feelings, for he had thought longingly of quitting his exile at Port Talbot before that time. But he looked forward to seeing the pretty Miss Sarah Harris at the ball. "I daresay," he told her mother, "that I shall not be able to dance with her (except the first waltz, which I now engage her for) as I have *so* much duty to do, in figuring with the farmers' daughters! I hope a good many will come over, and I should have liked exceedingly to have seen you there, but I suppose that is not possible. Keep constantly, though, trying to beat up recruits. . . . I hope we shall get some band or other because we poor *dancing bears* should at least have good music to perform our pranks by. And *I* do not admire four volunteer 'Musicianers' (I shall never be tired of that word, which I learnt last winter) playing their own compositions on wretched 'hurdy gurdies', each with admirable freedom following his own time, which would alone be sufficient to kill a whole herd of cattle, much less the solitary cow—but the four combined, is absolute homocide [*sic*]!"

The Anniversary went off much better than Julius had expected, chiefly due to the presence of Sarah and Amelia Harris. "We got there at a little after one," he informed Mrs. Harris two days later, "and I was luckily at the Burnhams when your girls came, with whom I laughed and fought till it was time for dinner. Becher and I shared a room, and I sat between him and Marriott at the Feast, which was dreadfully stupid, and lasted a fearful time. With the latter I talked a good deal but he has not a very *decided* affection for me, and I was sighing for Newcomen. After the dinner he and I teaed at the Parson's, and at nine I got Her Majesty, much against her will, to go to the Ball, but the ladies did stay such a time in the dressing room that I had lots of time to run about the town [St. Thomas], looking for some soda to remove the effects of about a thimble full of wine which I was foolish enough to offer the hospitality of my stomach to—(but it did not prove 'an angel unawares'). Thus, I daresay, it was ten when the ladies did make their entrée. I took in Miss Harris and taking her up to Col. T. left her with him, and she wanted to sit by his side all the evening, she was so much pleased with him. Besides she expected to have seen a man the height of Mr. Hagarman—the size of Acland, with the hair and eyes of Ermatinger, so she was a little disappointed, and did not recover her amazement during the evening. I did her the honor of dancing first with her, 'just as the gossips had said', but I never stand at the head of the *first* quadrille, for reasons you may guess, so we like humble folks stood at the side. We also waltzed together, and went to supper together and fought together quite enviably. . . . I danced too, with the beautiful Mrs. Gowman, Mrs. Ed. Warren—Miss Bale—Sarah Leonard—Askin, etc. etc. etc., and I think it must have been near four when it broke up. . . . Besides all my sparring with your two most amiable young ladies, I fought with Mademoiselles Williams, Nevels, and Douglas, to say nothing of smaller affairs with divers others, so that, altogether, I did pretty well."

Nevertheless, through it all, Julius could not forget the gnawing anxiety that beset him. "I amused myself a good deal," he wrote, "danced incessantly, talked wisdom to some, sentiment to others, nonsense to all, laughed at every thing —yet *within*—? I daresay every one thought me 'vastly amusing'—as a friend of mine used to say, and a perfect genius of gaiety, yet it did not penetrate much deeper than the rays of light which just glitter in the surface of the waters, and was like the tinselled mantle, with which the strolling player covers his rags. . . . I feel the recklessness of despair spreading over my heart, and every removal however temporary as an escape that I must enjoy to the utmost, as long as it lasts."

After the dance Julius rested for an hour in his room, then got up and performed his toilet by means of the pump and a horse pail. At half past six in the morning, as agreed upon with Amelia Harris, he was at the Rev. Mark Burnham's, where he found Marriott lying on the sofa wrapped in counterpanes, and attended by the girls. "There they were," Julius wrote, "one supporting the poor little fellow with her arm—the other pouring jorams of the delicious drink of China down his lilly white throat. 'Oh ho!' says I, 'this is very fine—I'm ill too'—whereupon dear Amelia—not the other, who 'cares not a farthing for—' and has 'a great affection for me'—went and got me cup after cup of the precious fluid, with sundry hunches of bread. . . . All this time, the Master and 'Missus' of the establishment were in a happy state of unconsciousness—quite ignorant of all the goings on —the two guests your daughters had at that early hour, and the food which they were so liberally regaling us with. At last, however, to my great and undissembled delight, Mr. Marriott turned tail and went off to London—and then Her Majesty and I talked by turns, with Amelia as a Moderator. . . . In the midst of all this Mrs. Burnham came in, and we were immediately as soft as the summer air—as bright as summer skies—yet as cold as if 'butter would not melt within our mouths!' I there breakfasted again, and then had to take my departure. . . . I do not feel very well, and I am going to try some calomel."

Marriott had said that Colonel Wetherall was coming out from London later in the week to visit Colonel Talbot, but Julius "devoutly" hoped he would not. The cook had the ague, Mrs. Hunter had been delivered of a child the night of the Anniversary, and Jeffrey was not in good health. On top of all they did not have a housemaid; and so the work of the house devolved on Julius and on George Macbeth, son of a neighbouring Scots settler, who had come to work for the Colonel the year before, at the age of thirteen. "I, therefore," Julius wrote, "have to make up the rooms, etc.—lay the table and all that—the which does not tend to make me look forward to a speedy retrial, as very disagreeable. Our little wood cutter boy finds himself suddenly transformed into *nurse*, cook, and the maker of the men's beds—and it is rather amusing to see him now, poring over the kitchen fire, and now, walking about, leading one child by the hand and with a *yearling* baby in his arms. He seems to like it too."

During the summer of 1840 Julius carried on his routine tasks, read the books which Mrs. Harris sent to him, and wrote long letters to his friends. Hating his exile, he yet found some solace in the beauties of nature about Port Talbot. One evening at the end of July he wrote to Mrs. Harris: "I am sitting nearly a third of the way down the cliff on the hard rough clay, weeds around me, a few trees in front—the lake, rolling its waves below—the leaden-colored waters spreading to the dark horizon—and to my left the far-spreading coast, illuminated here and there by some stray rays of the sun." Six months later, on the eve of his departure from Port Talbot, he wrote mournfully: "Now God knows, I have no reason to like this place, where really I have not passed one happy day, but I shall not leave the woods, and the hills—and the lake, upon which I have looked for upwards of seven years, without a sigh. Though, too, I have no reason to be attached to it and my several haunts are rather scenes of misery than of anything else, yet the places where, walking up and down, I have read particular books, recall to my mind those pages and their contents,—the very trees appearing almost to speak to me of the various incidents which the volumes contained. Thus, one little spot in the woods seems to breathe of one book, and another of another, so that I never pass through them that these works do not vividly open their pages before my eyes. Besides, too, from the want of fellow creatures to pour my affections upon, I have made friends of particular little places, or trees, or views, and perhaps wherever I go, or whatever may be my lot, I shall never forget them."

Meanwhile, the illness of Colonel Talbot continued throughout the summer of 1840. During July he had Colonel Dundas and several other officers from London to dinner. They arrived late, because of the pouring rain; and not expecting that they would come Julius and his uncle had finished their meal, even eating all the pudding that was intended for the guests. Julius found the visit "a dreadful bore", and Talbot was so unwell that he could scarcely sit up, "and was in misery all the time", while the officers "were rather merry, and talked of matters more interesting to themselves than to us." Julius did not appreciate Colonel Dundas: "He is good natured—gentlemanlike—a great man and all that—but he is not a sparkling gem, he is not a diamond." Rayner was "a terrible fellow 'quite orrid'—to turn his own word against himself", while Captain Stubbman did not labour under "the disease of superfluity of brains", and was very Irish. The other three officers were more to Julius' liking. Plunkett was quiet, very Irish in appearance, and not distinguished-looking, but his manners were those of a gentleman. Heset was "a good sort of person too, having more consideration for my poor Uncle" than any of the others. Julius liked Haddon best of all, "because he is honest—and plain—and manly—and sensible—but he is not the sort of man my Uncle likes, that is to say, in a tête à tête. When he is quiet he would do very well, but Colonel Talbot could not bear him, when he gets heated and exhilirated in Society—and becomes perfectly wild. . . ."

At this time Talbot was so ill and weak that he ate practically nothing, and his nights were disturbed and sleepless. It appeared evident that he had jaundice, but he refused to see a doctor or take medicine of any kind, and urging him to do so only annoyed and made him worse. By September, however, he was much improved, and glad to welcome the Allans, the Salmons, and other old friends who came to visit him. Julius was comforted by the arrival of his brother, Colonel Richard Airey, who remained for nine days. "We have now here," Julius wrote on October 3, "Mr. Allan of Toronto and his son, who arrived today from London. . . . He is, I think, an excellent, upright, honorable man, rough in manner but benevolent in heart; and his son is clever, well informed for his age, and far superior to the common run of the youths about him."

On January 16, 1841, Julius wrote to say good-bye to Mrs. Harris, before leaving Port Talbot forever. Whatever consideration had kept him there for a full year after his quarrel with his uncle no longer applied; he had decided to return to Ireland. "I cannot help smiling at the idea of people wondering," he declared. "I am not sorry! Is the prisoner sorry to escape from his dungeon?—or the slave from his fetters? . . . Even Mrs. Burwell and Mary could not help laughing, when they asked me the day I took leave of them, if I regretted my departure? and Leonidas said privately to me, and as if he was afraid he was guilty of some imprudence—'You will, at all events, be as well off anywhere you have bread and water! for what else have you here?'" He had, it is true, an affection for the place that had been his home for seven years, but what he could no longer endure was the "complete isolation during the spring time of life", not only from the society of many people, but from any single one of his own mind and tastes. "Days and days have succeeded one another," he wrote, "without much more conversation than formal salutations, while rarely have I had any one to whom I could talk on the subjects which interest me, and for years I have felt myself withering away, actually for the want of congenial communion!"

Julius did not anticipate a very pleasant journey to Toronto, for the rigours of winter were setting in after a mild week, the inns were wretched, and his uncle had a terrible cold that he blamed on the stoves in the Harrises' home in London, where he had been visiting during the holidays. "I leave here," Julius told Mrs. Harris, "Mr. Harris's umbrella, and my little model of a Swiss house, for your chimney-piece, which I hope you will value, as it was given me by my Mother." Two days later he and his uncle left in a sleigh, following the winding road through the Colonel's Wood that led to St. Thomas. Talbot stayed with Julius in Toronto for about two weeks, and when he left for home he gave him £200. Julius remained in Toronto until the middle of April before travelling to New York to take ship for England. He was being very gay, he wrote to Mrs. Harris in March, dining out and attending other social functions, but he could not rid himself of the thought of so many wasted years, and the uncertainty of the future.

For nearly two years Julius remained with his parents in Ireland, undecided what to do. In June, 1842, he wrote, despairingly, that his situation seemed hopeless. "I write regularly once a month to my Uncle," he told Mrs. Harris, "and always send my remembrances to you. Does he ever forward them to their destination? Do you think he *always* gets my letters. I am aware it looks idle my writing to him, and he may imagine that I wish to curry favor again, but would it not look worse my not doing so?" The following February he wrote to say that he was studying law at the Inner Temple in London, with five long years ahead of him before he would become a barrister. "Is my Uncle coming home or not?" he asked. "I never hear from him, but I write every month. I daresay he hates my letters, but I cannot help thinking that silence would be more offensive."

Julius could not forget his old associations. In the summer of 1843 he wrote to ask Mrs. Harris for news about the last Anniversary, and about all the people he knew, especially the Bechers, Cronyns, Wilsons, Leonards, and Burwells. He wished to know if the trees that he had planted at Port Talbot were thriving, and if they were large enough to make a show and give some shade. "They *ought*," he wrote, "to add greatly to the appearance of that southeast side of the hill which you see from the back windows of the house, and also on that which slopes to the mouth of the river." However, when he wrote again in December the nostalgia had passed; he was in love with the law. It was, he said, "a noble career—a lofty intellectual struggle and pursuit—and oh how much better than—pulling up thistles!!!! Now my eyes are always bright, my face always smiling. . . . I feel sometimes ready to jump with joy at my present happiness."

## CHAPTER XIX

# *Abdication*

WHILE Julius Airey advanced along the road that led to his future eminence in the common law, his uncle remained in his lonely farm house, surrounded only by servants—those whom Julius called menials and toadies. His health continued to be precarious. At the beginning of 1842 he took sick with one of his bad colds, which lasted for three weeks, forcing him to postpone his usual winter's visit to Toronto; but it was not so severe, he told William Allan, "as to require the panacea of Flax Seed Tea". The winter remained so open through January that he was unable to send to the mill, "and the consequence is, that starvation stares me in the face, for want of bread". He thanked Allan for investing another £1,000 for him, which made him feel he was growing rich. Colonel Burwell had just arrived for dinner, bringing "an invitation from the Bachelors of the Garrison of London to a fancy Ball on the 3rd of February".[1]

The Anniversary of 1842 fell in the fiftieth year, or jubilee, since Talbot first arrived in Upper Canada with Lieutenant-Governor John Graves Simcoe, and the Colonel looked forward to it with more than the usual anticipation. Writing to John B. Robinson early in January, he said that he planned to hold the Anniversary on May 23, as May 21, the proper day, fell on Saturday, which would limit the dancing to midnight. He only appeared "on the stage" once a year, he explained, and "the fuller the house the more gratifying".

Some time later he decided to hold it on Friday, May 20, "so that they can dance into the 21st, the proper day".[2]

"I cannot tell you," Talbot wrote to Allan the following year, "how much it would gratify me to have a gossip with Mrs. Allan and yourself, for the older I grow the more I value the society of those *I* consider my friends. Indeed, I am happy in being a philosopher in being so contented in my dignified retirement, as a very few of my standing would submit to the privations I do."[3] Sir Francis Head had expressed the same idea in a letter to the Colonial Secretary six years before. "Altho' the possessor of immense property," Head wrote, "he still lives in his log-house—still sits erect on his original hard-bottomed, strait-backed uncomfortable kitchen chair, his cell containing little furniture except sheep-skin sacks of corn and rude implements of husbandry. In short, taking his life altogether, it certainly forms the most extraordinary picture of practical philosophy it has ever been my fortune to witness."[4]

The old Colonel's political views remained as staunchly conservative as ever. He was convinced that the trend towards democracy, which appeared so alarming under the administration of Lord Sydenham, would lead ultimately to the separation of Canada from the British Empire. With the death of the first Governor of united Canada in the fall of 1841, and the appointment of Sir Charles Bagot, he waited anxiously for news as to the new Governor's policy. "However," he wrote to Allan in January 1842, "I have more faith in his character than I have had in many of his predecessors, at least I hope that he is an honest man."[5] But his disappointment was keen when Bagot accepted the "radical" Baldwin-Lafontaine ministry, and gave evidence, before his death in 1843, that he intended to further the growth of democracy.

In November, 1844, Talbot wrote to Lord Wharncliffe: "The country was actually on the brink of a revolution when the present Governor General, Sir Charles Metcalfe, commenced his administration, but thank God, it has been saved at least for the present, by his wise firm and prudent measures." The riotous elections, in which Metcalfe obtained a small majority in support of his ministry, had just ended. Opposed to any vestige of responsible government, he had gained his ends by arousing party strife to a pitch not seen since 1837. Talbot feared that his success was only temporary, and that "in a colony where radical feelings are not only encouraged but fostered, there cannot be any security for the future". The deplorable state of the province during the previous eight or nine years was the result of "the fickle and weak policy of the Home Government, in listening to, and giving into, the treasonable and Republican representations made under the name of Grievances".

Convinced that the North American provinces would "continue more or less in a state of anarchy", unless the British government resorted to "some bold system" to remodel their constitutions, Talbot described his own plan for Wharncliffe's consideration. It was, he believed, "the only alternative left to prevent our separation from the Mother Country", but he professed to be completely indifferent as to whether it met with censure or applause. His scheme was to have all the North American provinces united in a viceroyalty, with "the creation of a Peerage, for all Mankind are slaves to titles of distinction", to give it respectability. He thought that the appointment of the Duke of Cambridge as viceroy would give general satisfaction, as he was a discreet and capable person; and if it should be found expedient in the future to change the viceroyalty into an independent kingdom, it might be given to the duke.[6]

Talbot had been planning to leave for England in September, 1844, to visit the friends whom he had not seen in fifteen years, but the arrival of the district treasurer with a demand for the "monstrous sum" of nearly £600 as tax on his lands, knocked all his "Fairy dreams in the head". "This," he told Wharncliffe indignantly, "is the fruit of Lord Sydenham's tyrannical and odious Municipal Bill, and God only knows when 'The Lion of the West' can quit his den, for to appear before you all in the Old World as a Pauper would not correspond with my natural dignity."

The District Councils Act, of which the Colonel complained, had gone into effect at the beginning of 1842, vesting control of each district in an elected council to replace the magistrates assembled in quarter sessions, and giving each council the power to levy a wild land tax up to one and a half pence per acre. Until the end of the decade Thomas Gardiner Coyne, third son of Henry Coyne, represented Dunwich in the London District Council. It was he, according to a contemporary who wrote half a century later, who "moved a resolution that all land held by speculators should be taxed for the benefit of the municipalities in which such lands were located. Through his perseverance and influence in the council the resolution was carried. . . . I suppose there are today living in the neighbourhood of Tyrconnel many who can recall the treatment Mr. Coyne received at the hands of Colonel Talbot for the part he took in bringing about the change."[7] The growth of democracy, as Talbot had feared, provided an opportunity for the people to strike against privilege. Most of the people in Dunwich and Aldborough regarded the Colonel's vast holdings in those townships as a serious grievance; not only did they remain forest-covered and unproductive, a refuge for destructive animals, but until 1844 the tax upon them had been negligible.

One effect of the new tax was to force the Colonel to lease portions of his lands to tenants, to insure himself a larger income. In the process he discovered a number of discrepancies between the descriptions of lots given in the deeds, and their actual size. Burwell, whom he engaged to check all his property with the patents, soon found that four lots described therein did not exist, and that several others were much smaller than they were supposed to be. In all, Burwell discovered that the Colonel's patents showed 803 acres more than he actually possessed. Much disturbed by this, Talbot sought a new grant of land to make up for the deficiency, but he was told that the Land Act of 1841 put it out of the power of the Governor and Council to do so.[8] To Talbot this was another injustice that could be laid at Lord Sydenham's door.

His passion for land probably stemmed to a considerable extent from his feudal background, as did his desire to leave his name upon the countryside. He wanted the Talbot Settlement to remain as a memorial to himself and his family. Writing to Governor Metcalfe's secretary early in 1844, he told him that he had "for a long time been waiting to find a proper *spot* to give the title of the Head my family to, so as to complete the Talbot Country that I have for so many years labored to form. I have now found the Place, which is the new Town, about to be laid out at what is called the *Round O*, and if His Excellency will be pleased to call the Town Shrewsbury, I shall ever consider myself under a great obligation besides being highly flattered."[9] Metcalfe readily granted the request; and so the port on Rondeau Bay in Kent County was named after the head of the Talbot clan, the English Earl of Shrewsbury. Unfortunately, the coming of the railroads, which passed several miles to the north of

Shrewsbury, lessened the need for a port on Lake Erie, and it remained a small village, a haven of refuge for escaped slaves from the United States.

In the fall of 1845 the Colonel was seventy-four years old, but feeling quite well for his years. He was about to set off for Colonel Burwell's in Southwold, he informed William Allan on October 27, to attend the marriage of his daughter. No less than five Miss Harrises from London had been with him for nearly three weeks, "waiting for this very interesting undertaking". He hoped the excellent weather would last, "as all the amusement I have is in looking after my work on the Farm".[10] Burwell died the following January, which grieved him greatly. The old question of what was to happen to his great estate after his own death remained unanswered, and he felt the need of a companion of his own blood during his last years. In the fall of 1846 he wrote to his nephew Richard Airey, offering to make him his heir if he would come and live at Port Talbot. Airey was then Assistant Adjutant-General of the Horse Guards in London, England, and only the prospect of inheriting a rich estate could have induced him to give up his promising military career. He knew Port Talbot and his uncle well, having paid a number of visits to the log "castle" during the several years that he spent in Canada. But he accepted the offer and arranged to move with his family to Upper Canada. In the light of future events it appears doubtful that he could have made up his mind to remain there except for the few years that his uncle might live.

Julius Airey was greatly startled when he heard from Mrs. Harris about the Colonel's offer to his brother. "It was not that I had any hope blasted," he wrote to her, "or any vision dispelled. At least I think I had neither vision nor hope to be dispelled or blasted—and, on the contrary it is an unexpected gratification to me to hear, that after all he was not going to forget all his own kith and kin for menials and toadies about him—but still it did give me a shock. God knows! I have no rancorous feeling whatever against him, and still less of jealousy against my brother, in whose good fortune I shall ever sincerely rejoice. . . . The more I think over it, the more I feel that it was just a *natural* that he should be dissatisfied with me—as I was with that *dreadful* existence, the very thought and recollection of which still makes me shudder! I am getting too old—too frigid—too calm—and too careless about money—now, to heed very much any pecuniary loss—and not only is my present life incomparably preferable to the misery I endured in Canada, but would rather turn street-sweeper tomorrow than return to the same wretched state of mean and degrading dependency and thraldom. If too, any so near relation as a brother should ultimately come in for the spoils, what more could I wish?"[11]

The death of Jeffrey Hunter in November, 1846, had deprived the Colonel of his beloved personal servant, who had been with him, except for a few months in 1827, for twenty-eight years.* George Macbeth, the little wood-cutter boy who had helped Julius with the house work in 1840, was now about twenty years of age. One of the "menials and toadies", in Julius' eyes, he was kind and attentive to the old

* On October 12, four weeks before the death of his old servant, the Colonel conveyed to William Hunter, Jeffrey's three-year-old son, 200 acres of land, being lot 20 in the 10th concession of Dunwich, not far to the west of Port Talbot. He did this, the Colonel stated in the indenture, in consideration of Jeffrey's long and faithful service, "by means whereof" he had "become much attached to him, and interested in the welfare" of his son. It was probably on this property that Talbot later built a home for the Hunter family, and where he lived for a time after his return from England in 1851. Sheriff I. D. Cameron of St. Thomas has kindly loaned me a copy of the indenture.

man. Fairly well educated in the local schools, he was an intelligent youth who not only took Jeffrey's place but became the Colonel's constant companion and confidant. Nevertheless, pride of family still drew the Colonel to his blood relations in his search for a successor. Writing to William Allan in March, 1847, he told him that he expected Colonel and Mrs. Airey to arrive within two or three months, with their five children. "I anticipate much comfort from their society," he said.[12] It was September, however, before the Aireys left England, bringing with them a number of fruit trees and rose bushes for the Colonel's garden.[13]

The presence of the Aireys did not at first disturb the routine at Port Talbot, for they established themselves in Mahlon Burwell's old home a few miles away. The Harrises and others were frequent visitors. The previous June, when Talbot wrote to Judge William Salmon, to invite his brother George to stay with him for a few days, he told him that Mrs. Harris and three of her daughters and two of the officers of the 82nd Regiment had been at Port Talbot for a week, and he thought they intended to remain another week.[14] When he wrote to Judge Salmon again in March, 1848, he said he was anxious to have him come and meet the Aireys. Amelia and Eliza Harris had been with him for the last ten days, and Chief Justice Robinson and Captain Le Froy had recently left after a stay of three days.[15]

This way of life was soon ended when Colonel Airey insisted on living at Port Talbot, so that he could take over the management of the farm. On May 8 Talbot informed Judge Salmon that he had been "as busy as a bee building a log den for myself and servants, being obliged to give up my old house to Colonel Airey and family".[16] The Den, as it continued to be called by everyone, was built close to the house on the east, and it must have been of considerable size to accommodate Mrs. Hunter and her four children, the Colonel, and George Macbeth. Its rough-hewn construction, however, prompted a visitor the following year to describe it as a sort of shanty or Indian wigwam, which the Colonel was already proposing to enlarge.[17]

Talbot had told Salmon in March that he was thinking of visiting England that spring "should the old world last, but all appears convulsed". On May 20, 1848, despite some trouble with the gout in his right hand, he and George Macbeth set out for Quebec, where they took a steamboat for Liverpool. During the pleasant voyage of twenty-three days the old man was up on deck every day, and ate and slept well. From Liverpool they travelled by rail to London, where they obtained rooms at 26 Mount Street in Grosvenor Square and remained until late in July, while the Colonel visited friends. He soon decided that he preferred his "own quiet home Port Talbot, to the bustle of the great world", but he left about the end of July to spend the next two months with his brother in Ireland. He was pleased to find Lord Talbot "in wonderful good health and spirits", although in his 83rd year, and Malahide Castle "looking quite beautiful".

Most of October and November were spent with various of the Colonel's friends in Scotland and the northern part of England. Among these were the Duke of Argyll at Inverary, the Duke of Sutherland at Dunrobin, Lord Bellhaven in Lanarkshire, Lord Haddington at Tyringham near Dunbar, Lord Wharncliffe at Wortley Hall, and the Earl of Derby and his son Lord Edward Stanley at Knowsley Hall in Lancashire. Late in November Talbot went to stay with his brother James in Somersetshire for a few days, then back to Malahide Castle for ten days. After this he went to London, and from there to Lord Ellesmere's in Surrey, and the Duke of Sutherland's in Staffordshire. Having completed these visits he took a ten-day trip to Paris, where he was presented to Louis Napoleon, who had just been elected president of the new Republic of France following the revolution that dethroned King Louis Philippe. Despite his dislike of republics the old Colonel was pleased that the president was "very gracious" to him, and he enjoyed his stay in Paris, which was still "in a state of the greatest excitement". Returning to London, he remained there until March 6, when, as he wrote later, "I put myself and stock into the train for Liverpool, and to finish I gave two days farewell to Malahide and sailed on the 16th March." The stock, which he brought back with him to feast upon his "delicate pasture" at Port Talbot, consisted of a number of South Down sheep and Devonshire cattle. He also brought fifty varieties of roses and quantities of flower bulbs, most of which failed to grow, but he was more successful with a variety of fruit trees.[18]

On arriving back home the Colonel was surprised to find that the Aireys had greatly altered the old house and its surroundings. Many of the unsightly log buildings had been removed, the grounds were neatly kept, and the verandah was cleared of the implements of husbandry that had hung from its rafters. The house itself was almost unrecognizable. It had been extended to the westward by a frame construction of the same height and width and nearly half the length of the original squared-log building. The latter having been covered with clapboards, and its roof extended over the new frame section, the only appearance of irregularity was in the roof of the verandah, which was somewhat lower in front of the new part, to permit two small windows to be placed just below the eaves. At the west end of the building, and extending in the same direction, was a large kitchen, which was narrower and considerably lower than the rest of the house.

The Colonel's old sitting-room, and the store-room, had now been made into a large drawing-room, luxuriously furnished; and its four large front windows, extending to the floor, provided a magnificent view of the lake. Behind the drawing-room was a living-room of equal size, whose windows looked out over the ravine. The former kitchen was now a large entrance hall, with a small bedroom at the back. The new portion of the main house contained two bedrooms in front on the first floor, with a large dining-room behind, and four bedrooms upstairs. The decorations and furnishings were such as befitted the home of a country gentleman of wealth and taste. Lady Emmeline Stuart-Wortley was "quite enchanted with the place" when she and her daughter stayed there in the summer of 1849. They occupied the two front bedrooms downstairs, whose windows also extended to the floor and were framed with muslin curtains. The furniture was "so perfectly English that there is nothing wanting". In some respects the rooms were "quite luxuriously appointed". They had "some splendid decorations and draperies of beautiful old Greek lace" that Mrs. Airey had brought from the Ionian Islands, but everything had been so exquisitely arranged that there was nothing "unsuited to the general character of simplicity" of the house.

The Wortleys admired the beautiful situation, with the lake in front, several splendid groups of trees near by, and the thick forest to the north extending to the far horizon. The house appeared small from the front, with its long roof slanting down to the verandah, but it was actually very roomy and comfortable. There was now an air of true English refinement about it that must have amazed the Colonel.

"It is astonishing," Miss Wortley wrote, "in what a short time Colonel Airey has transformed a small, rough, log house into a comfortable country seat. A few months seemed to have been sufficient to alter the house so completely that Colonel Talbot himself hardly knew it again on returning from a short visit to England."

Talbot lived in the Den beside his former home, but he was on hand with the Aireys to receive the two ladies with the greatest cordiality. During the days that followed he sat with them for hours in the shade of the lilac and syringa bushes in the garden, entertaining them with stories of his life. He told them that he was really the last of the Mohicans, having been adopted into that tribe many years before. "In former days," Lady Wortley wrote, "he used to milk his own cows, and drive them home from their pasturing places, for many miles sometimes; and besides, he did all the household work in his establishment; cooked, churned butter, washed, etc. His energy and perseverance were finally rewarded with great success; and he is lord of almost a principality here, and of a very flourishing one, apparently, too."[19]

Talbot never tired of telling about his rise to wealth and power, by his own efforts and the use of his own hands. He seemed to derive as much satisfaction from describing the menial work he had done as in speaking in feudal terms of his lordship over a "principality". His whole history, as Sir Francis Head wrote in 1837, "forms a subject apparently suited to a romance rather than to an official despatch. Many people have been driven by necessity to live a life of hardship and seclusion, but it has seldom happened that a gentleman possessing the singular advantages which belonged to Colonel Talbot has voluntarily exchanged the enjoyments of the English Court for a solitary existence in the back woods of Upper Canada, where after remaining for some time the alpha and omega of human society, he gradually rose (as he himself declares) to become cook and milkman to his own workmen."[20]

Political events in Canada disturbed the Colonel as much as ever. Lord Elgin's introduction of responsible government, and his acceptance of the Rebellion Losses Bill which indemnified even the rebels, filled him with dismay. "Of course," he wrote to William Allan on October 8, 1849, "you will see by the papers that Lord Elgin has been prowling thro the West. He was in London on Wednesday last, no great demonstration in his favor, altho he was escorted from Oxford by 1500 Radicals. There were several triumphal arches erected for him in the streets of London, but before his Lordship reached the Town they were all cut down by the Tories and left on the ground for His Excellency and his respectable phalanx to drive over. For myself I remained quiet in my Den."[21]

Just two weeks later Talbot went to London as the guest of honour at the ceremony of breaking ground for the Great Western Railway. That evening he replied to a toast to his health: "I thank you, gentlemen, most heartily for the honor you have done me this day. I have witnessed a scene which I can never forget or hoped to behold in this settlement. It is an event never to be forgotten. I believe I am the oldest inhabitant. I have slept on this spot 55 years ago, when my best friend was a porcupine. We were often excessively hungry in those days, but we all used to declare that we were never so hungry as the night we ate the porcupine. What a change has occurred since then! Now I see different beings around me—no porcupine—no bristles—but in their place a company of half-civilized gentlemen. I wish you, gentlemen, all prosperity, and when I am laid under the sod, may you go on progressing."[22]

Finding that the Den was too close to the Aireys for comfort, in the fall of 1849 the Colonel built a new house across the ravine. Early in December the plaster was sufficiently dry for him to move into two of the rooms, but the chimneys smoked so much that he was forced to keep the doors and windows open. His spirits were greatly depressed by news of the death of his brother, Lord Talbot de Malahide, and by the "frightful state" of the country. "Little did I think," he wrote to John B. Robinson, "when I first arrived in Upper Canada with Govr. Simcoe in 1792, that I should live to see the present times. I believe that our friend Allan and myself are the only two left to witness the works of the D—l." He was "actually lonesome", he said, and he begged Robinson to come and see him as soon as the sleighing was good.[23]

Friction between Talbot and his nephew had been growing steadily since the former returned from his trip. He had been forced out of the home where he had spent so many years, and from the management of his own estate. While he lived in the Den beside the big house he found it difficult to carry on the peculiar manner of life to which he had become accustomed: the Aireys did not approve of his dress or habits.[24] These, however, were annoyances which were probably less important than Richard Airey's jealousy of George Macbeth, and his realization that his own position was not secure. "He is an excellent youth," Talbot wrote of Macbeth in October, "and has been a most faithful adherent to me since I took him under my care at the age of thirteen, ten years ago."[25] At his request William Allan invested £223 for George Macbeth.

The break between uncle and nephew came in March, 1850, apparently resulting from Airey's insistence that he be given title to the Talbot estate immediately. On March 15 Henry Becher, the Colonel's lawyer, arrived from London to settle "the differences between Col. Talbot and Col. Airey".[26] The following day an agreement was reached by which Talbot conveyed to his nephew about half of his landed estate, including Port Talbot and other lands in Dunwich amounting to 1,300 acres, as well as all his Aldborough property amounting to 27,650 acres. The instrument states that this was in lieu of Talbot's promise to devise "certain lands" to Airey, which indicates a definite agreement between the two prior to the nephew's arrival in Canada.[27] On the same day Talbot made his will, leaving the remainder of his property, real and personal, with the exception of a few individual bequests, to his "faithful young friend George Macbeth the younger". The bequests included the sum of £500 to Daniel Macbeth, younger brother of George, who also worked for the Colonel; the sum of £200 to each of the four Hunter children; and an annuity of £20 for life to Mrs. Jane Hunter. In repayment of a loan from Talbot's sister Frances, the sum of £1,000 was to be paid to her.[28]

The wax seals on these documents, opposite the Colonel's signatures, bear the impress of his signet ring, showing a "talbot" hound running, with his initials beneath. The talbot, an extinct breed of dogs from which the bloodhound is probably descended, is the ancient badge of the Talbot family.

## CHAPTER XX

# *The Exile*

The shock of the quarrel, and the loss of his beloved Port Talbot, so affected the old Colonel that for a time he was expected to die at any moment. Nine days later he was so emaciated and helpless that George Macbeth and his brother had to lift him from his bed and carry him in a chair to the living-room. Nevertheless he was determined to leave the place at once, and return to his native land. "Every moment he stays here is hastening his death," Macbeth informed Becher on March 25. "He is now scolding me to haste and pack up. I don't know what to do with him. I think it will be wrong to let him move in his present state. If I allowed him to travel in the way he is in England without medical advice (and he died), they would try me for my life as being accessory to his death."

Two days later Becher arrived from London, bringing with him a covered carriage for Talbot's conveyance. "Never mind the cost," Macbeth had written. "We need not let him know it and I can pay for it. It would be much warmer and comfortable—that we might induce him to take it to Hamilton—Daniel taking the luggage in our lumber waggon."[1] Talbot was now slightly improved in health, although only able to take a little wine as nourishment, and he was very irritable. But somehow he managed to survive the trip over almost impassable roads to St. Thomas, and from thence to London. Here he was forced to remain for nearly three months, an invalid at the home of the Harrises, the first seven weeks confined to bed with a severe attack of erysipelas.[2] Late in June he was sufficiently recovered to endure the long journey over the rough roads to Hamilton, where he embarked on a steamboat for the trip across the lake. An observer at Hamilton noted the great care given the "fine old Irish Gentleman" by his attendants, and the precautions taken to guard him against fatigue.[3]

By July 5, when the steamship which he and Macbeth had boarded at Quebec lay off Halifax, the Colonel was gaining fast. He was able to walk around by himself, even going up and down stairs with the assistance of one of the passengers. In fact, as Macbeth informed Becher, he was never still for five minutes, unless engaged in conversation with someone; as a result his feet remained swollen and he bathed them with warm salt water each morning and evening. At first the passengers and stewards were inclined to avoid him because of his eccentric appearance, but all this was changed when Mrs. Fanny Kemble, who had known him years before, asked to be introduced to him. Her attentions not only pleased the old man but made him the centre of attraction for all on board.

The steamer arrived at Liverpool on July 16, and after a night at the Stork Hotel, Macbeth and the Colonel took the train to London. Two days later Talbot was well enough to write to Becher from his room at Long's Hotel on Bond Street: "I want you to see my hand writing again. George will tell you all about me. I am certainly a little stronger but still very feeble, but can walk a little with the support and assistance of our friend George." On the 22nd he departed for St. Leonards in Sussex, having been told that the sea air might help him, but after a week's stay he returned to London, taking lodgings at 26 Mount Street in Grosvenor Square. "I flatter myself," he informed Becher on July 31, "that my health may be restored so long as to give me many years more of [Macbeth's] friendly assistance, for it can't be valued at my age—as yet I have not been able to walk out to see any of my old friends, indeed they are now going out of London as fast as they can, and as to my visiting them in the country it will not be in my power."[4]

Before leaving for England Talbot had given Mrs. Jeffrey Hunter the annuity of £20, and each of her four children the sum of £200, which had been provided for them in his will. In a letter dated August 14 Becher stated that he had paid a visit to Mrs. Hunter and advised her to use as little as possible of the money left by her late husband, "conceiving that her pension from you commencing on and after 1 July last, and the interest on the children's stock given them by me lately (of all which your generous provision I duly apprised her), would be enough for their wants". They were then living in a new house which Talbot had built for them some distance to the west of Port Talbot. Mrs. Hunter was also given the furniture that had been in the Den, with the exception of the Colonel's favourite armchair, and a picture of the Den, which had been given to Becher. "They have a very nice little house as clean as a new pin," Becher wrote, "and I was astonished at the parlor. Your old side board, carpet, etc., and some light blue paint Daniel said Jane could have, made it astonishingly neat and spruce."

Becher informed the Colonel that he had succeeded in selling his lot in Woodhouse, parts of those in Townsend, and one in London Township, amounting to 700 acres of land, for £1,525. The lot in Charlotteville was not yet sold, except for fifty acres that Talbot had disposed of long before;

the remainder was swampy and stripped of timber. In November, in answer to Talbot's request, Becher went to Dunwich in an effort to sell some of his lands there, but the people "seemed shocked at the price I asked for the land and seemed under the impression they were to get it for next to nothing". Convinced that he could sell little to them, Becher advised advertising in the Toronto papers in the spring, to attract the immigrants. He also reported that Shepherd, the London Mill tenant, had offered to buy the mill for £500, and that Archibald Hamilton wished to buy one of Talbot's village lots in Tyrconnel. Becher had engaged Deputy Surveyor Springer to lay out lots there, hoping, as he wrote the following spring, to have something "like a reputable and flourishing village in commencement at all events before your advent. I mean to make property in it high in the market in a few years."[5]

On his way to Mrs. Hunter's, in August, Becher had stopped at Port Talbot, where he found everything looking "very nice and pretty". Colonel Airey had left his uncle's deed of gift with Hercules Burwell to be registered, after demanding a receipt for it. "It must gratify you to know," Becher wrote to Talbot, "how he values your deed of gift, as indeed well he may!" Airey wrote to his uncle a few days later, giving him some news of the farm, and describing in detail the various roses, flowering bushes and trees that he had brought from England the previous year.[6] Talbot's bitterness was too deep to be forgotten, and he did not reply. Macbeth wrote that fall: "Col. Airey's letter is a gem—it is Airey all over—sent here to a Lady enclosed with a long apology for trouble, etc., and begging it might be forwarded to Col. T. as he was not aware what part of the world he was in—then there is a long account of the roses and garden, some attempts at pleasantry, some indignation at Daniel's taking away trunks full of old letters and refusing him (Col. A.) to nail them up and seal them to be kept till Col. T. returned etc.—and concluding with the favourable accounts to be heard from Mrs. Burwell (of Col. T.). The Colonel of course has not answered nor intends to do so—for I learnt at Harrowgate from Mrs. A's sister that Col. A. had weekly accounts from one or other of the family, who are well aware of the Col's residence and state of health."

Talbot had gone to High Harrogate, in Yorkshire, late in August, after much persuasion by Macbeth. Situated on an open plain, the place was bleak and cold, but the air was clear of smoke, and the waters were thought to be healthful; besides, the Colonel's sister Eliza, wife of Ellis Cunliffe Lister Kaye, was staying there. The Colonel stubbornly refused to drink the water, and Macbeth admitted that the smell and taste were dreadful. The hotel where they stayed, more than a mile from the springs, had from two to three hundred guests, each of whom had his own servant to wait on him, even at table. Talbot enjoyed being with his sister, and with the many old friends that he found there. When he grew tired he went to his room, which was warmed by a good fire. Although his legs remained swollen his appetite was good, and as the days passed his health and strength showed marked improvement. On each fine day he would walk about, but most of the time he sat in the hotel gardens, where, as Macbeth wrote, "he held his levees—being generally surrounded by a dozen at least of the visitors to Harrowgate, and the grass around his favourite seat had no need of mowing."

Nevertheless, Talbot soon grew tired of Harrogate, and after four weeks insisted on returning to London. Macbeth tried to get him to go to Richmond, but after some indecision he refused. Very few of his friends were in London and, not caring for the sights or amusements of the city, he remained in his room most of the time. The doctor prescribed a moderate amount of walking on grass or gravel walks, but Talbot would not hire a cab to get to the park or even take the carriages that were frequently put at his disposal. However, as Macbeth reported to Becher, "he is very well, the legs lessening, and his appetite good, the face plump, red and clear without a wrinkle, his clothes completely filled, and when any old Dowager (none else in Town) calls, his gallantry and efforts to walk up and down stairs are amusing enough."

The Colonel's concern about his income not only affected his health but prevented Macbeth from making any plans for the future. He had asked Becher in August to sell his Dunwich lands and invest the proceeds, so that he might have an income of not less than £800 or £1,000 per year. Everything in England was so much more expensive than at Port Talbot that he was worried about having enough to live on. Macbeth assured him that he had more than sufficient for the rest of his life, but he would not believe him:— "his dread of poverty was so vivid that he was ready to imagine anything". A letter from Becher arrived before the end of September, and although merely repeating the assurances given by Macbeth, it helped to quiet the Colonel's worries. He was even prevailed upon, "after a great many provisoes", to agree to go to Paris to avoid the London fogs. Macbeth was chiefly concerned with getting him away from his London rooms into the open air; travelling also kept his mind occupied, and he had less time to think of the old days. After a time Talbot became quite enthusiastic about the trip. He decided that they would go by way of Boulogne, staying at

Amiens and other places on the way to Paris if they found them to their liking. From Paris they would go to St. Germain-en-laye, which had been recommended to Talbot for his health. After a tour through Normandy and Brittany they would return by way of Havre de Grace and Southampton.

After two months spent in France, Talbot and his companion returned to London on New Year's Day, 1851. Two days later the Colonel wrote to tell Becher that his health was much improved, although he could not walk on the streets very much without tiring. "George is now out hunting up a lodging for me," he said, "for this Hotel, the Burlington in old Burlington Street, is most extravagant. I have not seen a soul as yet, in fact every person seems to be quite ruined in England." Macbeth enclosed a note of his own stating that Talbot was much better, the swelling in his legs was gone, and he was able "to trot about" quite well by himself; he had just gone out to Stultz's, where he had ordered a "new rig out" and bought a new hat. Macbeth liked the Burlington Hotel, but he could not induce Talbot to stay, although they could obtain apartments there at a reasonable price. Not long afterwards they moved into an apartment at 17 Mount Street.

The Colonel was still troubled about the state of his finances. He informed Becher that his letters did not give him quite what he wanted, which was a detailed statement of all his investments in stocks, with the amount of interest he was receiving from each. He had found living in England and Europe very expensive—"really a *York* sixpence will go further at Port Talbot than a Sovereign in London or Paris. . . . If I find that I can treat myself to a tour in the South of France in the summer, that is after the first of July, I shall do so, but all depends on my *pocket*. . . ." As for investments, he liked good honest ones that would "give a fair interest without being mixed up in Law", and he was opposed to "all *shipping* speculations such as railroads, steamboats and vaporings of every description".[7]

In a letter dated December 28, 1850, Becher informed Macbeth that Talbot's income, exclusive of his pension, amounted to almost £800 a year, and that this would be materially increased within a year, and in each succeeding year. "The Colonel could scarcely believe it," Macbeth replied, "until I pointed out the different items, at the same time telling him how much it would increase and how rich he would be in five years, which latter he said was like telling him 'live horse and you'll get clover'." He had recently acquired a bad cold, so was not feeling as well as before. "About ten days ago, feeling quite well and strong, he took advantage of my being out and walked to pay some visits. After walking and heating himself a good deal he returned in, when Lady Talbot called and insisted on taking him out in her carriage, when he must have got chilled, for ever since he has lost his appetite, is weak and has a most frightful cough."

Although refusing to reply to Richard Airey's letters, the Colonel was not indifferent to him. In his letter of January 3 he asked Becher how his nephew was "getting on, and how he is considered in my dear country—don't give your opinion half way, but the actual truth". It must have been a shock to him to learn, a few weeks later, that Airey was leaving Port Talbot to return to his old position with the Horse Guards. Now there would be no member of the Talbot family to carry on the management of the old farm, and it would pass to strangers. Nevertheless, he professed to have no interest in what Airey did. "As far as Col. Talbot is concerned," Macbeth wrote to Becher, "it is little matter now whether he comes or stays. Col. T. will not see him if he can help it."[8]

The Aireys left Port Talbot early in April, 1851, after renting the farm to an English gentleman named John Sanders. Becher informed Talbot that Sanders was "a thorough Englishman", who would "keep the place in great order", and would be not only a fine tenant for Colonel Airey but a great acquisition to the province. Before leaving, Airey had handed over to Becher all of Talbot's land books, and at the same time gave him the management of his own affairs in Canada. "I was not much impressed at the time with his value as a client," Becher wrote later, "but he is the best I ever had or ever shall have."[9] Macbeth was surprised when he learned that Becher had made up with Airey so amicably, but he was pleased, he told him, "for with your aid there is still a chance of keeping the old place in the hands of respectable people. Yet at first sight it looked very much like going over to the enemy."[10]

The Aireys arrived in England before the end of April. Two weeks later Talbot wrote to Becher: "Col. Airey is in London but that is all that I know about him, further than that he is unwell. He has not called on me yet, and hope that he may not. Amelia Harris wrote that he was going to sell all the fruit trees, shrubs and flowers that I was at the cost and trouble of taking to Port Talbot, but Mr. Sanders protested against this robbing the gardens, however Daniel told George that he had sold them or some of them." Some months before this, Macbeth had informed Becher that the Colonel wanted him to get from his home the portraits of his old friend Lord Wharncliffe and his son, and the ivory miniature of his sister Lady Barbara Young. But the Aireys wished to keep the picture of their aunt, and Becher did not insist that they give it up. Talbot now wrote that he was sorry to hear this, as he was convinced the Aireys intended "to make it their own, and I hate to have any communication with them".

Now that the Aireys had left Port Talbot, the Colonel was eager to return there. "I told you in my last," he wrote to Becher on April 3, "that it is not my intention to sell any of the land in the avenue between *old* Port Talbot and Burwell's, as my *hobby* now is, that myself and George shall employ ourselves there in making a snug little *Wigwam*, as my last retreat on this earth, and feel most desirous that George may be comfortably settled during my life. He is now in his 25th year of age and I am near 80, so that there's not much time for play." Becher had already written in reply to Talbot's previous letter: "Should you fulfil your intention of coming out next June you should give me three months notice to put up a little cottage for you in a pretty situation on the Lake, east of P. Talbot—or would you prefer living here? *You must not* winter in Canada however say I!!"[11]

The Colonel and George Macbeth arrived at Port Talbot late in July, saddened by the death of Daniel Macbeth, who had come to England not long before their departure and had drowned at Buffalo on the return trip. Until some provision could be made for their permanent residence they lodged at the home of Jane Hunter. "If it were painful," wrote his friend Edward Ermatinger, "to witness the departure of so distinguished a settler, after a residence of nearly half a century, from the shores of Canada, bowed down with age and infirmities, it was no less distressing to see him return, to seek a humble abode on the outskirts of the magnificent estate, which no longer belonged to him! Here those friends who had been in the habit of visiting him and partaking of his hospitality, while he remained the lordly proprietor of Port Talbot, found him after his return from England, cooped up in a small room, a lodger in the house of Mrs. Hunter, the widow of his old faithful servant Jeffry. This spot, with the house upon it, the Colonel had provided for Jeffry's family, and from this spot he could, through the woods, just catch a glimpse of the valuable property he had parted with to satisfy a debt due to honor only!"[12]

To most people the Colonel had always appeared indifferent to what others thought about him. As the eccentric "hermit of Port Talbot" he was almost a legendary figure, around whom a mass of folklore grew up, long before his death. Sir Francis Head wrote to Lord Glenelg in 1837, after describing his manner of living: "It is of course incomprehensible, some people declare him to be a misanthrope, others say he merely detests women, but all fear him—and I can truly assure your Lordship that this estimable and gentlemanly personage is looked upon rather as a wizzard than a man."[13] Edward Ermatinger, who visited Talbot at the Harrises' in London in the spring of 1850, when he was thought to be dying, found him much concerned that justice be done his memory. Learning that Ermatinger intended to write an account of his life, he talked to him "in a very feeling manner of his past career, and of his desire and endeavors to do right".[14] Published six years after the Colonel's death, Ermatinger's biography is on the whole sympathetic, although he attributes his faults and failures to a lack of religious guidance. Also sympathetic was the short account written by L. C. Kearney and published in 1857. "He possessed an excitable temperament, with a warm heart," Kearney wrote, "a repulsive hauteur, with the kindliest feelings of a generous nature. In fact he was an oddity unknown to himself, but who, when he had once gained a friend, never lost him by any caprice of a disposition not fashioned by nature, but by circumstances which surrounded him in his daily walks through life. He was generous by nature, more than from a love of ostentation; more of a cynic in his manners than he was willing to acknowledge, and viewed the world through a false medium. Hence a good deal of asperity was attributed to a man who possessed much of the sweetness and grace of manners peculiar to a soldier and a well-bred Irishman."[15]

Talbot was a member of the Anglo-Irish nobility, bred in the eighteenth century, some of whose habits of thought he could never discard, even after he had deserted the "follies and falsehoods and restrictions of artificial life" to work at menial tasks and live as a pioneer farmer in the Canadian wilderness. His political ideas were those of an age that was passing, and he fought fiercely the ideas and elements making for change. With an unbending faith in the rightness of aristocratic rule, he regarded democratic ideas as insidious enemies of the proper and orderly way of life. His early concern for the welfare of his settlers was sincere, but it was the concern of a benevolent despot who believed that he had a divine mandate to rule in the best interests of the people. He wished to be regarded as a patriarch, the "Father" of his settlement, surrounded by a grateful, respectful, and submissive populace. The tragedy of his life was that his "children" grew up and rebelled against the parental discipline, and in his unsuccessful efforts to force them into obedience, their respect, if not love, turned to hate. Derided and abused, his cloak of dignity torn to shreds, he shrank ever farther into a shell of choleric harshness, confirmed in the belief that he was beset by evil and self-seeking men, and that the world was disintegrating before the advance of mob rule.

Colonel Talbot was beloved by children, liked and admired by many ladies of wealth or rank, and his friends among the British aristocracy of both sexes were numerous. There are many testimonials to the kindness that he showed to his personal servants and to the labourers on his farm. Writing to Secretary Hillier in the spring of 1827 he told him that one of his men named John Bryers had fallen ill, and he urged him to send some special medicines without delay, "for John is a favourite, and I wish to relieve him as soon as possible".[16] But he could be capricious and harsh, unyielding and unforgiving; and he showed no mercy to his political and personal enemies. He was infuriated by any attempt to deceive him, or any suggestion that he could be influenced by designing men. "Master Cockburn is in luck," he told Hillier, referring to one of his settlers, "perhaps he may consider me under his control, if so he is d—ly mistaken."[17] He was self-righteous; he never admitted that he was in the wrong; he never forgave anyone with whom he quarrelled, even his nephews Julius and Richard Airey. Although rarely accused of unseemly conduct while intoxicated, it is true that, like many others of his time, he often drank to excess. "How often," inquired Sir Peregrine Maitland in the spring of 1826, "has the faithful Jeffry had to put you to bed? If you got to Salmon's on the night of the storm I have no doubt you wanted a little assistance in that way."[18]

The Colonel coveted land, wealth, and power. To achieve his goals he used methods that were sometimes devious, and he rode rough-shod over those who stood in his way; but he was never accused of dishonesty during many years of handling large sums of money derived from the sale of school and Crown lands, or in the location of hundreds of thousands of acres of the lands under his superintendence. Most of his work brought him no pecuniary compensation; his only recompense was in power, the satisfaction of settling the wilderness, and the certainty that his name would live in history. He was greatly disappointed, however, when the area south of the Thames River in Middlesex was made into a separate county in 1851 and given the name of Elgin, the Governor whose policies he abhorred. The previous year Becher had written to the Colonel, then in England, that the movement to divide Middlesex was likely to be successful, "and if I live I mean to try my small influence to get it called the 'County of Talbot', which will at all events be more complimentary to its Founder than naming it 'Elgin'!"[19] But this honour was not to be given the man who had made an unparalleled contribution to the settlement of Upper Canada during the preceding half century.

In the spring of 1852 the Colonel's long and active life was nearing its close. His neighbours sometimes caught glimpses of him, "a feeble old man, bent nearly double, and creeping about the old place, laboriously leaning on a stout walking-stick".[20] It is unlikely that he often left Mrs. Hunter's house to go to his former home, where the old associations stirred bitter memories. But his companion, George Macbeth, came frequently to enjoy the company of the Sanders, and especially that of Anne Gilbert Sanders, an attractive young lady nearly his own age. In a few months they were married. Taking the old man with them they settled in London, where on December 14, 1852, the Colonel made his last will and testament. Daniel Macbeth was now dead, the four Hunter children had received the sums mentioned in the first will, and the debt due Frances Talbot had been paid to her heir. Except for the life annuity to Jane Hunter, which was made a charge upon the estate, everything that Talbot possessed, estimated to be worth £50,000, was left to George Macbeth. None of the Colonel's relatives or friends was remembered in the will.[21]

John Rolph, now Commissioner of Crown Lands, had been trying for some time to obtain possession of Talbot's land records. In April, 1851, a few days after Richard Airey handed them over to Becher, the lawyer was approached by certain settlers who wished to make their annual payments on lands they had bought from the Colonel. Becher consulted Rolph, who said he thought that in the Colonel's absence this work should be done by John B. Askin, the land agent at London, and he asked Becher to give Askin all the necessary documents. A few days later Askin wrote requesting the records. But "all he got, and all he will get", Becher informed Talbot, "were three letters enclosed in a blank envelope with a certification that that was all!! He expected a bushel of books and maps—But they will get none unless you say so—I took care for you politely and properly to say to the department I was ready and willing to go on and finish the work if they had any desire—so the taking it out of my hands is their choosing—and I think it better where it is."[22]

In a memorandum to the Governor and Council, dated March 5, 1852, Rolph recommended that Talbot be required to turn over to his department all the township maps and other land records in his possession. A legislative act, passed in the previous session, which required all settlers to complete their settlement duties before the end of July, made this advisable, Rolph said, because the government had no information as to which locatees in the Talbot Settlement had not yet obtained their patents. The Colonel's advanced age made it even more advisable that he "should now be relieved from the onerous duty which he has so long, and with such manifest advantage to that section of Western Canada so efficiently and so impartially fulfilled, the evidence of which is to be found in the fact that notwithstanding the large numbers of locations in the numerous Townships which have been managed under his superintendence, complaints have been of the rarest possible occurrence."[23]

The Council approved Rolph's recommendation, and it seemed that the long Talbot regime would now end. That he had retained not only the records of his settlement, but also some remnants of his authority there, is apparent from the wording of the memorandum. It spoke of "relieving Colonel Talbot from the further charge" of the lands under his superintendence, and of "a transfer to this Department of the charge" of both lands and records. But the Colonel was too tenacious to give up these regalia while he lived. He still had them when he died on February 5, 1853, in his 82nd year, almost sixty years from the day he first visited the forested site of London in Simcoe's suite. Only his lawyer and friend Henry Becher appears to have visited him during the last weeks of his life. John B. Askin, who in Becher's words was "dying to get" the business of the Talbot Settlement, wrote to Commissioner Rolph on February 7 to inform him of the Colonel's death. He explained that, "as his demise might hereafter occasion difficulties with regard to the locations and public sales made by him in his life time, of the Lands of the Government, and as you perhaps might think it advisable to require the public papers and documents of which he had the possession of, to be placed within your controul [*sic*], I have taken the liberty of giving you the information of his demise."[24]

On February 8 the Colonel's body, alone and unattended except by the driver of the hearse, was borne through the winter's cold on its last journey to Port Talbot. Some of his faithful old settlers noted with sorrow that at St. Thomas the hearse stood outside a tavern while the driver warmed himself at the bar within, and that at Fingal it was left over night in a shed behind Lewis' Hotel. Next day the hearse moved slowly through the snow to Burwell's Corners, and thence through "The Colonel's Wood" to the old house at Port Talbot. For a short time the body rested there, before being taken to the cemetery of St. Peter's Church at Tyrconnel. Behind it came a procession of sleighs bearing a few of the leading men of London and elsewhere, as well as some of Talbot's settlers, who had gathered at Port Talbot. While the mourners stood quietly in the bitter cold the Rev. Mr. Holland of St. Peter's read a brief funeral service.[25] Then the last remains of the Colonel were laid to rest beside those of a young daughter of Colonel and Mrs. Airey, who had died on New Year's Day, 1849.

The graveyard where Talbot lies buried is beautifully situated on the cliff overlooking Lake Erie, and within sound of its waters. George Macbeth and his wife Anne now rest beside him within the wrought-iron fence enclosing the plot. Close by are the graves of Jeffrey and Jane Hunter and two of their children, as well as many of the Talbot settlers, including the Colonel's old enemy, Henry Coyne. Friend and foe, patrician and plebeian, all rest peacefully together, their work living after them in the fruitful countryside that they formed from the wilderness. Above the Colonel's grave a horizontal stone slab bears only the simple inscription:

SACRED
TO THE MEMORY
OF THE
HON. THOMAS TALBOT
FOUNDER OF THE
TALBOT SETTLEMENT

DIED
FEBRUARY 5 A D 1853
AGED 83 YEARS

"Let my soul live, and it shall praise thee; and let thy judgments help me." Psalm cxix, v. 175.

# *Notes*

## Chapter I

[1] Stephen Gwynn, *The Charm of Ireland* (Lond., 1934), pp. 27-31; John Carr, "The Stranger in Ireland; or a Tour . . . in the year 1805", *A Collection of Modern and Contemporary Voyages and Travels* (Lond., 1807), V, p. 24; W. H. Bartlett and M. Addey, *Ireland, Pictorial, Descriptive and Historical* (New York, c1882), II, pp. 59-63; C. L. Adams, *Castles of Ireland* (Lond., 1904), pp. 292-5; Ella MacMahon, *Historic Houses of the United Kingdom* (Lond., 1892), pp. 92-104; Constantia Maxwell, *Country and Town in Ireland under the Georges* (Dundalk, 1949).

[2] C. O. Ermatinger, *The Talbot Regime* (St. Thomas, 1904), p. 6.

[3] *Ibid.*, pp. 5-7; James H. Coyne, ed., *The Talbot Papers* (Trans. of the Royal Society of Canada, 3rd ser., 1907, 1909), I, p. 21.

[4] Arthur Young, A *Tour in Ireland* (Lond., 1780), p. 79.

[5] *Ibid.*, pp. 29 and *passim*. See also W. E. Lecky, A *History of Ireland in the Eighteenth Century* (New York, 1893), I, pp. 277-318; and Carr, *op. cit.*, pp. 34, 64.

[6] Singleton Gardiner to Hillier, Feb. 27, 1823, Public Archives of Canada (hereafter cited as P.A.C.), Upper Canada Sundries.

[7] Anna Jameson, *Winter Studies and Summer Rambles in Canada* (New York, n.d.), II, p. 10.

[8] "Talbot Family", *Encyclopaedia Britannica*, 11th edition.

[9] C. O. Ermatinger, *op. cit.*, p. 8; E. Ermatinger, *Life of Colonel Talbot* (St. Thomas, 1859), p. 1; "Manchester", *Encyclopaedia Britannica*, 11th edition.

[10] Duke of Buckingham and Chandos, *Memoirs of the Court and Cabinets of George the Third* (Lond., 1853), I, p. 339.

[11] *Ibid.*, p. 335.

[12] Phillip Guedalla, *Wellington* (N. Y., 1931), p. 28.

[13] Frances Gerard, *Picturesque Dublin* (Lond., 1898), pp. vii-viii. For the following account of Dublin and Dublin Castle see, in addition to the works on Ireland cited above: M. O. Morris, *Dublin Castle* (Lond., 1889); *Recollections of Dublin Castle and of Dublin Society* (N.Y., 1902); M. F. and B. M. Mansfield, *Romantic Ireland* (Bost., 1905), I, p. 198; Guedalla, *Wellington*, pp. 6-7; and Quebec *Herald*, Mar. 16, July 13, July 27, Oct. 5 (News from Ireland).

[14] Buckingham, *op. cit.*, I, p. 334.

[15] W. D. Powell, "Notice of Mr. Thomas Talbot", P.A.C., Powell Papers, M760.

[16] James A. Froude, *The English in Ireland in the Eighteenth Century* (N.Y., 1874), II, p. 520.

## CHAPTER II

[1] "Canadian Letters . . . 1792 and '93", reprinted from the *Canadian Antiquarian and Numismatic Journal* (Mont., 1912), p. 9.

[2] For the above account of Quebec and Montreal see the following: *Ibid.* pp. 5-23; Quebec *Herald,* Apr. 26, 1790; Quebec *Gazette,* July 9, July 23, Sept. 24, 1789, and Jan. 21, June 3, June 10, 1790, and May 19, May 26, June 2, 1791.

[3] *The Diary of Mrs. John Graves Simcoe,* ed. by J. R. Robertson (Tor., 1911), p. 62.

[4] *Ibid.,* pp. 78-9.

[5] *Ibid.,* pp. 89-92.

[6] Ermatinger, *Life of Colonel Talbot,* p. 14.

[7] Peter Russell to Elizabeth Russell, Aug. 6, 1792, Ontario Archives, Russell Papers.

[8] Mrs. Simcoe, *Diary, passim;* John White, Diary, Toronto Reference Library.

[9] Coyne, *Talbot Papers,* II, pp. 167-8.

[10] Mrs. Simcoe, *Diary,* p. 139; E. A. Cruikshank, ed., *The Corresp. of Lieut. Governor John Graves Simcoe,* 5 vols. (Tor., 1923-31), I, p. 256.

[11] Mrs. Simcoe, *Diary,* p. 148; Littlehales, "Journal from Niagara to Detroit", in *Simcoe Papers,* I, pp. 288-93; "Thames—Its Banks" (Journal of D. W. Smith), *Ontario History,* XLIV (1952), pp. 15-22.

[12] See p. 272 below.

[13] *Simcoe Papers,* I, pp. 308-9, 316, 349, 354, 373-4, 383; V, pp. 50,55, 60, 62, 72; Mrs. Simcoe, *Diary, passim.*

[14] *Simcoe Papers,* V, p. 50.

[15] Simcoe to Hobart, Feb. 11, 1803, P.A.C., Q Papers, Vol. 296, pp. 286-7.

[16] P.A.C., Upper Canada Land Petitions, G, 1 (1793-5), no. 5; Land Book D, Jan. 11, 1798.

[17] Mrs. Simcoe, *Diary, passim.*

[18] Talbot to Simcoe, July 17, 1803, Tor. Ref. Lib., Wolford Simcoe Papers, Vol. I, Bk. 9, p. 81.

[19] Mrs. Simcoe, *Diary,* pp. 211, 214-19.

[20] Ont. Arch., Russell Papers, Jan. 24, 1794.

[21] Mrs. Simcoe, *Diary,* pp. 219-21.

[22] James B. Brown, *Views of Canada* (Edin., 1851), p. 276.

[23] Mrs. Simcoe, *Diary,* p. 221.

[24] *Ibid.,* pp. 173, 227-8.

[25] Talbot to Simcoe, June 26, 1794, Wolford Simcoe Papers, Vol. I, Bk. 4, p. 222.

[26] P.A.C., Cole Simcoe Papers, Misc. (1763-95), Packet Oo.

CHAPTER III

[1] Gt. Brit., Hist. MSS. Com., App. to the 14th Report, Pt. 5, *The Manuscripts of J. B. Fortesque, Esq., Preserved at Dropmore* (Lond., 1894), II, pp. 402, 418, 425-8, 437, 450-3; Buckingham, *Memoirs*, II, p. 243.

[2] *Simcoe Papers*, II, pp. 280, 287.

[3] Talbot to Bathurst, Jan. 21, 1818, Q, Vol. 324, pt. II, p. 440; Ermatinger, *Life*, p. 4.

[4] Stevenson to Simcoe, Apr. 13, 1796, *Simcoe Papers*, IV, p. 244.

[5] "Notice of Mr. Thomas Talbot", Powell Papers, M760.

[6] W. R. Riddell, *The Life of John Graves Simcoe* (Tor., 1926), p. 297.

[7] Stevenson to Russell, Mar. 7, 1798, E. A. Cruikshank and A. F. Hunter, eds., *The Corresp. of the Hon. Peter Russell*, 3 Vols. (Tor., 1932-6), II, p. 114.

[8] P.A.C., Land Book D (1797-1802).

[9] Talbot's Diary, in Coyne, *Talbot Papers*, II, p. 180.

[10] Ermatinger, *The Talbot Regime*, p. 22.

[11] "Notice of Mr. Thomas Talbot", Powell Papers, M760.

[12] Talbot to Simcoe, Nov. 11, 1802, Wolford Simcoe Papers, I, Bk. 9, pp. 89-90.

[13] Ermatinger, *The Talbot Regime*, p. 12, footnote; Talbot to John B. Robinson, May 27, 1849, Robinson Papers, University of Toronto Library.

[14] James H. Coyne, "Address at the Unveiling of the Port Talbot Memorial Cairn", repr. from Ont. Hist. Soc., *Papers and Records*, XXIV (1927), p. 4.

[15] Q, Vol. 293, pp. 248-55.

[16] Jameson, *Winter Studies*, II, p. 11.

[17] Coyne, *Talbot Papers*, I, pp. 76-7.

[18] Ermatinger, *Life*, pp. 14-15. The story refers to Talbot Creek, but this was considered to be a mistake for Kettle Creek.

[19] Ont. Dept. Lands and Forests, Patent Office, Descriptions for patents 701 and 702.

[20] Talbot to Sullivan, Oct. 27, 1802, Q, Vol. 293, p. 255.

[21] Coyne, *Talbot Papers*, II, p. 181. Coyne dated these items 1805, but stated: "This date is not clearly written. It may be 1803 or 1801." Evidence clearly points to the date 1801.

[22] His name appears on these lots on a map of Niagara Township, tentatively dated 1784, in P.A.C.; see also W. Kirby, *Annals of Niagara* (Tor., 1927), p. 73. In the registry office the name M. Berringer (obviously a mistake for M. Bellinger) appears on Lots 68 and 69. Michael Bellinger was living in Niagara Township in 1806; *Upper Canada Gazette*, Nov. 15 and 22, 1806.

[23] P.A.C., Powell Papers, M762. Addison and Backhouse were then living in Niagara Township.

[24] Talbot to Simcoe, Nov. 11, 1802, Wolford Simcoe Papers, I, Bk. 9, pp. 89-90.

[25] Coyne, *Talbot Papers*, I, pp. 76-7.

[26] Nov. 11, 1802, Wolford Simcoe Papers, I, Bk. 9, p. 90.

[27] Simcoe to Hobart, Feb. 11, 1803, Q, Vol. 296, p. 290.

[28] G. C. Paterson, *Land Settlement in Upper Canada* (Ont. Arch., *16th Report*, 1920), p. 92. See also *U. C. Gazette*, May 9, June 30, Aug. 8, 22, and 29, 1801.

[29] Talbot to Simcoe, Nov. 11, 1802, Wolford Simcoe Papers, I, Bk. 9, pp. 89-90.

[30] P.A.C., Petitions, T, 5, no. 6; Ont. Patent Office Registers. He received the following lots: in Townsend, Lots 3 and 7 in the first conc. and Lots 4 and 6 in the second; in Woodhouse, Lot 13 in the third conc.; in Charlotteville, Lot 20 in the seventh conc.

[31] Coyne, *Talbot Papers*, I, pp. 75-7.

[32] Q, Vol. 293, p. 246.

[33] Coyne, *op. cit.*, pp. 77-8.

[34] Talbot to Simcoe, Nov. 11, 1802, Wolford Simcoe Papers, I, Bk. 9, pp. 89-90.

[35] Q, Vol. 293, pp. 248-55.

[36] Wolford Simcoe Papers, I, Bk. 9, pp. 89-90.

[37] Q, Vol. 296, pp. 286-92. See also "Memo. for Gen. Simcoe at his conference with Lord Hobart", in Wolford Simcoe Papers, I, Bk. 9, p. 94. Houghton then included the later townships of Bayham and Malahide.

[38] Q, Vol. 294, pp. 37-40.

[39] P.A.C., G Papers, Vol. 54, Pt. I, p. 90.

## Chapter IV

[1] Talbot to Simcoe, July 17, 1803, Wolford Simcoe Papers, I, Bk. 9, pp. 80-1.

[2] F. C. Hamil, ed., "Schenectady to Michilimackinac, 1765 & 1766; the Journal of John Porteous", Ont. Hist. Soc., *Papers and Records*, XXXIII (1940), p. 86.

[3] Wolford Simcoe Papers, I, Bk. 9, pp. 80-1.

[4] Upper Canada Sundries.

[5] Talbot to Green, Mar. 8, 1804, U. C. Sundries; P.A.C., Lieut. Gov.'s Office, Letter Book, 1802-1805, pp. 215-16.

[6] Mar. 2, 1804, Univ. of West. Ont. Library, Talbot Papers.

[7] Selkirk Diary, Nov. 19, 1803, P.A.C., Selkirk Papers, Vol. 75, p. 19623.

[8] F. C. Hamil, "Lord Selkirk in Upper Canada", Ont. Hist. Soc., *Papers and Records*, XXXVII (1945), pp. 35-48.

[9] Wolford Simcoe Papers, I, Bk. 9, p. 101.

[10] Land Book F, p. 25; Land Petitions, T, 7, no. 16; Ont. Dept. Lands and Forests, Survey Office, Letters Written, Vol. 17, p. 2669; Ermatinger, *Talbot Regime*, p. 34.

[11] Stores issued to Talbot, May 8, 1804, U. C. Sundries; Coyne, *Talbot Papers*, I, pp. 79, 88, 90-3.

[12] Wolford Simcoe Papers, I, Bk. 9, p. 101.

[13] Ont. Survey Office, Letters Written, Vol. 13, pp. 1708-9.

[14] F. C. Hamil, "Lord Selkirk in Upper Canada".

[15] Land Book D, pp. 60-2.

[16] *Ibid.*, p. 224.

[17] W. H. G. Armytage, "Thomas Talbot and Lord Wharncliffe: Some New Letters Hitherto Unpublished", *Ontario History*, XLV (1953), pp. 178-80. Hereafter cited as the *Talbot-Wharncliffe Letters*.

[18] Coyne, *Talbot Papers*, I, p. 97.

[19] J. J. Talman, *Loyalist Narratives from Upper Canada* (Tor., The Champlain Soc., 1946), p. 131.

[20] Ermatinger, *Life*, pp. 29-30.

[21] Land Book G, p. 43; Land Petitions, T, 8, no. 1.

[22] Land Book G, p. 437; Coyne, *Talbot Papers*, I, p. 84, note, II, p. 182; Gore to Russell, Jan. 26, 1808, Ont. Arch., Russell Papers.

[23] Land Book G, p. 331; Land Petitions, T, 8, no. 29; Russell Papers, May 20, 1807.

[24] Macdonell to Selkirk, May 30 and June 22, 1806, Selkirk Papers, Vol. LIV, pp. 14373-4.

[25] Land Petitions, T, 8, no. 39; Land Book G, p. 437. Four or five of these settlers were placed within his original grant.

[26] "Notice of Mr. Thomas Talbot", Powell Papers, M760.

[27] See Lieut.-Gov.'s Office, Letter Book, 1802-1805, pp. 176, 198, 215, 250; *ibid.*, 1806-1811, pp. 35, 63, 100; Ont. Arch., *Twenty-Second Report* (1933), pp. 87, 99, 139.

[28] Ont. Arch., *Eighth Report* (1911), p. 469; Coyne, *Talbot Papers*, I, p. 143.

[29] Q, Vol. 312, Pt. 1, pp. 34-8.

[30] Talbot to Simcoe, Sept. 21, 1804, Wolford Simcoe Papers, I, Bk. 9, p. 104.

[31] Strachan to Gore, May 22, 1817, G. Spragge, ed., *The John Strachan Letter Book* (Tor., 1946), p. 139.

## Chapter V

[1] "Notice of Mr. Thomas Talbot", Powell Papers, M760.

[2] Land Book H, p. 105.

[3] "Notice of Mr. Thomas Talbot", Powell Papers, M760.

[4] Land Book H, pp. 113-15.

[5] York *Gazette*, June 24, 1809, May 12, 1810; *Journals of the House of Assembly*, Ont. Arch., *Ninth Report* (1912), p. 40.

[6] Talbot to Goderich, July 29, 1831, Q, Vol. 358, Pt. 3, pp. 674-9; Land Book I, pp. 174-5.

[7] Burwell to Chewett and Ridout, June 8, 1809, Upper Canada Sundries (with Chewett's of June 20, 1809); Burwell to Chewett and Ridout, July 14, 1809, Ont. Survey Office, Burwell Papers, no. 4; Burwell's diary of Southwold, Yarmouth and Houghton, 1809, Ont. Arch., Crown Lands Papers, Shelf 73, Box 5 (under date June 14).

[8] U. C. Sundries, Dec. 10, 1809; Land Book H, pp. 223-5; Land Petitions, M, 9, no. 126, and R, 8, no. 27; Council notice May 1, 1807, in York *Gazette*, Jan. 6, 1808.

[9] Watson, "Statement of Facts", Mar. 22, 1811, Land Petitions, W, 10, no. 34.

[10] Land Book H, pp. 301-2.

[11] Diary of Survey of Westminster, by Watson, Ont. Arch., Crown Land Papers, Shelf 73, Box 7.

[12] Watson, "Statement of Facts".

[13] May 31, 1811, Coyne, *Talbot Papers*, I, p. 120.

[14] Land Book H, pp. 339-40.

[15] Land Petitions, S, 9, nos. 128-30.

[16] Nichol to Hillier, Oct. 19, 1820, U. C. Sundries.

[17] Talbot to Goderich, July 29, 1831, Q, Vol. 358, Pt. 3, pp. 674-9.

[18] Ont. Arch., Crown Lands Papers, Shelf 57, no. 8; see also Ridout to Brock, Apr. 13, 1812, Land Petitions, T, 10, no. 19.

[19] Watson, "Statement of Facts"; Land Petitions, W, 10, no. 1.

[20] *Ibid.*, no. 8; Land Book I, p. 7.

[21] Talbot to Watson, March 2, 1811, Coyne, *Talbot Papers*, I, p. 107. See also Watson's memorial, Land Book I, p. 67.

[22] Watson, "Statement of Facts".

[23] May 13, 1811, Coyne, *op. cit.*, I, p. 115. See also Nichol to Talbot, May 31, 1811, *ibid.*, p. 120.

[24] March 14, 1811, *ibid.*, p. 108.

[25] Mar. 8, 1811, Ont. Arch., Crown Lands Papers, Shelf 96.

[26] March 12, 1811, Coyne, *op. cit.*, I, pp. 107-8.

[27] March 16, 1811, *ibid.*, p. 110.

[28] March 15, 1811, *ibid.*

[29] April 27, 1811, *ibid.*, pp. 113-14.

[30] May 3, 1811, *ibid.*, p. 115.

[31] May 13, 1811, *ibid.*, p. 117.

[32] Land Book I, pp. 139-40.

[33] Ont. Survey Office, Letters Received, Vol. 17, pp. 4010-12.

[34] Coyne, *Talbot Papers*, I, p. 123; Land Petitions, B, 10, Pt. 1, no. 69.

[35] Coyne, *op. cit.*, I, p. 126.

[36] Land Book, I, pp. 192-6.

[37] Coyne, *op. cit.*, I, pp. 135-6; Land Book I, pp. 174-5; see also Talbot to Ridout, Mar. 22, 1812, Ont. Arch., Crown Lands Papers, Shelf 96.

[38] Coyne, *Talbot Papers*, I, pp. 144-5; Ridout to Brock, April 13, 1812, in Land Petitions, T, 10, no. 19.

[39] Coyne, *op. cit.*, pp. 148-9.
[40] Land Petitions, T, 10, no. 19.
[41] Coyne, *op. cit.*, I, p. 146.
[42] Land Book L, p. 197.
[43] Ridout's return of lands, Oct. 20, 1815, Q, Vol. 319; p. 132.
[44] Talbot to Gore, Mar. 20, 1813, Coyne, *op. cit.*, I, pp. 186-7.
[45] Mar. 20, 1813, Tor. Ref. Lib., Powell Papers, A27.

## Chapter VI

[1] Powell to Gore, Sept. 28, 1809, Gore Correspondence, Tor. Ref. Lib., Powell Papers, A30.
[2] Ermatinger, *Talbot Regime*, p. 50.
[3] Coyne, *Talbot Papers*, I, pp. 151-2.
[4] Powell to Gore, Apr. 12, 1820, Powell Papers, A30.
[5] Coyne, *op. cit.*, I, pp. 152-7.
[6] *Ibid.*, pp. 158-9.
[7] *Ibid.*, pp. 160-5.
[8] *Ibid.*, p. 189.
[9] *Ibid.*, pp. 189-90.
[10] *Ibid.*, p. 193.
[11] *Ibid.*, pp. 195-6.
[12] Ermatinger, *Talbot Regime*, pp. 79-80.
[13] *Ibid.*, pp. 73-8, 341-4.
[14] Frances Stewart, *Our Forest Home* (Mont., 1902), pp. 92-3.
[15] Sir James E. Alexander, *L'Acadie* (Lond., 1849), I, p. 146.
[16] Ermatinger, *Life*, pp. 48-9.
[17] P.A.C., C Papers, Vol. 685, p. 154.
[18] Ermatinger, *Talbot Regime*, pp. 83-6.
[19] *Upper Canada Gazette*, Suppl., June 3, 1824.
[20] Ermatinger, *Talbot Regime*, pp. 87, 340-6.
[21] York *Gazette*, June 3, 1815; Ont. Arch., *Twenty-Second Report* (1933), p. 139.

## Chapter VII

[1] Talbot memorial, Apr. 8, 1813, P.A.C., State Papers, Talbot portfolio; Q, Vol. 398, Pt. 1, p. 100; Land Book I, pp. 236, 241-3; Powell to Gore, Mar. 4, 1815, Tor. Ref. Lib., Powell Papers, A 30.
[2] Q, Vol. 319, pp. 126-30, 147-50.
[3] *Ibid.*, pp. 124-5.
[4] Land Book I, pp. 386-7.
[5] Ont. Survey Office, Burwell Papers, nos. 48-9.
[6] Land Book I, pp. 386-7.
[7] Gore to Talbot, June 7, 1817, U.C. Sundries; Bathurst to Smith, Feb. 28, 1818, Upper Canada, *Sessional Papers*, 1836, App. no. 22, p.7.
[8] Ridout to Loring, Mar. 13, 1815, U.C. Sundries.

[9] Ridout to Gore, Dec. 23, 1815, Q, Vol. 398, Pt. I, pp. 106-8.

[10] *Ibid.*, pp. 109-10; Ont. Survey Office, Letters Received, Vol. 17, pp. 3094-4000.

[11] McGill to Gore, Mar. 8, 1817, enclosed with Gore to Talbot, June 7, 1817, U. C. Sundries.

[12] Cameron to Talbot, Mar. 20, 1817, Q, Vol. 322, Pt. 2, p. 359.

[13] State Papers, Talbot portfolio.

[14] Land Petitions, T, 11, no. 32 (Aug. 5, 1817).

[15] Talbot to Hillier, Feb. 17, 1824, U. C. Sundries; Coyne, *Talbot Papers*, II, pp. 89-93; Petit. of T. Burgar, Nov. 14, 1833, Land Petitions, B, 18, no. 142.

[16] Memo. of McGill, Aug. 13, 1816, State Papers, Talbot portfolio; Land Book J, p. 1.

[17] Munro to Fuller, Nov. 28, 1879, Ont. Arch., Munro Papers; Land Petitions, B, 12, no. 235c (Jan. 3, 1820).

[18] Powell to Gore, Mar. 4, 1815, Tor. Ref. Lib., Powell Papers, A 30.

[19] May 5, 1845, Land Petitions, T, 3, no. 25.

[20] Land Book J, pp. 211-13, 217.

[21] Gore to Talbot, June 7, 1817, U. C. Sundries.

[22] Jan. 11, 1818, Powell Papers, A 27.

[23] Coyne, *Talbot Papers*, II, pp. 69-74, 185-90.

[24] John S. Brock to Daniel D. Brock, Sept. 22, 1817, Ont. Arch., Tupper Papers.

[25] Spragge, *Strachan Letter Book*, p. 146.

[26] Land Book J, p. 257.

[27] *Ibid.*, pp. 259-62.

[28] Gore to Powell, Jan. 11, 1818, Powell Papers, A 27; Jan. 18, 1818, *Talbot-Wharncliffe Letters*, p. 180.

[29] Halton to Claus, Oct. 12, 1818, P.A.C., Claus Papers, Vol. 17, pp. 450-1.

[30] Gore to Gordon, Jan. 26, 1818, Q, Vol. 324, Pt. 1, p. 112.

[31] Powell Papers, A 27.

[32] *Ibid.*

[33] Claus Papers, Vol. 17, pp. 450-1.

[34] Gore to Powell, Mar. 15 and Aug. 5, 1818, Powell Papers, A 27.

[35] *Ibid.*

[36] Fanny Kemble, "Old Woman's Gossip, XIX", *Atlantic Monthly*, XXXIX (Feb., 1877), p. 217.

[37] State Papers, Talbot portfolio; extract in Q, Vol. 358, Pt. 3, pp. 685-6.

[38] Land Book J, p. 320.

[39] MacMahon to Ridout, Apr. 30, 1818, Ont. Arch., Crown Lands Papers, Shelf 57, Box 8; McDonell to Jarvis, June 13, 1818, U. C. Sundries.

[40] Powell to Gore, Aug. 5, 1818, Powell Papers, A 30.

[41] Strachan to Gore, Dec. 8, 1818, Spragge, *Strachan Letter Book*, p. 182.

[42] Dec. 6, 1818, Powell Papers, A 27.

[43] Spragge, *op. cit.*, p. 139.

[44] Land Book K, pp. 344-5, 541-2; Talbot to Hillier, Aug. 13, and Dec. 20, 1822, U. C. Sundries.

[45] Land Book M, p. 34; Land Book N, pp. 81-2, 230; Land Petitions, M, 14, no. 29 (1824); Talbot to Hillier, Mar. 19, 1824, U. C. Sundries; Lieut.-Gov.'s Office, Letters of the Sec., July 1823-June 1824, p. 170; *ibid.*, 1826, pp. 88, 157.

[46] *U. C. Gazette*, Oct. 22, 1818.

[47] Q, Vol. 324, Pt. 1, p. 136, and Pt. 2, pp. 245-6; Maitland to Hillier, U. C. Sundries, Corresp., undated, M-Z; Land Petitions, T, 18, no. 66 (1834), and T, 20, no. 34 (1836); R. Talbot to Hillier, Nov. 27, 1822, U. C. Sundries; Burwell's Diary for Lond. Township, Ont. Arch., Crown Lands Papers, Shelf 72, Box 6; Ont. Survey Office, Burwell Papers, nos. 69-70.

[48] Burwell Papers, no. 65; Land Book K, pp. 13, 17.

[49] Burwell Papers, no. 82; Land Book K, p. 188; Talbot to Ridout, Apr. 22, 1819, Ont. Arch., Crown Lands Papers, Shelf 97.

[50] Talbot to Hillier, July 2, 1819, U. C. Sundries, Corresp., undated, M-Z; Burwell Papers, no. 71.

[51] Land Book K, p. 486.

[52] Ridout to Talbot, Feb. 24, 1817, Q, Vol. 324, Pt. 1, p. 178; Talbot to Ridout, Feb. 28, 1817, Ont. Arch., Crown Lands Papers, Shelf 96; Ridout to Cameron, Mar. 17, 1817, and Talbot to Ridout, Mar. 18, 1817, U. C. Sundries.

[53] Upper Canada, Assembly, *Sessional Papers*, 1836, App. no. 22, pp. 7-8.

[54] Land Book K, p. 379; Land Book L, p. 35; Talbot's memorial, Mar. 31, 1820, State Papers, Talbot portfolio; Powell to Hillier, Apr. 5, 1820, U. C. Sundries; draft in Powell Papers, M760.

[55] Upper Canada, Assembly, *Sessional Papers*, 1836, App. no. 22, pp. 7-8.

[56] Ridout to Hillier, Apr. 3, 1820, U. C. Sundries.

[57] Talbot to Hillier, Oct. 6, 1820, U. C. Sundries.

[58] Oct. 28, 1820, Q, Vol. 331, p. 169.

[59] Hillier to Clerk of Council, June 21, 1821, State Papers, Talbot portfolio.

[60] Land Book K, p. 487.

## Chapter VIII

[1] "Notice of Mr. Thomas Talbot", P.A.C., Powell Papers, M760.

[2] Munro to Fuller, Nov. 28, 1879, Ont. Arch., Munro Papers; A. McKellar, "The Old 'Bragh', or Hand Mill", Ont. Hist. Soc., *Papers and Records*, III (1901), pp. 170-9.

[3] Kingston *Chronicle*, Dec. 10, 1819.

[4] Robertson to Maitland, Nov. 27, 1819, U. C. Sundries; Land Petitions (1819), B, 12, no. 235h.

[5] *Ibid.*, nos. 235a and 235g.

[6] Draft of Powell's report for the Council, P.A.C., Powell Papers, M760.

[7] Land Book K, p. 357.

[8] Land Book J, pp. 259-62; Spragge, *Strachan Letter Book*, p. 146.

[9] Land Petitions, B, 12, no. 235, and A, 12, no. 111; Powell Papers, M760.

[10] Land Book K, p. 379; Land Book L, p. 35; Talbot's memorial, Mar. 31, 1820, State Papers, Talbot portfolio; Powell to Hillier, Apr. 5, 1820, U. C. Sundries.

[11] Land Petitions, A, 12, no. 111.

[12] Land Book L, pp. 35-9; Q, Vol. 331, p. 159; "Notice of Mr. Thomas Talbot", Powell Papers M760; Ont. Arch., Crown Lands Papers, Shelf 57, Box 8; Mar. 12 and 17, 1821, U. C. Sundries.

[13] State Papers, Talbot portfolio; Q, Vol. 331, pp. 161-7; Land Book L, pp. 96-9.

[14] U. C. Sundries, Aug. 29, 1821; McMahon to Talbot, Sept. 10, 1821, Lieut.-Gov.'s Office, Letter Book, 1821-1822, p. 86.

[15] Sept. 6 and 21, 1821, U. C. Sundries.

[16] Hillier to Talbot, Oct. 14, 1822, Lieut.-Gov.'s Office, Letter Book, 1822-1823, p. 77.

[17] Mar. 19, 1824, U. C. Sundries; Lieut.-Gov.'s Office, Letter Book, 1823-1824, p. 192.

[18] Talbot to Maitland, July 24, 1821, U. C. Sundries; Report of Receiver-General, July 27, 1821, State Papers, Talbot portfolio; Powell, Report on Talbot Settlement, Dec. 31, 1834, U. C. Sundries.

[19] Q, Vol. 332, Pt. 2, pp. 519-37.

[20] Gore to Powell, Apr. 10, 1822, Tor. Ref. Lib., Powell Papers, Gore Corresp. (1809-1828), A 28.

[21] Bathurst to Maitland, Apr. 9, 1822, P.A.C., State Book H, pp. 31-2.

[22] Powell to Mrs. Powell, Apr. 18 and 20, 1822, P.A.C., Powell Papers, M763.

[23] "Notice of Mr. Thomas Talbot", *ibid.*, M760.

[24] Anon. letter to Knox, Feb. 2, 1792, and Simcoe to Dundas, Sept. 27, 1792, P.A.C., Cole Simcoe Papers, Miscell. (1763-95), packet Ss; Littlehales to Powell, Simcoe Papers (MSS.), Vol. 5 (1796-1806), pp. 299-300.

## Chapter IX

[1] July 12, 1822, *Talbot-Wharncliffe Letters*, pp. 182-3.

[2] Oct. 24, 1822, *ibid.*, pp. 183-6.

[3] July 12, 1822, *ibid.*, pp. 182-3.

[4] July 12 and Oct. 24, 1822, *ibid.*, pp. 182-6.

[5] Maitland to Bathurst, June 29, 1822, Q, Vol. 331, pp. 145-56.

[6] Bathurst to Maitland (extract), U. C. Sundries, Feb. 10, 1823; letter in G, Vol. 60, pp. 78-81; Hillier to Talbot, Feb. 8, 1823, Lieut.-Gov.'s Office, Secretary's Letters, May 1822-July 1823, pp. 146-7.

[7] Bathurst to Maitland, G, Vol. 60, pp. 78-81; Land Petitions, T, 3, no. 25 (May 5, 1845).

[8] *Talbot-Wharncliffe Letters*, pp. 183-6.

[9] *Ibid.*, pp. 186-7.

[10] Gore to Powell, June 26, 1823, Tor. Ref. Lib., Powell Papers, A 28.

[11] *Talbot-Wharncliffe Letters*, pp. 188-9.

[12] *Ibid.*, pp. 186-7.

[13] *Ibid.*, p. 188.

[14] *Ibid.*, pp. 189-90.

[15] Q, Vol. 359, pp. 75-6.

[16] Q, Vol. 340, Pt. 2, pp. 422-3.

[17] G, Vol. 62, p. 163.

[18] Talbot to Hillier, Aug. 6, 1824, U. C. Sundries.

[19] *Colonial Advocate*, Aug. 5, 1824.

[20] *Ibid.*, July 29, Aug. 19 and 26, Sept. 2 and 16, 1824, and Apr. 7, 1825; Wolford Simcoe Papers, I, Bk. 9, p. 139. See also York *Weekly Register*, Dec. 30, 1824, and Mar. 3, 1825; *Talbot-Wharncliffe Letters*, p. 191.

[21] Talbot to Hillier, Feb. 7, 1827, U. C. Sundries.

[22] June 24, 1825, *ibid.*

[23] July 1, 1825, *ibid.*

[24] Talbot to Hillier, Mar. 7, 1826, U. C. Sundries.

[25] Nov. 23, 1826, *ibid.*

[26] Apr. 24, 1827, *ibid.*

[27] Sept. 13, (1827), U. C. Sundries, Corresp., undated, M-Z; Coyne, *Talbot Papers*, II, p. 170.

[28] *Colonial Advocate*, Jan. 10 and Feb. 21, 1828.

[29] Q, Vol. 350, Pt. 2, pp. 416-17, G, Suppl. Vol. (1794-1841), no. 66.

[30] Q, Vol. 353, Pt. 3, p. 420; G1, Vol. 65, pp. 404-7.

[31] Q, Vol. 352, pp. 136-7. See also Q, Vol. 351, p. 98.

[32] Q, Vol. 352, pp. 228, 237.

[33] Q, Vol. 352, pp. 235-41. See also *ibid.*, pp. 228-34.

[34] Nov. 9, 1829, State Papers, Talbot portfolio; Q, Vol. 352, pp. 242-3.

[35] Richard's Report, *Imperial Blue Books on Affairs Relating to Canada*, III (1830-1833), no. 334, p. 6; G1, Vol. 67, pp. 66-9.

[36] Q, Vol. 358, Pt. 3, pp. 680-4.

[37] *Ibid.*, pp. 674-9.

## Chapter X

[1] Land Petitions, T, 14, no. 58 (1821); Talbot to Hillier, July 26, 1821, U. C. Sundries; Ont. Survey Office, Burwell Papers, nos. 91-5; Burwell to Hillier, May 30 and July 26, 1820, U. C. Sundries.

[2] Land Book L, pp. 491-2; Lieut-Gov.'s Office, Secretary's Letters, July 1823-June 1824, p. 89; Talbot to Hillier, Dec. 12, 1823, U. C. Sundries.

[3] Talbot to Hillier, Feb. 20, 1824, U. C. Sundries.

[4] Matthews to Hillier, Jan. 25, 1823, Matthews' portfolio, U. C. Sundries.

[5] Feb. 20, 1824, U. C. Sundries.

[6] Hillier to Ridout, Mar. 2, 1824, Ont. Arch., Crown Lands Papers, Shelf 57, Box 8. See also Talbot to Hillier, Dec. 24, 1824, *ibid.*, Shelf 97.

[7] Talbot to Hillier, Mar. 4, 1824, U. C. Sundries; Maitland to Hillier, Mar. 17 (1824), U.C. Sundries, Corresp., undated, M-Z; Coyne, *Talbot Papers,* II, p. 94; Lieut.-Gov.'s Office, Secretary's Letters, July 1823-June 1824, p. 192.

[8] Talbot to Hillier, May 7, 1824, U. C. Sundries.

[9] Powell to Maitland, Oct. 9, 1824, *ibid.*

[10] Lieut.-Gov.'s Office, Secretary's Letters, July 1824-April 1825, pp. 85-6; Q, Vol. 336, Pt. 2, pp. 517-18.

[11] Talbot to Hillier, Nov. 24, 1824, U. C. Sundries.

[12] Coyne, *Talbot Papers,* II, p. 94; Lieut.-Gov.'s Office, Sec. Letters, July 1824-April 1825, pp. 115-19.

[13] Talbot to Colborne, Oct. 28, 1830, U. C. Sundries.

[14] Land Book O, p. 462.

[15] Chewett to McMahon, Dec. 27, 1832, U. C. Sundries.

[16] Talbot to Parke, Apr. 1, 1843, Crown Lands Papers, Shelf 100.

[17] June 27 and Aug. 6, 1824, U. C. Sundries.

[18] Nov. 8, 1824, and Jan. 14 and 26, 1825, *ibid.*

[19] Nov. 24, 1824, *ibid.*

[20] State Book H, pp. 30-2; Talbot to Hillier, June 24, 1825, U. C. Sundries; Talbot to Ridout, May 3, 1826, Crown Lands Papers, Shelf 97.

[21] Burwell Papers, no. 116.

[22] Talbot to Hillier, Aug. 6, 1824, U. C. Sundries.

[23] Lieut.-Gov.'s Office, Secretary's Letters, July 1824-April 1825, p. 223.

[24] July 1, 1825, U. C. Sundries.

[25] Talbot to Hillier, Aug. 31, 1825, Crown Lands Papers, Shelf 97; Talbot to Ridout, Dec. 2, 1825, *ibid.*

[26] Talbot to Hillier, Dec. 30, 1825, U. C. Sundries; Lieut.-Gov.'s Office, Sec. Letters, 1826, p. 15.

[27] Talbot to Colborne, Oct. 28, 1830, and Robinson to Mudge, Nov. 10, 1830, U. C. Sundries.

[28] Nov. 9, 1829, State Papers, Talbot portfolio.

[29] Coyne, *Talbot Papers,* II, pp. 108-9.

[30] Burwell Papers, Nos. 169-70.

[31] Coyne, *Talbot Papers,* II, p. 115.

[32] *Ibid.*, pp. 154-8. Elmsley finally decided not to buy.

[33] Talbot to Strachan, June 30, 1831, Ont. Arch., Strachan Papers.

[34] Coyne, *op. cit.*, p. 158; Talbot to Allan, July 21, 1833, Toronto Ref. Lib., William Allan Papers.

[35] Talbot to Colborne, Nov. 17, 1833, U. C. Sundries.

[36] Talbot to Allan, Aug. 7, 1835, William Allan Papers.

[37] Sandwich *Canadian Emigrant,* Aug. 22, 1835.

[38] John Robertson, Apr. 21, 1834, Ont. Arch., Miscell. Papers.

[39] Coyne, *Talbot Papers,* II, pp. 162-3.

[40] Sandwich *Canadian Emigrant,* Dec. 22, 1835.

[41] *Statutes of the Province of Upper Canada,* Revised by J. Nickalls (Kingston, 1831), pp. 412-13; Matthews to Ridout, Mar. 8, 1826, Crown

Lands Papers, Shelf 97; *Colonial Advocate*, Mar. 23, 1826; Talbot to Hillier, Mar. 7, 1826, U. C. Sundries.

42 Burwell's Diary of Survey, Crown Lands Papers, Shelf 72, Box 6; Burwell to Ridout, June 29, 1826, U. C. Sundries; Coyne, *Talbot Papers*, II, p. 103; Talbot to Hillier, Apr. 15, 1827, U. C. Sundries.

43 Talbot to Hillier, Apr. 24, 1827, *ibid.*

47 Sandwich *Canadian Emigrant*, Feb. 1, 1834.

45 Land Book N, p. 136.

46 *Gore Gazette*, Nov. 24, 1827.

47 Sandwich *Canadian Emigrant*, Feb 1, 1834.

48 Toronto *Patriot*, July 10, 1835.

49 F. C. Hamil, "Colonel Talbot and the Early History of London", *Ontario History*, XLIII (1951), 159-75.

50 Jameson, *Winter Studies*, II, p. 14.

## Chapter XI

1 G. F. Plant, *Oversea Settlement* . . . (Lond., 1951), pp. 24-6; Norman Macdonald, *Canada, 1763-1841* (Lond., 1939), pp. 19-22.

2 *Talbot-Wharncliffe Letters*, pp. 186-7.

3 *Ibid.*, pp. 189-90; Coyne, *Talbot Papers*, II, pp. 92-3.

4 Report of the Select Committee on Emigration, May 26, 1826, Kingston *Chronicle*, Sept. 1 and 8, 1826; Edwin C. Guillet, *The Great Migration* (Tor., 1937), pp. 22-3, 209, 225.

5 Quoted in the Report of the Select Committee on Emigration, 1826, Kingston *Chronicle*, Sept. 8, 1826.

6 Guillet, *op. cit.*, pp. 168-9, 209. See also Kingston *Chronicle*, June 24, 1825.

7 Plant, *op. cit.*, pp. 29-31; Reports of the Select Committee on Emigration, 1826, 1827; Macdonald, *op. cit.*, pp. 19-21.

8 Mackenzie to Goderich, printed in York *Patriot*, Jan. 4, 1833; Kingston *Chronicle*, Dec. 12, 1829, June 19 and 26, July 24, 1830.

9 Kingston *Patriot*, May 1, 1832.

10 *Talbot-Wharncliffe Letters*, pp. 192-5.

11 Kingston *Chronicle*, July 2, 1831.

12 Coyne, *Talbot Papers*, II, pp. 111-12.

13 *Ibid.*, pp. 112-14.

14 Kingston *Chronicle*, May 14 and 28, July 23, Aug. 20, Sept. 3 and 17, 1831; Macdonald, *Canada*, p. 24.

15 Lieut.-Gov.'s Office, Sec. Letters, Jan.-Oct., 1831, p. 179.

16 Sandwich *Canadian Emigrant*, Sept. 29, 1832.

17 *Ibid.*, Sept. 29, 1832. See also Report of the Emigration Commissioners, Mar. 30, 1832, in Kingston *Chronicle*, May 19, 1832.

18 Sandwich *Canadian Emigrant*, Sept. 29, 1832.

19 Kingston *Chronicle*, May 12, 1832; Coyne, *op. cit.*, II, pp. 115, 139.

20 *Upper Canada Gazette*, July 12, 1832.

21 Kingston *Patriot*, June 19, 1832.

[22] Colborne to Goderich, Jan. 10, 1833, in *Colonial Advocate*, Oct. 10, 1835; Sandwich *Canadian Emigrant*, Mar. 8, 1832.

[23] Kingston *Chronicle*, May 19, 1832.

[24] Kingston *Patriot*, Apr. 24, 1832; Kingston *Chronicle*, May 26, 1832; Guillet, *op. cit.*, pp. 25-7.

[25] Kingston *Chronicle*, May 26, June 2, 9, and 16, 1832.

[26] *Ibid.*, June 2, 16, 23, 1832; Guillet, *op. cit.*, p. 158; Kingston *Patriot*, June 5, 1832.

[27] *Ibid.*, June 19, 1832; Kingston *Chronicle*, June 12 and 23, 1832.

[28] Coyne, *Talbot Papers*, II, p. 140.

[29] *Ibid.*, pp. 140-3.

[30] Robinson to Rowan, Aug. 13, 1832, U. C. Sundries.

[31] Reprinted in York *Canadian Freeman*, Oct. 26, 1832.

[32] Colborne to Goderich, Jan. 10, 1833, in *Colonial Advocate*, Oct. 10, 1833.

[33] Coyne, *op. cit.*, II, p. 111.

[34] *Ibid.*, pp. 115-16.

[35] *Ibid.*, pp. 141, 144; Evidence before the Committee on Grievances, York *Correspondence and Advocate*, June 11, 1835.

[36] Coyne, *Talbot Papers*, II, pp. 150-1.

[37] *Ibid.*, p. 152.

[38] Sandwich *Canadian Emigrant*, Nov. 30, 1833.

[39] *Correspondent and Advocate*, June 11, 1835.

[40] Sandwich *Canadian Emigrant*, Nov. 15, 1834.

[41] *Upper Canada Gazette*, May 29, 1834.

## Chapter XII

[1] John S. Brock to Daniel D. Brock, Sept., 1817, Ont. Arch., Tupper Papers.

[2] Quoted in Ermatinger, *Life*, pp. 64-5.

[3] Univ. of Western Ont., Library, Autobiography of Joseph Elson.

[4] Q, Vol. 398, Pt. 1, pp. 44-5.

[5] William Baby, *Souvenirs of the Past* (Windsor, 1896), p. 152.

[6] *Kent County Commemorative Biographical Record* (Tor., 1904), p. 837.

[7] Wm. Proudfoot, "Diary", Ont. Hist. Soc., *Papers and Records*, XXVII (1931), under date Sept. 1, 1834.

[8] St. Thomas *Liberal*, Mar. 14, 1833.

[9] For the following anecdotes see Ermatinger, *Talbot Regime*, ch. 36, and L. C. Kearney, *The Life of Colonel the Late Honorable Thomas Talbot* (Chatham, 1857).

[10] Talbot to Hillier, Oct. 6, 1820, U. C. Sundries.

[11] Q, Vol. 398, Pt. 1, pp. 44-5.

[12] Talbot to Hillier, Aug. 13 and Dec. 20, 1822, U. C. Sundries.

[13] Talbot to Hillier, June 24, 1825, *ibid.*

[14] Talbot to Hillier, Nov. 16, 1826, and Mar. 1, 1827, *ibid.*; Robinson to Hillier, Nov. 27, 1826, *ibid.*

[15] Land Petitions, T, 14, no. 81.

[16] Q, Vol. 378, Pt. 1, p. 92.

[17] Munro to Fuller, Nov. 28, 1879, Ont. Arch., Munro Papers.

CHAPTER XIII

[1] R. Gourlay, *Statistical Account of Upper Canada* (Lond., 1822), I, p. 577. For complaints see *ibid.*, pp. 340-7, etc.

[2] John Howison, *Sketches of Upper Canada* (Edinburgh, 1822), pp. 184, 188-90.

[3] Boulton to Hillier, Jan. 23, 1823, enclosed with Jan. 27, 1823, U.C. Sundries; Burwell to Hillier, Jan. 27, Gardiner to Hillier, Feb. 27, and Gardiner to Maitland, May 15, 1823, *ibid.*

[4] Robinson to Maitland, Dec. 2, 1824, *ibid.*

[5] Petit. of G. Willson, Nov. 4, 1824, *ibid.*

[6] D. F. McOuat, ed., "The Diary of William Graves", *Ont. Hist.*, XLIII (1951), p. 15.

[7] W. L. Mackenzie, *Sketches of Canada* (Lond., 1833), p. 112.

[8] Matthews to Hillier, Nov. 24, 1820, Matthews' portfolio, U.C. Sundries. See also his of Oct. 31 and Dec. 23, *ibid.*

[9] Matthews to Ridout, May 14, 1821, Crown Lands Papers, Shelf 97; Matthews to Maitland, Oct. 14, 1822, Matthews' portfolio, U.C. Sundries; *U.C. Gazette*, May 21, 1821.

[10] Matthews to Ridout, May 19, 1821, Crown Lands Papers, Shelf 97.

[11] Matthews to Hillier, Nov. 27, 1820, and May 8, 1823, Matthews' portfolio, U.C. Sundries.

[12] York *Weekly Register*, July 17, Aug. 9, Sept. 4 and 11, Oct. 2, Nov. 20, 1823, and Jan. 1, 1824.

[13] *U.C. Gazette*, Apr. 22, 1824.

[14] Coyne, *Talbot Papers*, I, p. 110.

[15] *Ibid.*, pp. 90-1.

[16] Matthews to Hillier, Dec. 23, 1820, Matthews' portfolio, U.C. Sundries.

[17] *Colonial Advocate*, July 1, 1824.

[18] St. Thomas *Liberal*, Nov. 29, 1832.

[19] Mar. 19, 1824, U.C. Sundries.

[20] For the following account of the election see W. L. Mackenzie, "Recollections of the West on a trip to the Talbot Settlement", *Colonial Advocate*, Sept. 2, 1824.

[21] *Ibid.*, July 29, 1824.

[22] *Ibid.*, Sept. 2, 1824.

[23] Talbot to Hillier, July 23, 1824, U.C. Sundries.

[24] Talbot to Hillier, Aug. 6, 1824, *ibid.*

[25] Talbot to Hillier, Nov. 26, 1824, Matthews' portfolio, *ibid.*

[26] *Colonial Advocate*, Apr. 18, 1825.

[27] Talbot to Hillier, Apr. 15 (1825), Corresp. undated, M-Z, U.C. Sundries.

[28] *Colonial Advocate,* Dec. 29, 1825, Jan. 5 and 19, 1826.

[29] *Ibid.,* Jan. 4, Feb. 8, Sept. 6, 1827; *Upper Canada Loyalist,* Dec. 30, 1826; Kingston *Chronicle,* Mar. 9 and 16, 1827; Matthews to Bayham, Feb. 7, 1827, Matthews' portfolio, U.C. Sundries.

[30] Talbot to Hillier, Apr. 11, 1827, U.C. Sundries.

[31] Matthews to Mudge, Jan. 27, 1828, *ibid.*

[32] *Colonial Advocate,* May 22, June 6, and Dec. 11, 1828.

[33] York *Canadian Freeman,* Apr. 16, 1829.

## Chapter XIV

[1] St. Thomas *Liberal,* Nov. 29, 1832.

[2] *Talbot-Wharncliffe Letters,* pp. 192-5.

[3] See the biography of Wharncliffe in *Dictionary of National Biography.*

[4] Coyne, *Talbot Papers,* II, pp. 140-1.

[5] A. Dunham, *Political Unrest in Upper Canada, 1815-1836* (Lond., 1927), p. 132.

[6] Kingston *Patriot,* Mar. 6, 1832.

[7] Coyne, *Talbot Papers,* II, p. 134.

[8] *Colonial Advocate,* Mar. 15, 1832.

[9] Coyne, *op. cit.,* II, p. 117; Sandwich *Canadian Emigrant,* Apr. 7, 1832; *Colonial Advocate,* Mar. 28, 1832.

[10] *Ibid.,* Apr. 5, 1832.

[11] *Ibid.,* Mar. 28, 1832.

[12] *Ibid.,* Sept. 26, 1833. See also Sandwich *Can. Emigrant,* Apr. 7, 1832.

[13] This and the following account of the St. George's Day meeting is based on documents in Coyne, *Talbot Papers,* II, pp. 117-38.

[14] Q, Vol. 374, Pt. 3, p. 608.

[15] York *Can. Freeman,* May 10, 1832.

[16] Reprinted in Coyne, *op. cit.,* p. 136.

[17] Reprinted in *Colonial Advocate,* June 14, 1832.

[18] St. Thomas *Liberal,* Nov. 29, 1832.

[19] *Ibid.,* Nov. 29, 1832.

[20] *Ibid.,* Dec. 13, 1832.

## Chapter XV

[1] Thomas Need, *Six Years in the Bush . . .* (Lond., 1838), p. 17.

[2] St. Thomas *Liberal,* Jan. 10, 1833.

[3] Coyne, *Talbot Papers,* II, p. 151.

[4] St. Thomas *Liberal,* Jan. 24, 1833.

[5] *Ibid.,* Feb. 14, 1833.

[6] *Ibid.,* Mar. 14, 1833.

[7] *Colonial Advocate,* Feb. 20, Apr. 3, May 22, 1834; *Canadian Correspondent,* Oct. 18, 1834.

[8] St. Thomas *Liberal*, Nov. 29, 1832.

[9] *Correspondent and Advocate*, May 18, 1836.

[10] *Ibid.*, Mar. 24, 1836.

[11] Feb. 28, 1836, Tor. Ref. Lib., William Allan Papers.

[12] *Corresp. and Advocate*, Mar. 31, 1836.

[13] *Ibid.*, Apr. 27, 1836.

[14] *Ibid.*, May 18, 1836.

[15] *Ibid.*

[16] Editorials in the St. Thomas *Liberal*, reprinted in *Corresp. and Advocate*, May, 11, 18, 25, June 1, 1836.

[17] Dunham, *Polit. Unrest*, pp. 184-5; *Corresp. and Advocate*, July 13, 1836.

[18] Ross to Joseph, June 22, 1836, U. C. Sundries.

[19] Quoted in *Corresp. and Advocate*, July 26, 1836.

[20] *Ibid.*, June 1, 1836.

[21] Quoted in Fred Landon, *Western Ontario and the American Frontier* (Tor., 1941), p. 160; St. Thomas *Liberal*, quoted in *Corresp. and Advocate*, July 20, 1836.

[22] *Ibid.*, July 2, 20, 26, 1836, Jan. 11, and Mar. 1, 1837.

[23] *Ibid.*, July 20, Dec. 21, 1836.

[24] *Ibid.*, Aug. 10, 1836; *Patriot*, Aug. 16, 1836.

[25] Duncombe's petition, in the *Patriot*, Nov. 18, 1836.

[26] *Ibid.*, Feb. 10, 1837. See also *ibid.*, Nov. 18, 1836, and Head to Glenelg, Feb. 4, 1837, in *ibid.*, Sept. 19, 1837.

[27] *Corresp. and Advocate*, Aug. 3, 1836.

[28] Reprinted in *ibid.*, Sept. 7, 1836.

[29] Reprinted in *ibid.*, Feb. 8, and Suppl., Apr. 19, 1837, etc.

[30] *Patriot*, Sept. 8, Oct. 17, 20, 24, 1837.

[31] *Ibid.*, Oct. 6, 1837.

[32] Landon, *Western Ontario*, pp. 165-6.

[33] *Patriot*, Oct. 17, Nov. 3, 1837.

[34] F. C. Hamil, ed., "Another Letter from John Talbot, 1838", *Ont. History*, XLIII (1951), pp. 81-2.

## Chapter XVI

[1] Q, Vol. 378, Pt. 1, pp. 99, 101.

[2] *Ibid.*, pp. 67-71.

[3] *Ibid.*, pp. 57-60.

[4] *Ibid.*, pp. 93-5.

[5] *Ibid.*, pp. 82-7; Talbot to Mudge, Oct. 13, 1830, U. C. Sundries.

[6] Q, Vol. 378, Pt. 1, pp. 100-2.

[7] Lieut.-Gov.'s Office, Sec. Letters, Aug. 1832-Mar. 1833, pp. 111-12.

[8] G1, Vol. 70, pp. 409-15.

[9] Land Book Q, pp. 374-5; Q, Vol. 378, Pt. 1, p. 80.

[10] Parke to Colborne, May 4, 1835, Land Petitions, P, 19, no. 13.

[11] Address of the House, Mar. 28, 1835, Crown Lands Papers, Shelf 57, Box 6; *Journal of the Assembly*, 1st sess., 12th parl., (1835), pp. 316, 325, and Appendix, Vol. 1, pp. 40, 54, 58. Talbot replied to Colborne's request for a return of all lots settled by him, that it could not be made, because no location was final until the settlement duties were completed. See also Talbot to Rowan, Apr. 11, 1835, U. C. Sundries.

[12] Q, Vol. 390, Pt. 2, pp. 436-51.

[13] Talbot to Head, Mar. 26, 1836, U. C. Sundries; Q, Vol. 390, Pt. 2, pp. 386-94.

[14] Q, Vol. 395A, pp. 123-8.

[15] Q, Vol. 398, Pt. 1, pp. 48-99.

[16] *Ibid.*, pp. 37-47.

[17] *Ibid.*; and G1, Vol. 83, pp. 56-8.

[18] Q, Vol. 402, Pt. 2, pp. 258-63.

[19] Q, Vol. 403, Pt. 1, pp. 103-7.

[20] *Ibid.*, p. 108.

[21] *Ibid.*, pp. 103-7.

[22] P.A.C., Canada West, Prov. Sec. Office, no. 1343.

[23] *Ibid.*

[24] Ont. Arch., Price Papers, Apr. 13, 1846.

[25] *Ibid.*, Sept. 30, 1847.

[26] Renwick to Macdonald, Feb. 2, 1848, Crown Lands Papers, Shelf 101.

[27] Ermatinger, *Talbot Regime*, p. 292.

## Chapter XVII

[1] Brown, *Views of Canada*, pp. 268-9.

[2] Jameson, *Winter Studies*, II, pp. 7-9.

[3] Talbot to Hillier, Apr. 15, 1827, U. C. Sundries.

[4] Frances Stewart, *Our Forest Home*, p. 91.

[5] Talbot to Hillier, Apr. 11, 1827, U. C. Sundries; and May 30, 1827, State Papers, Talbot portfolio.

[6] Talbot to Hillier, Sept. 13 (1827), U. C. Sundries, Corresp. undated, M-Z.

[7] Kearney, *Life*, p. 9.

[8] Ermatinger, *Talbot Regime*, p. 301.

[9] Coyne, *Talbot Papers*, II, pp. 117-18, 139.

[10] *Ibid.*, p. 151.

[11] *Ibid.*, p. 115.

[12] *Ibid.*, p. 144.

[13] Talbot to Allan, May 27, 1833, Tor. Ref. Lib., William Allan Papers.

[14] Talbot to Allan, July 21, 1833, *ibid.*

[15] Coyne, *op. cit.*, II, pp. 160, 162.

[16] Baby, *Souvenirs*, p. 152; Jameson, *Winter Studies*, I, pp. 340-1, II, pp. 7-9; Coyne, *op. cit.*, II, pp. 159-62.

[17] Talbot's squared-log house, completed in 1833, is the main part of the enlarged house completed by Col. Airey in 1849, which still stands essen-

tially unchanged. The old cellar and the attic rooms are much the same as in Talbot's time.

[18] Jameson, *op. cit.*, II, pp. 9-10.

[19] Aug. 17, 1821, and Mar. 1, 1827, U. C. Sundries.

[20] Alexander, *L'Acadie*, I, p. 146.

[21] Lady Emmeline Stuart-Wortley, *Travels in the United States, etc., during 1849 and 1850* (N. Y., 1851), p. 30.

[22] Jameson, *op. cit.*, II, p. 13.

[23] Ont. Arch., Munro to Bishop Fuller (1879).

[24] Autobiography of Joseph Elson, p. 4.

[25] *Talbot-Wharncliffe Papers*, pp. 182-6.

[26] Kearney, *Life*, p. 16.

[27] *Gore Gazette*, May 31, 1828.

[28] Munro to Fuller (1879).

[29] Reprinted in Toronto *Correspondent and Advocate*, May 7, 1835.

[30] Baby, *Souvenirs*, p. 152; J. E. Middleton and F. Landon, *The Province of Ontario* (Tor., 1927), I, p. 299; Alexander, *L'Acadie*, I, p. 146.

[31] *Colonial Advocate*, June 4, 1829.

[32] Munro to Fuller (1879). See also the story about Sir Richard in Kearney, *op. cit.*, p. 10.

[33] *St. Peter's Church, Tyrconnell* (St. Thomas, 1928), p. 19; J. J. Talman, ed., *Report of a Missionary Journey made by the Hon. and Rev. Charles James Stewart through Upper Canada in 1820* (Lond., Univ. West. Ont., 1942), pp. 7-8.

[34] *Talbot-Wharncliffe Papers*, p. 182.

[35] *St. Peter's Church*, p. 35; Becher to Talbot, Aug. 14, 1850, Univ. West. Ont. Library, Talbot Papers.

[36] Kearney, *op. cit.*, pp. 8, 10; Ermatinger, *Talbot Regime*, p. 137.

[37] Kearney, *op. cit.*, pp. 19-20; Ermatinger, *op. cit.*, p. 306.

[38] June 17, 1825, U. C. Sundries.

[39] Kearney, *op. cit.*, p. 21.

[40] Talbot to Hillier, Apr. 15 (1825), U. C. Sundries, Corresp. undated, M-Z.

[41] *Gore Gazette*, May 31, 1828.

[42] Coyne, *Talbot Papers*, I, Intro., p. 57. This picture is in the Library of the University of Western Ontario.

[43] Frances Stewart, *Our Forest Home*, pp. 90-3.

[44] Middleton and Landon, *Ontario*, I, p. 299.

[45] Jameson, *Winter Studies*, II, p. 2.

[46] Alexander, *L'Acadie*, I, p. 145.

[47] Ermatinger, *Talbot Regime*, p. 151.

[48] Baby, *Souvenirs*, pp. 148-9.

## Chapter XVIII

[1] Coyne, *Talbot Papers*, II, pp. 115, 159.

[2] Letter signed by Paul Pry, in *Colonial Advocate*, Sept. 26, 1833.

[3] Coyne, *op. cit.*, p. 162.

[4] Ermatinger, *Talbot Regime*, pp. 210-11, 356, 359.

[5] Q, Vol. 403, Pt. I, p. 106.

[6] Tor. Ref. Lib., William Allan Papers.

[7] *Talbot-Wharncliffe Letters*, p. 195, footnote.

[8] The following is based on Julius Airey's letters to Mrs. John Harris, in the Library of the University of Western Ontario.

## Chapter XIX

[1] Coyne, *Talbot Papers*, II, p. 169.

[2] C. W. Robinson, *Life of Sir John B. Robinson* (Edin., 1904), p. 337.

[3] July 31, 1843, William Allan Papers.

[4] Q, Vol. 398, Pt. I, pp. 43-4.

[5] Coyne, *Talbot Papers*, II, p. 169.

[6] *Talbot-Wharncliffe Letters*, pp. 195-7.

[7] St. Thomas *Journal*, Jan. 30, 1901. See also *History of the County of Middlesex, Canada* (Tor., 1889), pp. 74-7.

[8] Land Petitions, T, 3, no. 25 (1844).

[9] Canada West, Prov. Sec. Office, no. 7037.

[10] Tor. Ref. Lib., William Allan Papers.

[11] Julius Airey to Mrs. Harris, Jan. 9, 1847, Library of the Univ. of West. Ont., Harris Papers.

[12] Coyne, *Talbot Papers*, II, p. 172.

[13] *Ibid.*, p. 173; Ermatinger, *Talbot Regime*, p. 291.

[14] *Ibid.*

[15] *Ibid.*, p. 292.

[16] *Ibid.*, p. 293.

[17] Lady Emmeline Wortley, *Travels*, p. 29.

[18] Talbot to John B. Robinson, May 27, 1849, Univ. of Toronto Library, Robinson Papers. I am indebted to Miss Julia Jarvis for a copy of this letter. See also Ermatinger, *op. cit.*, pp. 364-5; and Coyne, *op. cit.*, II, p. 174.

[19] Lady Emmeline Wortley, *op. cit.*, pp. 28-9; Ella N. Lewis, *Sidelights on the Talbot Settlement* (St. Thomas, Elgin Hist. Soc., 1938), pp. 15-19.

[20] Q, Vol. 398, Pt. 1, pp. 42-3.

[21] Coyne, *Talbot Papers*, pp. 174-5.

[22] "The Great Western Railway", comp. by Miss Gilkison, London and Middlesex Historical Society, *Transactions*, II (1909), p. 34.

[23] Coyne, *op. cit.*, II, pp. 176-7.

[24] Ermatinger, *Talbot Regime*, p. 294.

[25] Coyne, *op. cit.*, II, pp. 174-5; Talbot to Allan, Oct. 26, 1849, William Allan Papers.

[26] H. C. R. Becher, "Diary", ed. by M. A. Garland and Orlo Miller, Ont. Hist. Soc., *Papers and Records*, XXXIII (1939), under date Mar. 15, 1850.

[27] Coyne, *Talbot Papers*, II, pp. 192-4.

[28] Library of the Univ. of West. Ont., Talbot Papers.

## Chapter XX

[1] Ermatinger, *Talbot Regime*, pp. 365-6.

[2] Talbot to Strachan, July 30, 1850, Ont. Arch., Strachan Papers.

[3] *Kent Advertiser*, July 11, 1850, reprinted from the *Dundas Warder*.

[4] Ermatinger, *op. cit.*, pp. 366-9; Talbot to Strachan, July 30, 1850, Strachan Papers.

[5] Becher to Talbot, Aug. 14, Oct. 30, Dec. 3, 1850, and Apr. 17, 1851, Lib. of Univ. of West. Ont., Talbot Papers.

[6] R. Airey to Talbot, Aug. 17, 1850, with the Becher letters, *ibid.*

[7] Ermatinger, *Talbot Regime*, pp. 369-72; Coyne, *Talbot Papers*, II, pp. 177-8.

[8] Ermatinger, *op. cit.*, pp. 371-4.

[9] Becher to Talbot, Apr. 17, 1851, Lib. of Univ. of West. Ont., Talbot Papers; Becher, *Diary*, p. 123.

[10] Ermatinger, *op. cit.*, p. 376.

[11] *Ibid.*, p. 374; Becher to Talbot, Apr. 17, 1851, Becher letters, with Talbot Papers.

[12] Ermatinger, *Life*, pp. 213-14.

[13] Q, Vol. 398, Pt. 1, p. 44.

[14] Ermatinger, *Life*, preface.

[15] Kearney, *Life*, pp. 24-5.

[16] Talbot to Hillier, Apr. 24, 1827, U. C. Sundries.

[17] Apr. 15, 1827, *ibid.*

[18] Coyne, *Talbot Papers*, II, p. 101.

[19] Becher to Talbot, Aug. 14, 1850, Becher Letters, with Talbot Papers.

[20] Coyne, *op. cit.*, I, p. 57.

[21] *Ibid.*, II, pp. 195-6.

[22] Becher to Talbot, Apr. 17, 1851, Becher letters, with Talbot Papers, Lib. of Univ. West. Ont.

[23] Land Petitions, T, 6, no. 36 (1852); Land Book F, p. 411.

[24] Attached to front of Book E of Talbot's Township Maps, in Ontario Archives.

[25] Ermatinger, *Talbot Regime*, pp. 298-9; Coyne, *Talbot Papers*, I, Introd., p. 56.

# *Bibliography*

## MANUSCRIPT SOURCES

Many letters, petitions, and reports, written by Colonel Talbot to the Lieutenant-Governors of Upper Canada, or to their private secretaries, are to be found in the Upper Canada Sundries, the Land Petitions, and the Talbot portfolio in the State Papers, in the Public Archives of Canada at Ottawa. These collections also include letters and reports addressed to the Surveyor-General and other officers of the government by Talbot, as well as various documents pertaining to the Talbot Settlement written by others. Transcripts of many of these, with some not available elsewhere, are included in the minutes of the Land Committee of the Executive Council recorded in the Land Books, which constitute an invaluable source of information on the affairs of the Settlement throughout; and in the Q series, which consists of despatches and enclosures from the Lieutenant-Governors to the Secretaries of State for the Colonies. The despatches from the Secretaries of State to the Lieutenant-Governors are kept in the G series. The Letter Books of the Lieutenant-Governor's Office contain copies or abstracts of many letters written to Talbot from that office. Much valuable material concerning the Colonel is contained in the William Dummer Powell Papers, the Simcoe Papers, the Claus Papers, the Selkirk Papers, and the Papers of the Provincial Secretary's Office. All of these are to be found in the Public Archives of Canada.

Extensive use was made of the Crown Lands Papers, and to a lesser extent of the Munro, Russell, Strachan, and Tupper Papers, in the Public Archives of Ontario at Toronto. In the Surveyor-General's Office of the Department of Lands and Forests of Ontario, the principal sources used were the volumes of Letters Written, and Letters Received, and the Papers of Mahlon Burwell. The Registers of Lands, and the Descriptions, in the Patent Office, yielded some details of value. Much information was obtained from the William Dummer Powell Papers, the William Allan Papers, and the transcripts of the Simcoe Papers, in the Toronto Public Reference Library. The bulk of the original Simcoe Papers, recently transferred from the University of Toronto Library to the Public Archives of Ontario, from which transcripts were made for the Toronto Public Reference Library and the Public Archives of Canada, were also examined.

At the University of Western Ontario Library are the Talbot Papers, which include a number of letters and documents formerly belonging to H. C. R. Becher, the Colonel's lawyer. Most of these, with the exception of the Becher Papers, were published by James H. Coyne in the Transactions of the Royal Society of Canada. The University of Western Ontario Library also has the valuable collection of letters written by Julius Airey to Mrs. John Harris; and the manuscript autobiography of Joseph Elson.

## PRINTED SOURCES: LETTERS AND RECORDS

Armytage, W. H. G., ed. "Thomas Talbot and Lord Wharncliffe: Some New Letters Hitherto Unpublished". *Ontario History*, XLV (1953), pp. 177-97.

Coyne, James H., ed. *The Talbot Papers.* 2 Vols. Transactions of the Royal Society of Canada, 1907, 1909.

Cruikshank, E. A., ed. "Additional Correspondence of Robert Nichol", Ontario Historical Society, *Papers and Records*, XXVI (1930).

Cruikshank, E. A., ed. *The Correspondence of Lieut. Governor John Graves Simcoe.* 5 Vols. Toronto, 1923-31.

Cruikshank, E. A., and Hunter, A. F., eds. *The Correspondence of the Honourable Peter Russell.* 3 Vols. Toronto, 1932-6.

Great Britain. Historical Manuscripts Commission. 14th Report, Appendix, Part V. *The Manuscripts of J. B. Fortesque, Esq., Preserved at Dropmore.* Vol. II. London, 1894.

Hamil, F.C., ed. "Another Letter from John Talbot, 1838", *Ontario History*, XLIII (1951), pp. 81-2.

Ontario. Bureau of Archives. *Reports.* Toronto, 1903-33.

Spragge, G., ed. *The John Strachan Letter Book.* Toronto, 1946.

Upper Canada. *Journals of the Legislative Assembly, and Appendices*, 1835, 1836.

## PRINTED SOURCES: NEWSPAPERS

Particular use was made of a number of newspapers of the Province, not only for material dealing directly with Colonel Talbot and the Talbot Settlement, but for background information on immigration and political affairs. The file of the St. Thomas *Liberal* (1832-4), in the Public Archives of Canada, yielded a great deal of material on the Colonel's venture into the political arena. The *Colonial Advocate*, begun by William Lyon Mackenzie at Queenston in May, 1824, and moved to York later in the year, was also extremely important. In November, 1834, it was joined with the York *Canadian Correspondent* to become the *Correspondent and Advocate*, which continued publication until the summer of 1837. The Kingston *Patriot*, which in 1833 also moved to York, was used from the beginning of 1832 to June, 1841, yielding much information on political affairs in the Talbot Settlement and throughout the Province. The *Gore Gazette* (1827-9) provided much of interest for the London District; and the Sandwich *Canadian Emigrant* (1831-6) for the Western District. The Kingston *Chronicle* (1819-31), and the Kingston *Gazette* (1810-19) were especially valuable for material on immigration. The *Upper Canada Gazette* was searched from the beginning in 1793 through 1833 for occasional items of interest. More important were the files of the *Weekly Post* (1821), the *Weekly Register* (1822-6), and the *U. E. Loyalist* (1826-9), all of which were published in conjunction with the *Upper Canada Gazette*. The York *Canadian Freeman* (1825-34) was of occasional value. All of these newspapers are available in microfilm.

## PRINTED SOURCES: TRAVELLERS' ACCOUNTS, JOURNALS, ETC.

Alexander, Sir. James E. *L'Acadie, or Seven Years' Explorations in British America.* 2 Vols. London, 1849.

Baby, William L. *Souvenirs of the Past.* Windsor, 1896.

Becher, H. C. R. "Diary of", ed. by M. A. Garland and Orlo Miller, Ontario Historical Society, *Papers and Records,* XXXIII (1939).

Brown, James B. *Views of Canada and the Colonists.* Edinburgh, 1851.

Buckingham and Chandos, Duke of. *Memoirs of the Court and Cabinets of George the Third.* Vol. 1. London, 1853.

Carr, John. "The Stranger in Ireland, or, a Tour . . . in the year 1805", *A Collection of Modern and Contemporary Voyages and Travels,* V. London, 1807.

Carruthers, J. *Retrospect of Thirty-Six Years' Residence in Canada West.* Hamilton, 1861.

Graves, William. "The Diary of", ed. by D. F. McOuat, *Ontario History,* XLIII (1951), pp. 1-28.

Great Britain. Parliament. *Imperial Blue Books on Affairs Relating to Canada,* III. 1830-3.

Hamil, F. C., ed. "Schenectady to Michilimackinac, 1765 & 1766; the Journal of John Porteous", Ontario Historical Society, *Papers and Records,* XXXIII (1940), pp. 75-98.

Howison, John. *Sketches of Upper Canada.* 2nd ed. Edinburgh, 1822.

Jameson, Anna. *Winter Studies and Summer Rambles in Canada.* 2 Vols. in 1. New York, Wiley and Putnam, n. d.

Kemble, Fanny. "Old Woman's Gossip, XIX", *Atlantic Monthly,* XXXIX (Feb. 1877), p. 217.

Mackenzie, W. L. *Sketches of Canada.* London, 1833.

Need, Thomas. *Six Years in the Bush . . . 1832-1838.* London, 1838.

Proudfoot, William. "Papers and Diary", Ontario Historical Society, *Papers and Records,* XXVII (1931).

Simcoe, Mrs. John Graves. *Diary* Edited by J. Ross Robertson. Toronto, 1911.

Smith, David W. "Thames—Its Banks", transcribed by R. M. Lewis, *Ontario History,* XLIV (1952), pp. 15-22.

Stewart, Frances. *Our Forest Home.* Montreal, 1902.

Sullivan, Edward. *Rambles and Scrambles in North and South America.* London, 1852.

Talman, J. J., ed. *Loyalist Narratives from Upper Canada.* Toronto, Champlain Society, 1946.

Wortley, Lady Emmeline Stuart. *Travels in the United States, etc., during 1849-1850*. New York, 1851.

Young, Arthur. *A Tour in Ireland*. London, 1780.

## PRINTED SOURCES: SECONDARY

Adams, C. L. *Castles of Ireland*. London, 1904.

Bartlett, W. H., and M. Addey. *Ireland, Pictorial, Descriptive and Historical*. New York, c1882.

Campbell, T. *Pioneer Days in London*. London, 1921.

Coyne, James H. "Address at the Unveiling of the Port Talbot Memorial Cairn", Ontario Historical Society, *Papers and Records*, XXIV (1927).

Dunham, Aileen. *Political Unrest in Upper Canada 1815-1836*. London, 1927.

Ermatinger, C. O. *The Talbot Regime*. St. Thomas, 1904.

Ermatinger, Edward. *Life of Colonel Talbot*. St. Thomas, 1859.

Froude, James A. *The English in Ireland in the Eighteenth Century*. Vol. II. New York, 1874.

Gerard, Frances. *Picturesque Dublin*. London, 1898.

Gourlay, R. *Statistical Account of Upper Canada*. Vol. I. London, 1822.

Guedalla, P. *Wellington*. New York, 1931.

Guillet, Edwin C. *The Great Migration*. Toronto, 1937.

Gwynn, Stephen. *The Charm of Ireland*. London, 1934.

Hamil, F. C. "Colonel Talbot and the Early History of London", *Ontario History*, XLIII (1951), pp. 159-75.

Hamil, F. C. "Colonel Talbot's Principality", *Ontario History*, XLIV (1952), pp. 183-93.

Hamil, F. C. "Lord Selkirk in Upper Canada", Ontario Historical Society, *Papers and Records*, XXXVII (1945), pp. 35-48.

Hamil, F. C. *The Valley of the Lower Thames, 1640 to 1850*. Toronto, 1951.

Kearney, L. C. *The Life of Colonel the late Honorable Thomas Talbot*. Chatham, 1857.

Kent County. *Commemorative Biographical Record of the County of Kent, Ontario*. Toronto, 1904.

Kirby, William. *Annals of Niagara*. Toronto, 1927.

Landon, Fred. "The Talbot Settlement", in Middleton, Jesse E., and Landon, Fred. *The Province of Ontario, a History, 1615-1927*, I. Toronto, 1927.

Landon, Fred. *Western Ontario and the American Frontier*. Toronto, 1941.

Lecky, W. E. *A History of Ireland in the Eighteenth Century*. Vol. I. New York, 1893.

Lewis, Ella N. *Sidelights on the Talbot Settlement*. St. Thomas, Elgin Historical Society, 1938.

Macdonald, Norman. *Canada 1763-1841, Immigration and Settlement*, London, 1939.

McKellar, A. "The Old 'Bragh', or Hand Mill", Ontario Historical Society, *Papers and Records*, III (1901), pp. 170-9.
MacMahon, Ella. *Historic Houses of the United Kingdom*. London, 1892.
Mansfield, M. F. and B. M. *Romantic Ireland*. Boston, 1905.
Middlesex. *History of the County of Middlesex, Canada*. Toronto, 1889.
Morris, M. O. *Dublin Castle*. London, 1889.
Paterson, Gilbert C. *Land Settlement in Upper Canada, 1783-1840*. Ontario Archives, 16th Report, 1920.
Plant, G. F. *Oversea Settlement, Migration from the United Kingdom to the Dominions*. London, 1951.
*Recollection of Dublin Castle and of Dublin Society*. New York, 1902.
Riddell, W. R. *The Life of John Graves Simcoe*, Toronto, 1926.
Riddell, W. R. *The Life of William Dummer Powell*. Lansing, Michigan, 1924.
Robinson, C. W. *Life of Sir John B. Robinson*. Edinburgh, 1904.
*St. Peter's Church, Tyrconnell, Ontario, 1827-28*. St. Thomas, 1928.

# Index

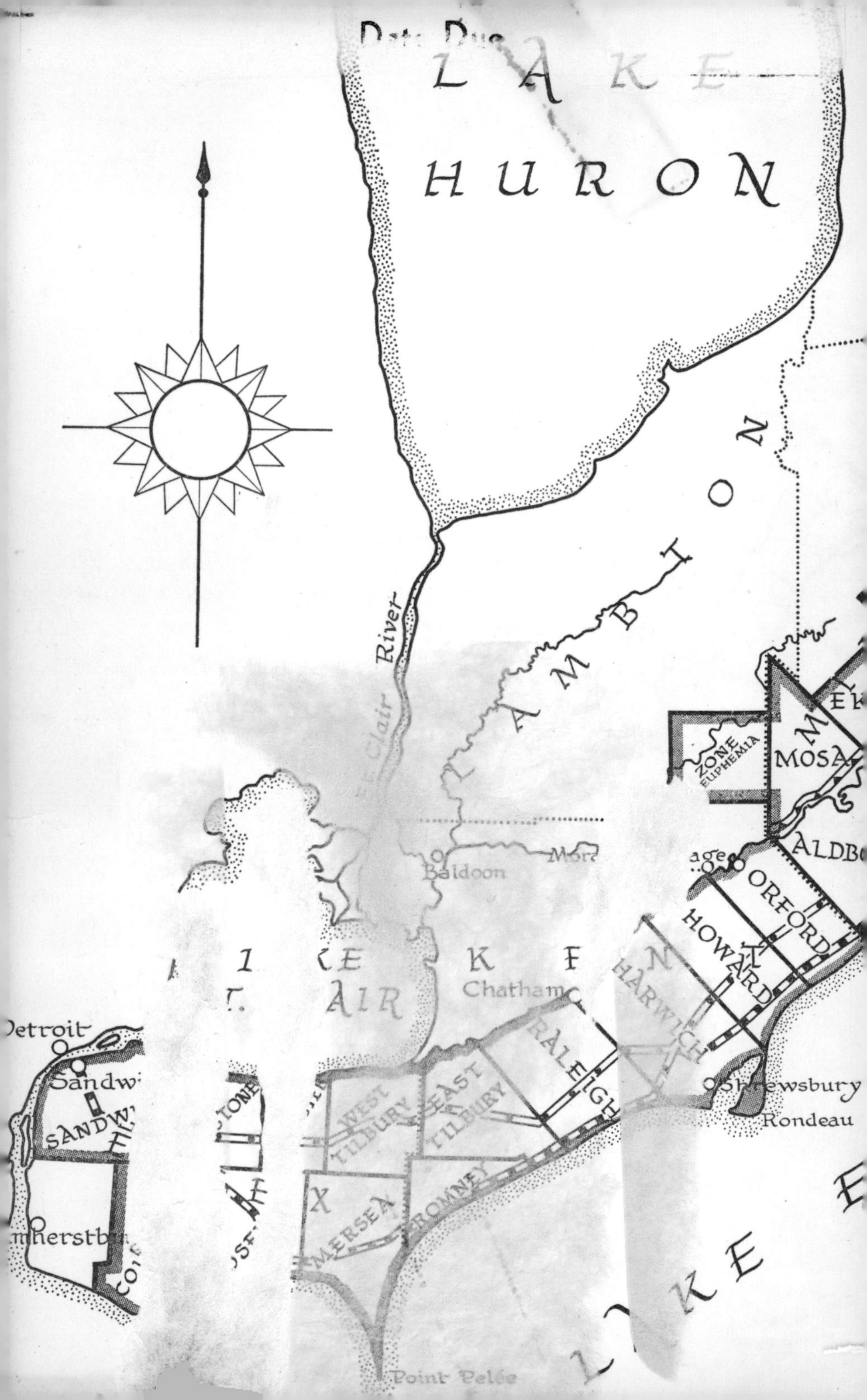

LAKE
HURON
LAMBTON
St. Clair River
Baldoon
Chatham
Detroit
ZONE
EUPHEMIA
MOSA
ORFORD
HOWARD
HARWICH
RALEIGH
WEST TILBURY
EAST TILBURY
MERSEA
ROMNEY
Shrewsbury
Rondeau
Point Pelée